The Thunder Tree

BOOKS BY ROBERT MICHAEL PYLE

Wintergreen: Rambles in a Ravaged Land
The Thunder Tree: Lessons from an Urban Wildland
Where Bigfoot Walks: Crossing the Dark Divide
Chasing Monarchs: Migrating with the Butterflies of Passage
Nabokov's Butterflies (with Brian Boyd and Dmitri Nabokov)
Walking the High Ridge: Life as Field Trip
Sky Time in Gray's River: Living for Keeps in a Forgotten Place
Mariposa Road: The First Butterfly Big Year

ON ENTOMOLOGY
Watching Washington Butterflies
Handbook for Butterfly Watchers
The Audubon Society Field Guide to North American Butterflies
The IUCN Invertebrate Red Data Book (with S. M. Wells and N. M. Collins)
Butterflies: A Peterson Color-In Book (with Roger Tory Peterson and Sarah
    Anne Hughes)
Insects: A Peterson Field Guide Coloring Book (with Kristin Kest)
The Butterflies of Cascadia

The Thunder Tree

LESSONS FROM AN URBAN WILDLAND

Robert Michael Pyle

Oregon State University Press • Corvallis

The paper in this book meets the guidelines for permanence and
durability of the Committee on Production Guidelines for Book
Longevity of the Council on Library Resources and the minimum
requirements of the American National Standard for Permanence of
Paper for Printed Library Materials Z39.48-1984.

Library of Congress Cataloging-in-Publication Data
Pyle, Robert Michael.
The thunder tree: lessons from an urban wildland/Robert Michael Pyle.
p. cm.
Originally published: Boston: Houghton Mifflin, 1993.
ISBN 978-087071-602-7 (pbk.)
1. Natural history—Colorado—High Line Canal. 2. Pyle, Robert Michael.
3. High Line Canal (Colo.) I. Title.
[QH105.C6P88 1998]
508.788—dc21   98-14030
CIP

First published in 1993 by Houghton Mifflin
This edition first published in 2011 by Oregon State University Press.
Printed in the United States of America

Oregon State University Press
121 The Valley Library
Corvallis OR 97331-4501
541-737-3166 • fax 541-737-3170
http://oregonstate.edu/dept/press

For Tom, who found the Thunder Tree,
and for his family,
Mary Margaret, Michael, Heather, Pete, Grant, and Jerrod

and in memory of Lois Webster,
conservationist, naturalist, and lover of the High Line

In my time, a man can't discover a river, but he can always be on the lookout for an unexplored ditch.

—Sam McKinney, *Reach of Tide, Ring of History*

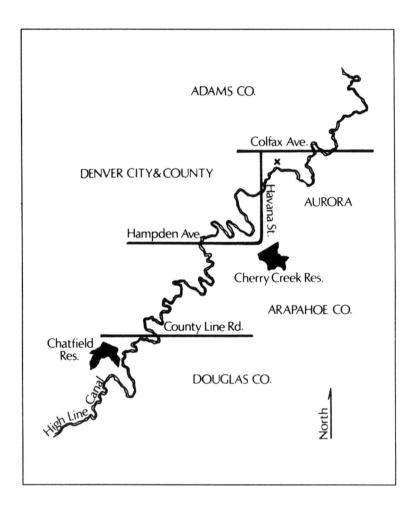

The general situation of the High Line Canal in Colorado
(with kind permission of the Denver Board of Water Commissioners)

The Front Range of the Rocky Mountains lies to the west, the western edge of the Great Plains to the east. X marks the Thunder Tree. For a more detailed representation of topography, roads, and towns, see U.S. Geological Survey map "Front Range Urban Corridor, sheet 2 of 3 (Greater Denver Area, Colorado)" :100,000 scale, 1972, also available at http://nationalmap.gov/ustopo/index.html (in the Fitzsimons 7.5-minute quadrangle or the Denver east 30-minute quadrangle).

CONTENTS

Foreword

A few years ago, at a small conference sponsored by Yale University, I met Robert Michael Pyle for the first time, and I've not been the same since. The topic of that conference, biophilic design, was uplifting. So was the presence of E. O. Wilson and David Orr and other luminaries in the worlds of ecology. But Bob cast a spell all his own.

His face is framed by flowing white hair and beard. He looks like a cross between a mountain man and Santa Claus. His eyes are filled with wonder, intelligence, and generosity.

Imagine Bob placing a butterfly on a child's nose. "Noses seem to make perfectly good perches or basking spots, and the insect often remains for some time," he writes, in the book that you're holding. "Almost everyone is delighted by this: the light tickle, the close-up colors, the thread of a tongue probing for droplets of perspiration. But somewhere beyond delight lies enlightenment. I have been astonished at the small epiphanies I see in the eyes of a child in truly close contact with nature, perhaps for the first time. This can happen to grown-ups too, reminding them of something they never knew they had forgotten."

That essence, which still exists at the edge of memory, is the special place in nature that we discovered when we were children, and if we're lucky, still exists in our hearts.

In *The Thunder Tree*, Bob revealed the intense relationship that can develop—that should develop—between a child and such a special place. As an adult, Henry David Thoreau may have had his Walden. Annie Dillard inhabited her Tinker Creek. But as a child, Bob Pyle *became* his High Line Canal—an accidental wilderness, he called it, surrounded by urban wasteland.

A ditch, a ravine, a cluster of trees at the end of the cul de sac, an empty (filled!) lot; to an adult's eyes, such nearby nature may seem insignificant. But to a child, these places can be doorways into whole galaxies. They're as important to human experience as wilderness, and formative to nearly every conservationist's consciousness. As of 2008, for the first time in human history, more people live in cities than in rural areas. As this trend continues, nearby nature will either disappear or come to be valued as essential to human development.

We need new mechanisms to protect these places. Why not encourage neighborhoods to establish their own neighborhood land trusts to protect them for their children and grandchildren and future generations? In Detroit and other cities people are already turning wasteland into parkland and community gardens. We should, in fact, not only conserve but *create* more of these special places—on reclaimed land, on green roofs, in front and back and side yards. These places offer protection from what Bob called the "extinction of experience."

"What is the extinction of a condor to a child who has never seen a wren?" he asks. That sentence alone is reason to celebrate the republication of *The Thunder Tree*, a classic in the literature of the human relationship with the natural world.

Bob would be the first to say that leading a nature-balanced life is challenging in cities or countryside. New communications technology has upped the ante. In 2007, in one of his *Orion* magazine columns, Bob announced that he was thinking about going cold turkey on e-mail.

"Time will tell whether I can make a living without e-mail," he wrote. "In the meantime, I'm going back to the post, and the virtues of patience and silence. My loss, you'll say. Maybe so. We'll see." Two years later, I e-mailed Bob and asked him how his life was going since he swore off e-mail. It was a bad sign when he answered, quickly. "I have backslid. You could say I had a hiatus, but I haven't yet fully succeeded in achieving the ideal. I try to spend as little time as I can on the machine away from writing, however, and do as little as possible on the Web." When he must spend time before a screen to do his daily work of writing, he gets up and goes outside as soon as possible, to balance screen time with "scintillating butterflies, fish, or lizards."

He works at it and sets a fine example. I can see him now, running through a summer field, waving his net at clouds of butterflies, followed by children and adults. Perhaps each of them hopes that the big guy with the flowing white mane will stop and turn and place a butterfly on their nose. That's exactly what Bob does with his writing.

Richard Louv

author of *Last Child in the Woods: Saving Our Children from Nature-Deficit Disorder* and chairman of the Children & Nature Network

PROLOGUE

Everybody's Ditch

And in time there's no more telling which is which between them, no sharp distinction, no clear edge of difference where it can be said that here the land ends and here the man begins.

— Don Berry, *Trask*

A green ravine creases northeast Seattle, draining into Lake Union near the University of Washington. My mother grew up in a white shingle house beside this ravine and it became her constant haunt. Whenever she was able to return to Seattle, Mother's first impulse was to visit "her" ravine. On one of these pilgrimages she took me along, and I saw in her face the meaning of place. At Ravenna Park she made a personal connection that transformed the way she looked at the land for the rest of her life.

When people connect with nature, it happens *somewhere*. Almost everyone who cares deeply about the outdoors can identify a particular place where contact occurred. This may have been a wilderness, a national park, or a stretch of unbounded countryside, but more often the place that makes a difference is unspectacular: a vacant lot, a scruffy patch of woods, a weedy field, a stream, a green ravine like Ravenna—or a ditch.

My own point of intimate contact with the land was a ditch. Growing up on the wrong side of Denver to reach the mountains easily or often, I resorted to the tattered edges of the Great Plains on the back side of town. There I encountered a century-old irrigation channel known as the High Line Canal. Without a doubt, most of the elements of my life flowed from that canal.

From the time I was six, this weedy watercourse had been my sanctuary, playground, and sulking walk. It was also my imaginary wilderness, escape hatch, and birthplace as a naturalist. Later the canal served as lovers' lane, research site, and holy ground of solace. Over the years I studied its natural history, explored much of its length, watched its habitats shrink as the suburbs grew up around it, and tried to help save some of its best bits. Despite the losses, the High Line remained a place to which I would often return. Even when living in national parks, in exotic lands, in truly rural countryside, and in Seattle near Mother's ravine, I've hankered to get back to the old ditch whenever I could.

Around dry Denver, the canal has many adherents. Since the public trail along the canal service road was opened in the seventies, tens of thousands have taken their pleasure there. But even before that, in the days of its unofficial access, I was not alone in finding it. A young woman named Laura Corliss wrote her "Study of the High Line Canal" for school in 1975, telling of her family's longtime dependence on the ditch for recreation. The Corlisses lived along the canal in Denver, between Eisenhower and Bible parks. Laura's dad, Charles, rafted significant portions of the canal, and his children tubed, biked, chased frogs and crawdads, swung, dived, and swam all summer long. It was all against water department rules, but "without the canal I don't know what I would have done," Laura told me, "or what growing up would have been like." She spoke for many kids and many ditches when she wrote, "During those hot and long summer days, I would have been bored stiff if it weren't for that High Line Canal."

It isn't difficult to find lovers of the High Line around Denver, but I've been surprised by the number of people from elsewhere who care for this particular ditch. Three women I've met in the Pacific Northwest exemplify this phenomenon. Evelyn Iritani, a Seattle journalist whose father spent a lot of his time on the ditch when he lived near it in the forties, knows it through his tales. Ellen Lanier-Phelps, a land planner in Portland, gained her appreciation for urban greenspaces from growing up beside the canal in a Denver suburb. Norma Walker now lives in Ocean Park, Washington, near my home, but the High Line was her sons' "safety net" when her family lived in Colorado and she was mayor of Aurora. I am no longer surprised, no matter where I am, when conversation comes around to a common affection for the High Line Canal.

Even if they don't know "my" ditch, most people I speak with seem to have a ditch somewhere—or a creek, meadow, wood-lot, or marsh—that they hold in similar regard. These are places of initiation, where the borders between ourselves and other creatures break down, where the earth gets under our nails and a sense of place gets under our skin. They are the secondhand lands, the hand-me-down habitats where you have to look hard to find something to love.

This book is my love song to damaged lands, a serenade for all such places. I want to ask: What do shreds and scraps of the natural scene mean, after all, in the shadow of the citified whole? What can one patch of leftover land mean to one person's life, or to the lives of all who dwell in the postindustrial wasteland? In the end, this is not a book about *a* ditch. It is a book about everybody's ditch, and what Kim Stafford, with perfect pitch of place, calls "weaving a rooted companionship with home ground."

The Thunder Tree is neither a guidebook to the High Line Canal nor a complete historical chronicle of this venerable watercourse. There is a need for both types of books, which I hope will someday be satisfied. In the meantime, I trust that this very different book will awaken interest in places like the High Line in every community.

Nor is this a personal history. The ditch made the man, yet this is a memoir of a place, not a person. My life stories are meant to illuminate the land, not the other way around. As for sequence, I agree with Vladimir Nabokov, writing in *Speak, Memory:* "I confess I do not believe in time. I like to fold my magic carpet, after use, in such a way as to superimpose one part of the pattern upon another. Let visitors trip." Just as recollection and current events mingle in the stew of our awareness, history and happenstance trade places frequently in this narrative. Readers looking for a linear chronology will surely trip.

Instead, I have sought to draw a dense but light-permeable portrait of a changing countryside and the people who depend on it in different ways. The first part, "Lifeline," introduces the ditch through intense personal experience, follows it from top to bottom, and tells of the illimitable importance of water in the West. "Landmarks," the second part, examines the face of the near-urban countryside as a habitat for hope, change, and continuity. Part III, "City Limits," considers the consequences of growth when natural limitations are ignored. The last section, "Still Life," speaks of loss and what's left when trees, people, and landscapes pass from the scene. Leaflike, the book hopes to honor and emulate the woven canopy of the namesake tree.

Nearly forty years have elapsed since I first saw the High Line Canal. The landscape that so touched me has changed almost beyond recognition in those years—until I get down inside the ditch. Except for the proliferation of plastic among the flotsam in the bottom, the scene between the bank grass and the cottonwoods remains much the same as that which first enchanted me so long ago. As a ditchwalker in that silty bed, I have had none of the rights the farmers enjoy, no responsibilities such as the ditch-riders bear—just the exercise of my free senses in company with the wind, the rain, and the place. What follows is my experience of that place.

It is through close and intimate contact with a particular patch of ground that we learn to respond to the earth, to see that it really matters. We need to recognize the humble places where this alchemy occurs, and treat them as well as we treat our parks and preserves—or better, with less interference.

Everybody has a ditch, or ought to. For only the ditches—and the fields, the woods, the ravines—can teach us to care enough for all the land.

PART I

Lifeline

The Hailstorm

These are the ice nuclei, which come to lie like secret seeds at the heart of every pearl of hail.

— Lyall Watson, *Heaven's Breath*

"Wake up, Bobby."

My brother nudged my shoulder until I opened my eyes. His flannel pajamas and messed-up brown hair told me he'd just gotten up. Cool, fresh air drifted in through the window I'd cranked open beside my pillow. Blue sky filled in the mesh of the screen. That and the gentle air promised a fine day, but I wanted to sleep. I closed my eyes again.

"Come on," Tom insisted, poking me. "Let's head over to the canal before it gets too hot."

The breeze smelled faintly of window screen and irises. Then it shifted and the sweet stink of fertilizer took over, until that was smothered by the acrid odor of roofer's tar. These smells would be with us all summer, field marks of a new suburb still under construction.

I rolled out from under my brown Space Cadets bedspread and into my slippers, keeping the cold asphalt tiles from my feet. To get me moving, Tom chased me down the hall to the kitchen. Mother was already outside in the yard, having laid breakfast things out on the table for us. We toasted white bread and slathered it with butter and grape jelly to have with our Cheerios. When the oat circles were gone, we dredged the yellow bowls loudly with our spoons for the thick sediment of sugar and milk in the bottom.

Our spoons and bowls chinked on the blue Formica tabletop. Finished, we scooted back the chrome chairs of our dinette set, rinsed our dishes, and left them to dry. If we were lucky, we should be able to make a clean getaway—our room was relatively tidy, the lawn had recently been mowed, and the dandelions were in hand.

We dressed quickly in the light cotton print shirts, jeans, and black engineer boots that we wore all that summer of 1954. It being a weekday, Dad was at his office in downtown Denver, or making sales calls for the Mutual Office Supply Company. Mom was working in her embryonic garden, her tan deepening as our bare new yard began to fill with plants. Before she could think of something for us to do, we asked if we could go to the canal. "Okay," she called through the back door, "but stay out of the water and come home for dinner. Have fun!"

Free to wander, we strode the concrete sidewalk to its slanted curb and entered the odor of new asphalt heating up with the day, then crossed Revere Street into the Jefferses' yard. Beside the little tower of their standard backyard incinerator, a chain link fence opened onto Hoffman Heights Park. The gate clanked shut, and we left the built world behind.

We had lived in Hoffman Heights for a little over a year. The rows of brick homes like ours were beginning to acquire the softening influence of grass, gardens, and small trees. Our house was built of rose-yellow bricks, topped with a red roof of bright asphalt shingles speckled with white. The Jeffers house was almost identical to ours except for its brown roof, its garage, and the fact that it backed onto the park.

The park was donated by Sam Hoffman, a developer who used assembly-line methods to build solid but low-priced housing tracts across the country. Hoffman Estates, Illinois, destined to become the home of Sears, Roebuck in later years, and Hoffman Heights, Colorado, were two of his largest and best-known projects. On the square mile of old Cottonwood Farm, between Peoria and Potomac streets, Sixth and Thirteenth avenues, Hoffman built 1,705 new homes. Brick or shingled frame, set on concrete pads, they had one story and no basement. Variations in brick color (blond or red), style, number of bedrooms, and garaging (one car or no garage) made the subdivision seem less like a tract than most. The streets curved gently. Here and there a court or circle sliced across the pattern to break it up and confound kids on their way to piano lessons. Concrete sidewalks with sloped curbs and gutters ran beside the broad oiled-and-graveled streets that smacked in summer with the sound of swelling tar bubbles.

Hoffman's plan to build "way out beyond Aurora," as doubters put it, made sense to couples who wanted to raise their families outside the aging city, yet within commuting range of Denver. When Dad went off to World War II in the merchant marine, his family numbered only three. After Susan came Tom, then me. We grew to six when Bud was born in 1952. Our North Denver bungalow wasn't a shoe, but it was bulging. Like many another veteran coming home to cramped quarters that quickly grew more so, Dad found the new suburban alternative appealing. Mother, anticipating more bedrooms and a larger garden, agreed. They decided to buy a Hoffman Deluxe Brick for $11,450, plus $250 extra for the fourth bedroom. We moved "way out beyond Aurora" in June 1953.

Our antecedents had come from small farming and ranching towns with names like Fancy Farm and Steamboat Springs and from big cities like Detroit, Denver, and Seattle. Sam Hoffman promised that his suburb would combine the best of the country and the city in a pleasant setting more livable than either. But town and country never married easily in my family, any more than they did in Hoffman Heights. Aurora would eventually become larger than Denver itself, a vast clutter of subdivisions full of motorists bound daily for real city or real countryside.

The living was not, in fact, unpleasant, but the suburb, neither urban nor rural, left many of its residents hungry for one or the other rather than satisfying their need for both. In those early days, however, genuine rural countryside still survived within walking distance of the vanguard tracts. Now Tom and I set out to reach just such a leftover landscape.

We crossed the open park, still just an old weedy field. Backyards bordered it along Revere Street, Del Mar Circle, and Seventh Avenue; the volunteer fire station and Hoffman Boulevard lined the north side. Ball fields had been plunked down in the dirt and tumbleweeds, and a county crew mowed the stiff farm grasses into a semblance of lawn. The only big trees around, a few plains cottonwoods along filled-in ditches, gave away the sites of old farmsteads. One of the biggest stood in the middle of the presumptive park. All the local kids made forts in the dirt and brush around the base of that old cottonwood and in the small grove of Chinese elms surrounding it.

Years later there would be tennis courts, playgrounds, and a mothballed trainer jet in Hoffman Park, but we made do with the ghost farm's shady grove. Our games and bivouacs beat the place barren, leaving it muddy in winter and dusty in summer. Then, like nomads abandoning a used-up oasis, we left the tatty grove behind and took to rambling the fields and ditches beyond the last platted streets.

We passed our favorite part of the nascent park, the so-called sanitary landfill, which was anything but. A long slot in the raw ground, it was where the developer disposed of the generous effluvium from the building of hundreds of houses. It was good for salvage. With Dad, we would carry a load of garbage to the fill and return with a box of nails or a few bricks for the patio barbecue pit. He finished our bathrooms with ceramic tiles from the sanitary landfill.

We were forbidden to visit the fill by ourselves because of its real or imagined dangers. The deep canyon of the landfill oozed a sour nosegay of thrilling stinks and smokes. Methane vapors swirled in the shadows. Since the slit cut into lakefill beneath the water table, dark pools of polluted water collected in the bottom. Outcrops of trash, old clothing, splintered wood, and half-rotted garbage made lurid strata in the crumbly walls. Of course, it was irresistible. There were trophies to be found, adventures to be enacted. But the attraction had paled the day we buried our deceased hamsters in holy ground on the bank of the fill. The older, tougher Yourtz boys, Gary and Ian, violated their grave, gaily hurling their furry corpses into the smoking pit. When we objected, they beat us up.

This bright morning we hurried past. The pit, nearly full, was soon to be covered over and a playground installed on top, but we had somewhere better to go. One day the previous fall, Tom had come home on his bike and breathlessly announced, "There's an old canal. It's neat. Come on!"

Only seven years old, I hadn't yet shed my training wheels, so I followed as best as I could on foot. Tom had led me across the park, past the fire station and the bulldozed and graded site of the future shopping center, over a railroad track, then across Sixth Avenue, through a cornfield to a ditch, and along it to a bigger one. It was nearly a mile, and I panted to keep up. How far was Tom taking me? When we arrived at the High Line Canal,

I took a long look up and down the winding watercourse and agreed: "It *is* neat."

Brimful with muddy water in midsummer, the High Line Canal spanned some twenty feet from bank to bank. Ranks of tall cottonwoods, like the one marooned in the park but less lonesome, lined the ditch as far as we could see in either direction. The canal, the dirt road beside it, and the vegetation twined into a sublime tangle. Peachleaf willows nudged old homestead locusts at the headgates of feeder canals. Fields of unruly weeds ran up to banks of yellow-flowered rabbitbrush. Long grass overhung the canal, swaying with the current in a summer-long hula. Screaming black and white birds fanned overhead, their colors echoed by big butterflies darting out from the willows, gliding back to the same perches again and again. After the barrenness of our ordered young tract, this wild green clutter promised rich pickings.

At our old house in North Denver, the city limits lay just a block away. There, Tejon Street shed its macadam hide and became "the Dusty Road." In the first years of the fifties, Susan and Tom and I had taken to the Dusty Road daily, a borrowed cocker in tow, to explore its fields, its brook, its raccoon-and-crawdad-filled marsh. Along the road was a dairy farm. Between its great barn and the roadside ditch grew gleaming mountains of discarded milk bottle caps. Their bright foil, printed with the dairy's red and blue badge, seemed like some magical ore deposit. Tom and I flung the crinkled disks at each other until the road sparkled with silver circles. Queenie the cocker followed us as far as we walked, bouncing back and forth and off to the side like a paddleball. In the evening we would urge the spaniel, by then a bedraggled and filthy marsh beast, back into her own yard. We fancied that her owners never knew how she got so muddy.

Moving to Hoffman Heights, we missed the Dusty Road. The weedy park, with its boundaries, scarcely made up for a country lane that could take you forever. Not that our new streets were all paved at first. Mounds of gravel lay in rows down the middle of each block, like camels resting in some suburban caravan. On their humps sat lanterns—round black kerosene pots with wicks—to show motorists the obstacles after dark fell. As rainy afternoons faded into dusk, the ozone aroma of damp gravel blended with the oily smell of the smudge pots. These roads were dusty, too—they just didn't go anywhere. So when we discovered the High Line Canal, with its dirt service road stretching away for miles and miles in either direction, the borders of possibility fell away.

On this sunny Tuesday in July, almost a year later, we trekked to the canal for perhaps the fiftieth time. We had followed our usual route along the Sand Creek Lateral, the broad side ditch that ran off to the north. Its headgates were closed, so the lateral was dry, but it was lush with growth from the slosh of its full flow against the banks. The morning that had begun so cool and moist was already growing torrid. When we felt the shady breath of the ditch we sucked it up like the air in the chocolate aisle of Hested's dime store. Turning into it, we walked west along the canal service road, past old farmhouses with rickety barns and bridges and rusting farm implements. No Trespassing signs, posted by landowners and the Water Department, drew us on.

The heat of the day began to build in earnest. Ragweed flagged in the wilting rays, and magpies took to the thickets. We shuffled more slowly, plucking succulent shoots of pigweed and rubbing them until our fingers were green. Our engineer boots were hot and covered with dust. Cumulonimbus climbed the eastern sky. "Think this is far enough?" I asked after a long, treeless stretch.

"I haven't seen the ditchrider," Tom said. "He'd kick us out if he came along, but if we're lucky, he won't." We couldn't see any houses from here, either.

We longed to get off the griddle of the road. Dropping into the shade of a spreading willow, we stripped down to the swimsuits we wore underneath our jeans and slithered into the current. Some fifty miles from its mountain source in the Platte River Canyon, the water was still cool, almost cold.

Denizens of the Great American Desert, we were drawn to water wherever it was to be found. We gravitated to plastic wading pools. We sought out lawn sprinklers, broken hydrants, and warm rainwater running ankle-deep in the concrete gutters of the streets. But the slippery brown flow of the canal was best.

Parents worried about drownings, and rightly so—from time to time some kid would indeed drown somewhere along the canal. They worried about broken glass, and now and then we did bring home a bloody toe. And they warned us of the dangers of polio, supposedly transmitted in dirty water. But that seemed like double jeopardy to us: if we had to have those unpleasant polio shots at school, why should we have to skip the ditch as well? Generations of farm kids had used the High Line as their swimming hole, and we did the same.

We hadn't been in the water long before the cottonwood tops began to rustle, announcing the arrival of a summer squall. The morning's easy breeze came up in a wind that sucked the heat out of the day as clouds crowded the blue. Soon raindrops speckled the surface of the ditchwater. Tom and I half hoped for a cool afternoon thunderstorm, but this one was coming a little early. Usually we made it home first, or met the rain on the way.

Lightning scratched the western sky. We were leery of lightning, both in the open and beneath the cottonwoods. A kid we knew claimed he knew someone whose cousin's friend had been struck while caddying. Everyone knew you weren't supposed to get under a tree, which could act as a lightning rod. And Dad had told us that rainwater could carry the jolt along the earth or into a stream, through what he called ground flash. It seemed nowhere was safe.

Willow leaves blew off the tree as we scrambled wet into our boots and jeans. No longer hot, we were getting damn cold as the ditchwater evaporated off our skin in the wind. By the time we reached the Sand Creek Lateral, cottonwood leaves clattered like rattlesnakes and their boughs creaked close to breaking in the rising gale. This was no ordinary afternoon shower. Then the first hail came.

At first it just stung. Hail wasn't uncommon with our summer thunderstorms. Normally pea-size, it could smart, but it wasn't a big deal. We knew from school that hail occurred when hot air near the ground rose rapidly in powerful updrafts, carrying ice crystals into supercooled vapor in the heights of the towering clouds. Layers of ice formed around the nucleus, making a hailstone that eventually fell to earth. GrandPop had told us of hailstorms that ruined crops on family places farther east, but the most we'd ever seen hail do was break off a few flowers. We were still more worried about the lightning. Thunder growled and lightning rent the dark fabric of the cloud bank.

But the thunderclaps and lightning strikes were far apart—we counted "One thousand one, one thousand two, one thousand three"—while the hail was here and now. The stones had grown to the size of marbles and were pounding down like a giant bag of aggies emptied overhead. The hail didn't pass quickly by as it usually did, and it was beginning to hurt. Confused by the rough touch of weather I'd never known before, I fell behind.

"Come on, Bobby! We're almost there."

I could barely hear Tom over the thunder, the wind's wail, and the hail thudding all around us. Hailstones bouncing up met those coming down, creating a percussive curtain that kept us from seeing our feet. But I could see Tom's face, which had gone terribly pale. The wind whipped his cotton shirt, exposing his tanned back already red with welts. Tumbling on the slippery sediment of hailstones, I tried to catch up.

Iceballs pounded down, bruising our elbows, knuckles, knees, and heads. They were bigger than any hail we'd ever seen, bigger than our marbles, and getting bigger. "Tommeee," I wailed as a stone the size of a shooter struck me on the collarbone. I squatted beside a locust tree, uselessly: a shattered magpie nest fell from its branches and disintegrated around me, its sticks mixing with the white rubble. Mesmerized by white and out of breath from crying, I felt the blows on my back and watched pellucid eggs of ice roll down toward the ditch.

Tom came back and hauled me to my feet. He said nothing, just clamped his mouth shut with his lips sucked in. I knew that look from Grammy's face when she battled weeds, a turkey on a platter, or shiftless grandsons, and I knew it meant business. I stopped crying and let myself be pulled. Dragging me behind him, Tom dove into the ditchbed of the Sand Creek Lateral. Had the headgate been open to the lateral we would have been stuck in the open field. We sought shelter behind a concrete check dam, but it gave no lee. The smells of chopped weeds and rotting leaves filled my nostrils, the pungency of pulverized earth mixed with the wild ozone.

Walnut-size hailstones smashed against the dam and ricocheted into our faces. Between sobs I saw that Tom was red all over. His brown hair was plastered over his eyes; he still had his glasses, but he was crying, too.

We tried to run again. Dad sometimes brought ball bearings home for us to play with and now it felt as if we were running on them. I slipped over and over and fell into the mud. Struggling up, I huddled against Tom, hanging on his arm. A great hailstone struck his forehead. He staggered and fell.

When he looked up again, without his glasses, Tom squinted toward a gray-green shape looming in the dull light. "There it is," he cried, but I could barely hear him over the din of the storm. Tom scrambled up the ditchbank and called for me to follow. But the bare slope had turned to mud, and I kept sliding down. The ice bullets drilled the air and drove me back. My boots slipped, my stinging fingers found nothing to grip. I landed in a bed of hail and mud and whimpered, "I can't do it. We're gonna die."

Tom's hand, wet and cold, grabbed mine and yanked me up the bank. "No, we're not," he hollered. "Come on, the hollow tree is right up here. See?"

I did see it. I stumbled to the old hollow cottonwood and clutched at its furrowed brown bark, the smooth white edge of its heartwood cleft, glassy wet. Its tattered leaves slapped our faces. We crawled inside the punky charred hollow, and I dropped to my knees, whining and gasping. Tom coughed, choking on ice and dust. He pulled me up, packed me deep into the blackened hold, and fell across me, covering me as best he could. He tried to block the gape with his body, using his battered back like the operculum of a snail. But he was too skinny, and the wind got past him. The storm shifted to the north, blew directly at the hollow, and pummeled us afresh.

Then Tom went heavy and loose against me, and I saw that his forehead was bright blue. I thought he might be dead, after all. A friend of mine, Patrick Ramsey, had died of bone cancer, and in his coffin he had looked this pale and still. That was the first death I'd ever known, and it left me feeling hollow, scared, and guilty: he was my friend, and I was supposed to deliver his *Weekly Reader*. But near the end, I'd stayed away.

Unable to move under Tom's limp body, I hoped he was only knocked out. We'd often played at knocking each other out with the butts of our cap guns, as our cowboy heroes did in the comics and movies. But here he was out for real and not coming to right away, as the cowboys did. The ice continued to pound the tree and shatter like shrapnel. Broken stones collected at our feet in a cold white crust, like strange snow in midsummer. I felt alone and very cold. Tom moved, then moaned.

Gray rainwater ran down the ditch in a torrent studded by floating hailstones like so many clouded fisheyes. The cornstalks we'd often squatted among, gnawing on stolen ears, lay threshed by the hail. Tom could see little of this without his glasses. Then lightning struck close by, and I was blinded, too. Through the flash behind my eyes I could hear the thunder banging nearer. I no longer worried about lightning. Though I knew this hollow tree had been struck in the past, nothing could get me out of there. My sight returned, but there was only gray. Over the thunder I heard the hail's tattoo on the cottonwood drum, and beneath that my own small voice, pleading for it to end.

Then, after a last punishing volley slipped past Tom's shield to strike me over the kidneys, where a slap hurts most, it did end. The hail faded into the summer storm that spawned it. Wind dropped; the nimbus died. Soft rain began to fall, the kind we'd expected when the clouds sneaked up on that sultry afternoon. Final thunder thrummed across the eastern plain. The storm passed.

We clung to each other, reluctant to leave the hollow tree in case the hail came back. Slowly, along with the air outside, we were becalmed. Realizing where I was, I felt my old dread of spiders almost as relief. Normally they scared me half to death in such places. Here, scared much closer to death, I'd forgotten the spiders as I embraced the walls of our blessed den. The damp, off-sweet smell of the burned and rotting wood filled my nostrils and left a permanent brand of scent.

After a few more minutes it seemed safe to go. We uncoiled our stiff limbs and scrambled out of the hollow tree, through the skerried waves of toe-chilling nuggets, over to Sixth Avenue. There were no cars in sight. Hail covered the fields, the road, everything, in drifts and sheets, like a winterscape. For a moment it was easy to believe that everyone else was dead and we were the only survivors.

A farmer, out surveying his devastated fields, found us and took us to his home. We recognized the place as the last farm in the neighborhood, kitty-corner from the bulldozed mire of the future shopping center. Tom and I had often slipped across Sixth Avenue to play in DeLaney's barn, keeping an eye out for the farmer, who was sure to chase us off. But today Farmer DeLaney led us into his house, where his wife gave us cocoa and blankets, looked to our knots and welts, and called our mother. I heard her voice, delirious with relief.

Mother came for us right away in our old Packard. When she arrived, her fine black hair was disheveled, her gray eyes red with crying, but she looked steady and amazed. She thanked the farm couple as she knelt to hold her sons. When she stood again, Mother looked from Tom to me and back again as she stroked our bruised foreheads lightly and made soft sounds. Her full lips maintained their will as she said, "There's been so much damage . . ." Her already high cheeks rose in a smile that became a muffled sob. She cried and embraced us both for a long time. When she opened her purse to find her hanky, the familiar smell of leather, lipstick, and Pall Malls erased the fierce freshness of the hailstorm's breath.

Mother and the farmer talked about the storm as we finished our cocoa and she dried her eyes. Then we were home, beneath our ruined red roof. I found myself still dazed, safe in a warm bath to ward off bruises and chilblains. Tom went to Dr. Rowan's office, concussed. There, and ever after, Tom described the experience with pithy concision: "It started hailing," he said. "Then, *bam bam bam* on the ol' head."

When I climbed out of my bath and into my bed, I asked for Blackie, our kitten. "He doesn't seem to be around," Mother said. I suspected, but it was long before I learned for sure, that he'd been battered to death by the hail. Searching frantically, Susan had found him lying in a puddle behind the ash-pit.

Blackie wasn't the only casualty of the great Hoffman Heights hailstorm. Cows had their backs broken by hailstones the size of grapefruits. Damage to homes and businesses ran to several hundred thousand dollars. At the peak of the maelstrom, the driving rain and hail had short-circuited the fire department's siren. According to the *Denver Post*, "The siren wailed for five minutes while housewives cowered behind furniture to escape flying glass from broken windows." Grammy and I looked up "hail" in her *Encyclopaedia Britannica* and learned that we lived in "Hail Alley," where "on the New York–Denver airway one thunderstorm in 800 produces hail as large as walnuts and one in 5,000 as large as baseballs." It didn't mention softballs. A friend later sent a clipping that did, from up the alley in Woonsocket, South Dakota, where hail "like baseballs and softballs" shredded all the roofs. So we were not the sole victims of such a freak. But to us, ours seemed the only storm in the world.

The young gardens of the new town, so recently carved from the bare prairie, were largely destroyed. My mother agonized over hers, which she had lovingly coaxed from farmed-out soil—her slaughtered chard, her maimed zinnias. The *Denver Post* asked her what it was like: "'It was like a swarm of grasshoppers passing through,' said Mrs. Pyle, surveying her battered yard. 'But there won't be any more getting up at five A.M. to water.'"

If Mother was able to laugh about her garden, she never could about us. During the height of the storm, her heart was in her throat and her mind ran to the High Line Canal. There, she knew, her sons were playing when the squall arose. Afterward, when we went back to look for Tom's glasses, the most we could find was a small fragment of hammered gray plastic. When she saw that, she choked an "Oh!" and praised the hollow tree instead of yelling at us for being out there. A spanking, in any case, would have been redundant.

All the ruined roofs were eventually repaired, the gardens replanted. Order restored itself to the fresh settlement on the edge of the High Plains, its neat rows broken only by occasional great relics of cottonwoods left behind from Cottonwood Farm in the backyards of a few lucky families. We had no big trees in our yard, just the stripling Chinese elms my mother had stuck in the ground. But Tom and I shared in the luck of the cottonwoods just the same, for that old hollow poplar, which we came to call the Thunder Tree, surely saved our lives.

The Thunder Tree itself was the survivor of countless prairie tempests. Had it not been there, had Tom not known about it and found it for us through the screen of hail, the papers might have recorded two boys lost to the big hailstorm of July 27, 1954—just a week after the younger lad's seventh birthday.

For a long time I believed that a farm boy had been killed in the field next to us, battered to death by the hail as he tried to take shelter beneath his tractor. But studying the newspapers years later, I can find no mention of any fatality. They rightly report our adventure and that of my schoolmates Dennis Christie and Rich Bolenbaker getting caught in the hail close to home. They ended up with scars on their shoulders, but definitely alive.

Did someone make up the story of the dead farm kid to scare or impress us? Or was there such a boy—perhaps the son or nephew of our rescuer— who, like us, was caught out and hurt, but survived, and we, to make a better story, later killed him off in the telling? Who knows. Sometimes I wonder whether Tom and I between us didn't spawn the whole story of the boy and canonize it as part of our large body of canal apocrypha, just to remind ourselves how close we'd come.

I remember the small clipping taped to our kitchen cupboard for years, and what it actually did say. It's long gone, but I found the article in the library's microfilms of the *Denver Post*:

"Tommy Pyle, 11, and his brother, Bobby, 7 . . . suffered dollar-sized bruises on their backs, heads, and shoulders before finding refuge in a hollow tree."

The story goes on to tell of Blackie the kitten's fate, but that part had been censored from the cupboard-door version so we wouldn't be reminded of our pet's ordeal every time we reached for the Cheerios.

2

Watercourse

*This sleek, sinuous, full-bodied animal. . . . a babbling procession of the
best stories in the world, sent from the heart of the earth to be told at last
to the insatiable sea.*

—Kenneth Grahame, *The Wind in the Willows*

Tom braked his brown Schwinn with its handlebars turned up and said,
"Hey, Bobby, you wanna go flying?"

We often made believe about flying. I figured this was just another game
for "Bill" and "Joe," our adventurous alter egos. "Sure," I said. "What do we
use for an airplane this time?"

"Really," he said. "I can get us a ride in a real plane."

"Sure," I said again. "And how do you plan to do that?"

"Just bike out to the airport with me," he said. "You'll see."

Tom ranged widely all over the town. There was hardly a corner of
Aurora, Altura, or East Denver that he and big Billy Rose hadn't explored
on their bikes. I knew he'd often been out to both the little private Sky
Ranch and Denver's Stapleton Field to watch the planes. So when he
claimed to have found a pilot who would take us up, it was at least plausible.
Still, I was dubious when I set out with him early the following Saturday.

When we arrived at Coombs Aircraft and went inside the office, I
hung back while Tom asked questions. Then we went outside, and Tom
approached a man standing by a little blue Piper Tri-Pacer on the tarmac
and, as he put it, "did some blabbin'." He gestured impatiently for me to
come; soon we were inside the single-engine plane, seat belts fastened. The
pilot, a middle-aged man with a grin, radioed the squat tower and began
the takeoff.

I was shoved back in my seat as we sped down the runway, faster than
I'd ever gone. I tugged forward to see between Tom and the pilot, trying

to peer over the prop and out the side windows. We took off to the east, then banked right. The Aztec-deco monument of Fitzsimons Hospital came into view, its red-checked water tank and smokestack standing out against the green blanket of the watered grounds. Banking right over downtown Aurora, we could see the Denver skyline, such as it was in 1957. And beyond that the Rockies, unhazed by smog. Another right brought us in line with the main north–south runway of Stapleton, and we landed. We'd been in the air about five minutes. Tom, who'd also cadged flights out at the Sky Ranch, said that was plenty long, the cost of running aircraft being what it was.

I was wide-eyed the whole time and all the way home. I'd often imagined soaring with the magpies, and now I knew what they saw up there. What most caught my eye was the High Line Canal. From walking it often I knew it was loopy, but I never knew how much. Passing over Sixth Avenue at a thousand feet or so, I saw the ditch strung out from southwest to northeast. It looked like a ball of brown and green twine unraveled across the countryside by some cosmic cat.

In those days I lacked a notion of the nature of the canal. After seeing part of it from the air, I wanted to know all about it—where it started, where it ended, what it did in between. I watched the water flow in and out, and I reckoned it must come from somewhere and end up somewhere else, but I had no clear sense of what constituted a watercourse. The wheres were imponderable to a young animal of small home range.

Next bends always beckon, and the High Line Canal has many bends. In the years after that first aerial view, I walked many of them, but I was never satisfied at the end of a walk, for there was always more ditch beyond. As I grew and my territory expanded, the bounds of the watercourse seemed to shrink into the imaginable, to resemble a real stream, with a source and a mouth and a middle. It became important to me to find them, to know the whole extent of that sinuous shore.

Hiking in the rain at Mount Rainier some years ago, I met a man walking the opposite way along the Wonderland Trail, which circles the great mountain. He was elderly and limited in his abilities, but he was determined to hike the whole thing, bit by bit. One of my companions thought this a silly goal. "Why should it matter if he goes all the way around the mountain, just so he enjoys his hikes?" he asked. But I understood perfectly. For years I'd had the same objective for the High Line Canal.

Every year someone treks the length of the Pacific Crest Trail from Canada to Mexico, bicycles across North America on U.S. 6, or canoes the entire Mississippi River from headwater to bayou. It seems to be a common compulsion to travel the entirety of a way, once it captures the imagination. This was certainly the case with me and my ditch. The Wonderland Trail it was not: it was just an old dirt track. But for me, it was always, in novelist/poet David Wagoner's phrase, "the road to many a wonder." And I wanted to see them all, no matter how humble or subtle.

I doubted that anyone had ever walked the entire canal. Even the ditchmen rode as much as they walked. In later years there were those who claimed to have done so, but I was skeptical, for the ends and some of the middle bits are quite challenging, with pipes and flumes and tunnels. Not that I cared whether I would be the first. Firsts are ephemeral and hard to prove, and they have little attraction for me. Nor was it the feat that attracted me. What feat? To walk eighty or ninety almost-level miles? The great wilderness advocate Bob Marshall used to walk that far in a day, in steep terrain.

No, my desire to go the whole of the High Line had more to do with learning and seeing than meeting challenges. Hardly high adventure, my serial trek falls squarely into what Harvey Manning calls "low adventure" in his enchanting book *Walking the Beach to Bellingham*. Harvey watches ants and travels with spiders while nibbling kipper snacks and swigging Rainier Beer, as he wanders the shoreline that has bounded his life. This is the kind of adventure the High Line offered—to ply a set course in one's own time and style, start to finish.

My early explorations didn't get too far. The source was somewhere in the mountains, far too far across Denver to reach on my own. The mouth wasn't actually in Kansas, as kid myth had it, but it was still too distant to find on foot. When I got wheels—first a bike, then an aged Vespa, finally a succession of wizened autos—I ranged farther from home. Many failed searches for the terminus followed. One of these, with friends

Chuck Dudley and Tim Hartman, produced the memorable misnomer "four-legged hawk" for a common winter raptor when Tim misheard my pronunciation, but not the mouth of the ditch. Eventually, taking shortcuts, lopping off the loops, I found both ends. But working piecemeal, I failed to knit the bits into a pattern of the whole.

Inevitably, I decided to attempt a hike of the full length. During the summer of 1973, between college stints on the West and East coasts, I set out with a heavy pack containing clothes, camping gear, field equipment, notebooks, maps, fruit, a big bag of roasted soybeans, vitamins, and water. I carried a staff-cum-butterfly net, appropriated from my younger brother, Bud, who had fashioned it from a High Line cottonwood branch.

I set out as close to the mouth as I could get in Waterton Canyon, southwest of Denver. The first night I camped above the Platte River with my Water Board letter of safe passage next to me in my sleeping bag. The next day I walked the wildest, most beautiful stretch of the canal, through the olive foothills and Neapolitan hogbacks, over Willow Creek, across the Douglas County uplands, all the way to the dramatic crossing of Plum Creek. Here I was obliged to go around, since the former redwood flume had been replaced by a siphon beneath the quick-sandy creek. I took a ditch swim in the hot early evening, skimming miles worth of sweat from my dusty skin. On the banks, creamy white clematis draped bleached cottonwood logs, like lace over old bones. I decided to camp here. It was a lovely spot.

But the mosquitoes were coming on strong. It was still eighty-five degrees at six o'clock. This wasn't like the backpacking I'd become accustomed to in the Cascades and the Sierra Nevada. The way was flat, but it was a skillet on high. I'd consumed all my potable water, my pack was too heavy, and I was already getting tired of soybeans. Besides, I was beginning to get concerned about where I might camp in the more populated stretches of the canal. Mostly, I was thirsty.

Reluctantly I shouldered my pack, hiked to a log cabin tavern on the Sedalia road, and ordered icewater and a beer. My friend Chuck Dudley came to join me for another beer or two, and when he left for town, I went with him. That concluded my great canal trek. I went back to walking it bit by bit, which I still do. I have yet to fill in the last blank spots in my ditch picture.

By now, though, the pattern of the place has come clearer. From any bridge, I can look upstream and down and receive a sense of where I am, where the ditch has been, and where it's going next. Sometimes I throw a cottonwood twig into the flow, Pooh-stick style, and imagine the check dams it will drop over, the flumes it will shoot, before falling on mud where it might take root. Or I will drop a single leaf into the middle and try to follow it as far as I can before it disappears around a bend or an eddy sucks it into the long bank grass. When I do these things I feel I am working on an integrated field theory of ditches.

A ditch differs from a river chiefly in the fact that it has been dug by humans. But since many rivers have been channelized, this distinction blurs. In the end, canals and rivers are both watercourses. So what is a watercourse? Some would include the entire path of a given water drop, from cloud to cloud through the hydrological cycle. Others might insist it means no more than a gutter, inlet to outlet, dam to dam. What to one person is a poem and a living thing is to another a mere tube for transporting water and whatever effluent it can carry. The latter attitude found its form in the thousands of streams that were sunk into underground storm drains as our cities grew, the former in the present practice (and delightful term) of "daylighting" such streams. In barest terms, a watercourse is defined by the discrete point of the beginning of flow, the clear confluence with another body, and the nature of the basin that it drains in between. The moisture it carries gives a stream its character, but it is the movement of water over territory that makes it a place.

Suppose a creature with eyes, say a toad, were to raft the full distance of the High Line. What would it see that would set this linear place apart from all others? This could happen. The headwaters of the South Platte River arise in the Mosquito Range of the Colorado Rockies, one of four big-river beginnings that spring from these high peaks, each draining a different corner of the state. In the upland bogs and snowfields where the trickles pour forth lives the western toad, *Bufo boreas*. It would be possible for a shag of sphagnum tugged loose by the fast spring current to harbor a toadlet coming forth from its winter hibernation. True, it would meet a strong challenge in surviving the spillways of the three dams that give pause to the Platte as it cuts across the Front Range. But suspend disbelief for the passage of the reservoirs, and your toad finds itself floating the spectacular Waterton Canyon toward the low country. Like Grahame's Toad of Toad Hall, it's in for quite a ride.

The golden eye of the toad opens on a small diversion dam near the mouth of the gorge. The river rolls over the low wood and stone structure, then shrugs aside to dodge around the last crystalline ridge before plunging onto the plains for the much easier ride home. Across the small forebay gapes a failed railroad tunnel that in 1880 became the takeout for the High Line Canal. Early summer flow at its peak, the big wooden headgates have just been wheeled open, sucking a portion of the river, and the toad, under the round arch of the tunnel.

The toad is not alone. Townsend's solitaires hawk insects around the tunnel mouth, flashing their salmon wing patches against the salmon-colored quartzite of the rock face. Cliff and barn swallows dash in to their pots and cups of nests that line the tunnel for a hundred feet into the hole, and out again. Just within the inner lip, a dipper's moss-ball nest occupies a chink between the stone and concrete of the arch. Bats sleep overhead. Then, dark. The walls glow from a mat of spiderwebs catching the light at the end of the six-hundred-foot bore. Then the raft, bigger now, having caught needles and twigs in its hems, bursts out into that light through a locomotive-size gape—rough here, with no arch.

The first half-mile of the seventy-one to come runs through a concrete flume, from the tunnel down to the canyon mouth. Ragged orange hoodoos and twisted blue junipers guard the ridge above, gray rabbitbrush and scrub oak daub the steep hillsides. Pebble-furred, big-tailed rock squirrels navigate the fissures and watch from pink promontories, causing pink-pebble slides that splash into the cool, fast flow. Canyon wrens warble from the walls and a bighorn ram stands rampant on the rampart above the craggy rocks. The toad is oblivious to these, though they are among the last of its montane neighbors to be seen on a voyage soon to strike the flatlands. The ponderosa pine and Douglas fir have been left behind. The flume, a hundred times longer than its twenty-eight-foot width, passes instead through a shelterbelt of willows, chokecherries, box elders, and sumac. A kingfisher bolts into the flow to snatch a fish from the toad's elevation. Both Steller's and eastern blue jays haunt and screech in the scrub, giving away the canal's role as an east–west biological corridor to the human observer but only startling the small toad.

The flume ends as the canyon walls drop away. The Rocky Mountains are over, their load lying in the floor of the dug ditch: a few yards of cobbles, then pebbles, gravel, and sand, sorted by the current. Sand and silt will underlie the journey for the rest of the way, seldom bedrock. But the ditch has not quite left the hills behind. All along the Front Range, creeks drop out of the mountains through their canyons, dissecting the foothills into a thousand brushy creases such as this. The South Platte River, rushing alongside some twenty feet downslope, cut this outlet. The broad blue canal follows along, looking for this mile just like an actual stream.

Then the creeks and rivers and ditches must cross the hogbacks. These dipped strata of Mesozoic shales and sand-stones put up pointy barricades all along the front, as if the first defense against the advancing plains. Where they are the reddest and tallest and most baroquely eroded, they make fabulous formations such as Roxborough Park, just south of the High Line's crossing. Here my great-uncle Amos Whetstone built a brick plant whose maroon kiln still stands; my grandmother and great-aunt played among the red rocks with sons of the local ranchers. Elsewhere the beds run to white, are high in silicates, and bear dinosaur tracks. The canal punches through the hogback at Waterton with little ado, the ridge long ago crashed by the Platte and whittled by a silica-clay company whose white bricks contrasted with the Roxborough reds. Still, our toad should take a look, as this is the last mountain to be seen up close from its moss-green boat.

Now the canal parts company from the river that spawned it. The Platte hugs the hogback for a way, feeding a succession of reservoirs, before diving into Denver's industrial deeps. Winding north and east, the canal broadly parallels the Platte; then, clinging to the high line of the land, the ditch begins to diverge. It rounds Kassler, a green-roofed, white-clapboard water company village where the first slow-sand filtration system in the West was built in 1900, feeding water to Denver by gravity. Here, emerging from the hills, the canal runs some forty feet wide and eight deep. Its shores grow rich with mountain mahogany, whose last year's seeds are curly feathers. Reddish sandstone outcrops bracket its banks backed by rocky montane vistas, rippling green fields, and the cottonwoods and box elders of the river bottoms.

Toad swoops past the gauging station and little Platte Canyon Reservoir, from which the canal's flow can be adjusted up or down. The raft spins through an intricate sand trap looking like the J-shaped scoring runnels in a penny arcade ball-throw game. In honor of its designer, longtime waterman George Swan, this structure is known in house as the Swan Trap, the reservoir as Swan Lake. But there are no swans here, just kestrels and kingbirds. Then a long, gentle swoop and a loop across the oasis of a farm on Willow Creek, which enters the ditch. This stretch is drawn in the generous greens of grass, trees, meadow, and wild carrot, where black swallowtails hover to lay their round yellow eggs.

Now the route swings around a peninsula jutting into the belly of another reservoir, called Chatfield. Here, in the sometime-flooded bottomlands, a cougar appeared not long ago. Dams can create as well as consume habitat. Another thing they do is prevent the old joinery of streams at their accustomed meeting places. A sluggish impoundment, Chatfield swallows half a dozen streams that would otherwise find their confluences with the Platte in this valley. One of these, Plum Creek, stirred up by a tornado, caused the great flood of 1965. For that it was amputated above the mouth, a harsh fate for any watercourse.

Sweet clover, fluffy foxtail grass, and veronica (like chips of blue Delft) grow against the algal backwater, beneath a jungle of chokecherry, wild plum, and willow. Meadowlarks and lazuli buntings color the floodplain, flying up at a killdeer's alarm call. It might as well have been issued for the toad, about to undergo a dangerous passage. What once would have been a scenic ride across Plum Creek in a long redwood flume now amounts to a deep and rapid plunge beneath the bed, through a gravity siphon. The flume went out with the flood. The toad clings to its moss mat as it is sucked through the bars of the debris dam, steeply down beneath the sandy channel, through the swooshing jet of water, to be shot back up on the other side. It had a good hold, and held its breath well, as amphibians do. The voyage continues.

The illusion of wildness departs as the ditch curves north to parallel two railroads, the Denver and Rio Grande Western and the Atchison, Topeka, and Santa Fe. The toad plies a busy Platte Valley in company with the river, the canal, freight trains, and a highway. If the ditch seems the least part of the system now, a hamlet-turned-container-facility remembers history well enough: its name is Acequia, Spanish for "irrigation ditch." John Nichols's *Milagro Beanfield War* was fought over the acequias in New Mexico. Once this ditch, too, was important.

Changing human use dominates the next miles. Power pylons overhead clash with the wooden stubs of an old bridge built into a massive cottonwood root and a venerable wooden barn with tractor-trailers on either side. A graveyard for old graders lines up along the Rio Grande tracks, across the ditch from a ChemLawn depot overshadowing a dozen plucky beehives. The toad abides.

Green returns as the route encounters a series of gulches running down off Cherokee Mountain and Wildcat Point, ranchette territory on the plateau to the southeast that has seen neither Cherokee nor wildcats for quite a while. An old concrete plug, orange-lichened, like the base of a Mayan temple ruin, tries to block the water diverted by the railroad. But this flowage is named Spring Gulch for a reason: it lies on a spring line. Green algae and lush shrubs suggest the plug's failure. The marsh below is alive with fox, raccoon, and beaver, orioles and flycatchers, green darner dragonflies and yellow swallowtails. Assassin bugs wait in the lupines and big silver-spotted skippers roller-coaster court all over the marsh. A frog calls, then a toad croaks softly; ours, jumping ship, might feel at home here. But it's too late; the current carries it along as fast as old Mr. Toad's motorcar.

Northeasterly, past Plum Creek School and the old crossroads settlement of Blakeland, the canal runs across the tracks from City Ditch. This even older canal was Denver's first water supply. It flows north along the Platte all the way into town. The High Line jogs east in a broad loop around green Marcy Gulch, which it crosses by a surviving flume. The toad might notice the difference in the sound of the slosh as the water passes from earthen banks into steel aqueduct. After Marcy, the High Line passes the last real ranch with a right to its water before striking into the suburbs. The toad might as easily be swept through the headgate here, or the next one into McClellan Reservoir, which impounds Dad Clark Gulch and tops up from the ditch.

Slipping around the reservoir the canal gathers a pair of small streams. Their valleys in June wear a shade of verdure that the toad might recognize from its alpine home. But this once-peaceful stretch has undergone great change: E-470, Greater Denver's turnpike ring road, now lines the shore below the canal. The streams and gulches in its culverts drain the uplands where the major High Line irrigator once resided. Highlands Ranch is an upmarket subdivision instead of the real and working ranch it once was.

Once the toad flumes over Dad Clark and burrows beneath the freeway, it leaves Douglas County and enters Arapahoe and the outer walls of the city. Not that the rural idyll ends here, but settlement definitely grows more dense within the ring road. South Suburban Parks takes over care of the canal path from State Parks, as evidenced by fancy signs and footbridges. This stretch passes through Littleton and unincorporated county land prior to affluent Greenwood and Cherry Hills villages. Senescent farms and neopastoral estates blend with industrial parks and office blocks as countryside holds on by its nails. Cottonwoods line the curves. Their leaves, loosed by a thunderstorm, alight upright, stems stuck in the dried mud of the path. A dog barks, a gray cat basks in a dry lateral ditchbed; a white cat and a white collie seem to ignore the wild asparagus, poison ivy, goldenrod, and sand plum clothing the ditchbank while guarding some weekend squire's pumpkins. A cool cloud makes a breeze.

The toad, by now an old hand, tightens its grip on the raft, lately enlarged by a few cottonwood leaves, and shoots the long wooden flume over Lee Gulch. Cornflower spatters the meadow blue below the flume; copses of currant, snowberry, and plum fill the valley. A mountain biker says, "Now *this* is the High Line Canal!" Beyond the gulch, very large houses with chicken houses out back close in. A patch of alfalfa in a vacant lot quivers with nectaring butterflies. Then comes busy South Broadway. A racket of grackles batters the air, contesting Broadway's roar.

The culvert brings toad out beside a gargantuan cottonwood with a city of fox squirrels in its branches. The dogleg that follows encloses not the flowery, spring-fed meadow I once knew but a dense development of apartments already aging. The signs of kids using the canal for pleasure have evolved from ladders and ropes into graffiti sprayed on the broken doors of garages facing the ditch: "Motley Crue," "Twisted Sister," "I love big tits." Oblivious, an ambush bug catches a checkered white on an aster by one leg, and a big blue hunting wasp tugs a sphinx-moth caterpillar into a hole between an anthill and its negative image, an ant-lion crater. There is still quite a show off Broadway, but the toad, like the kids, can't see it.

The path saunters through established neighborhoods with schools, shopping centers, radio towers—modest communities with little rural pretense, yet once known as Pickletown for all the truck farms they supported. One of the pioneer families donated the next big oxbow loop of land to the town in hopes that it would remain natural. The DeKoevends got their name attached to the resulting park, but not their wish: South Suburban Parks has developed it almost completely, replacing prairie grass and rabbitbrush with bluegrass and playing fields.

Denver Post columnist Joanne Ditmer, longtime champion of the canal, argued for one wild green space here at Big Dry Creek, along what she affectionately dubbed "the old wriggly snake." "When much of the surrounding land looked just like it, the natural state of the park was not essentially unique," wrote Ms. Ditmer, "though blessed topographically with streams and hillocks. But soon there will be housing or buildings on all sides."

Over the bank, the toad glimpses the angular roof lines of an ice arena, tennis court fences and lights, a big recreation center, maintenance sheds, and a church. They are foreign, and it shifts its gaze back between the green banks and hangs on tighter.

No flume this time, nor a siphon. Big Dry Creek, unlike the canal, is seldom dry. When they both run, they share a common stretch, then diverge again. All the lawn watering in the area keeps the water table artificially high, and the creeks run dry less often than before. Overflow can be shunted from creek to canal, or vice versa, to regulate the overall flow.

Had the toad's craft slipped between the bars of the floodgate, it would have ridden Big Dry Creek some four miles to its confluence with the Platte and to its probable demise in the river's industrial core.

Two more loops and the channel meets Little Dry Creek, whose crossing is just as dangerous. Instead of a flume or a shared stream, it consists of a deep gravity siphon, or conduit. The flow plunges underground, as at Plum Creek, and up again through a grated gate across the canyon. Toad too emerges, disoriented but unharmed, bobbing in the muddy current beside the nerve center for the entire canal.

Now, if it wished, our batrachian could hop out for a visit with the men who run the whole show. Their headquarters sits beside the canal at Orchard Road, a cluster of modest brown buildings blending easily into the canal scene. The ditchrider's house, one of six along the High Line, is doubtless the most unassuming dwelling for miles, but it has more flowers than any of the nearby mansions. The High Line Canal Field Office is situated in the heart of Greenwood Village, an exclusive domain of the leisured. The new development by Little Dry Creek is signposted The Village on the Meadow—one more village, one less meadow. It is a land of paddocks and horse barns arrayed around landscaped ponds and bridges. One of the watermen's chief challenges in this stretch concerns the moneyed horse folk who consider the ditch their own and resist all vegetation removal. South Suburban, meanwhile, moderates the war between the riders, who like the dirt path, and the cyclers, who prefer it paved. Neither clientele seems to realize that the main business of the ditch is still the conveyance of water. The canal flows by its HQ, like the toad it carries, entirely unbiased in the matter.

Styles in Greenwood vary from Spanish stucco and Cotswold cottage to pseudo-Moorish and Northwest redwood. Elegance and taste butt up against embarrassments like Astroturf and Pepsi machines by the pool. The common element is a species of green not found on trees. Yet bits of bucolic countryside survive in pumpkin fields and pastures. Among them, the estates of the privileged probably preserve more habitat than all the parks, even if, as the canal's managers confide, their owners are the most likely to be rude to them and to block headgates with grass clippings. Several pairs of Canada geese with clutches of goslings swim the canal, graze the bank. A heron eyes the toad, but remembers from a previous attempt what such a morsel tastes like and turns away again. On the bank, clearwing hummingbird moths drink at purple vetch.

The little raft spins beneath a graceful footbridge into Cherry Hills Village, the model of gentrified rusticity. For five miles, all the way to the Denver frontier, it serpentines through a particularly pretty reach, embracing within its curves an expansive prep school campus and the compounds of the old and new well-to-do: some mature and graceful, others just profanely huge. Extensive spinneys are watered by spring, creek, canal, pond, and Blackmer Lake. In spring, apple and crabapple trees paint the banks with white and pink petals, and wild plum blossoms cloud the bottoms, promising their small sweet fruit in the fall. Beyond East Hampden Avenue the flowage carves Wellshire Golf Course, whose mock-Tudor clubhouse and green setting might almost be taken for the real thing deep in Wiltshire. Golf balls plunk into the ditch, disturbing the cottonwood fluff that furs the surface, but missing the rafting toad.

Now eastering, the route borders Mamie Doud Eisenhower Park and enters its namesake's erstwhile neighborhood. The country villas give way to ordinary neighborhoods between quiet banks. Then comes the long, noisy culvert beneath the Valley Highway (I-25), Denver's first freeway. If the ring road was the outer rampart, this is the inner wall, as the canal enters Denver proper. Briefly it runs alongside the interstate, about as fast as the traffic that makes the toad burrow into the soggy sphagnum as deep as it can get.

Passing through Holly Hills, more loops, more parks, another gulch. The nature of the terrain requires the High Line to follow a snaky course parallel to the mile-high contour of the land. Only slowly does it drop, and the course it follows is anything but direct. After the deep bite of Goldsmith Gulch comes the biggest loop of all, through the broad, sandy valley of Cherry Creek.

The major tributary of the Platte draining the plateau southeast of Denver, Cherry Creek used to flood regularly. The urban portion was long ago channelized, becoming an emerald necklace for Mayor Robert W. Speer's 1930s scheme to beautify the "Queen City of the Plains."

Castlewood Dam, built in 1890, burst in August 1933, scouring the channel through the city and taking out many bridges, buildings, and businesses. The second try at containing Cherry Creek, the seven-mile earthen dam for Cherry Creek Reservoir completed in 1950, allowed Denver to rest easier with the sometimes surging stream.

The canal used to cross Cherry Creek's sandy bottoms in a high wooden flume, but one of the floods took it out for good. A pair of great redwood-stave pipes, left over from a competing canal that never held water, already lay beneath the creek bed. Water managers appropriated these for the High Line, later lining the leaky wood with concrete. According to ditchrider George Swan, that was "a hell of a job." Now it promises a hell of a trip for toad.

For a while the soggy raft enrolls in the bright swirling flotsam behind the intake grate. Styrofoam, leaves, green tennis balls, and red apples rotate like molecular models of heavy water; softballs, beer cans, pop bottles, spray cans, broken wood, plastic, and more Styrofoam cups all rotate in a matrix of branches and twigs. A prairie dog sentry barks like a shrill metronome in the prickly-pear grassland beside the path, catching the toad's attention before it finds itself tugged below for another long, tubular passage.

Overhead, blue willows clutch plastic debris, today's river wrack. Pink gravel and brown roots bind the hard mud beside a purple swatch of blooming cleome: the offerings of the arid land given the benediction of water. The canal and the creek give theme to this latter-day realm of golf course, condominium, and office park, called, respectively, Los Verdes, Wild Stream, and The Greens.

Two men in business suits emerge from The Greens to take a break among the green, forgetting to leave their minds behind: "Less money?" "Yeah." "Well, with us if they say that, we just say, 'No deal.'" The golfers across the canal seem more relaxed, old guys chipping onto a green, young guys bantering with women. Trimmed fairway runs into the rough of thatched bank grass and milkweed, as the canal runs pretty past "Luxury French Townhouses from the 170's" and the overgrazed but open remnants of a farm with horses still in residence. An Oz-like scarecrow graces a backyard, and a rope hangs limp from a cottonwood branch. All of this escapes the notice of the drowsy toad, lulled off by the longest straight stretch on the entire course.

Northward, the canal wends between Parker Road and Cherry Creek as walkers, riders, cyclists, joggers of all ages and ethnicities go by in denim and colorful skimpsuits, denizens of the many apartments nearby. Past the last one, the canal enters the green precincts of the historic Fairmount Cemetery. A curtain of blue spruce separates the quick and the dead, the lively runners from Denver's departed. Beyond shimmers Windsor Lake, where my father sneaked swims back in Mayor Speer's day. The lake that irrigated sumptuous Windsor Farms now waters the Windsor Gardens golf course and the gravesites of Denver pioneers, Masons, and war dead. Golf balls and bones are the new produce.

Past Windsor, a last old farm survives on pumpkins, petunias, and firewood. Then comes Havana Street and the grid of mile roads I grew up among. But what the toad beholds is a changed landscape signposted Chrysler, Toyota, Volvo, Jeep; U-Haul, Midas, Suzuki, Avis; Bonanza, Red Lobster, Dunkin' Donuts; and all the rest. Information overload: the toad turns aside to face the soft mud.

The U-shaped ditchbed wears a flowing green fringe of grass, wreathing Aurora for the next several miles. Despite the massive alterations brought by human population growth, life goes on in odd curves and corners left behind. Little of it is life the toad would know from its mountain fastness. Here live the plants and animals of the prairie edge. A gnarled willow draped in wild clematis hosts a pair of nesting kestrels in a cavity, magpies in its tangled crown. Red-shafted flickers hammer hollows into the cottonwoods that bind the banks wherever they are allowed to stand. Bluet damselflies occupy weed-stalk perches, as monarchs and mourning cloaks engage in the latter's willow-branch territory. Both beavers and muskrats ply the waters, and the toad's raft ripples over a submerged beaver dam built right across the ditch.

Barbecue smells mingle with blue willow scent, baseball broadcasts with magpie announcements. Bolstered by a beaver-chewed twig, the raft passes modern waferboard cartons of recent erection, then the solid old brick box of pioneer William Smith's home. A little farther and it just misses being drawn down the intake of the one-time Sand Creek Branch of the High Line, at the point known as the Great Bifurcation. Once this would have meant a pleasant side trip in the open, past the Thunder Tree, on to a crossing of Sand Creek, and deposition in First Creek a few miles short of the Platte. Now it would certainly prove fatal to any passenger but a fish, since the water is piped underground for a mile to Mount Nebo Cemetery and Fitzsimons Army Hospital's grounds before dumping into Sand Creek. But the fortunate young toad sweeps onward into white-water instead, then plunges over the six-foot Niagara of a drop-check dam, without a barrel.

High banks lined with sandbar willow shield the floater from the town that has consumed the fields I knew as a youth. Where vegetation permits an open prospect, traveling the high line of the land makes for an inclusive and unforgiving view of your surroundings: you don't miss much. There is the freeway, I-225, that took out the farms of my boyhood friends; condos on three corners at Sable Road, the abandoned homestead and woods on the fourth now occupied by a homeless camp; the mall, the jail, and the new city center. The toad sees it all, making nothing of it but smelling the familiar scent of cold water on stone as the canal sloshes over another check dam onto shaly bedrock beside the outtake of the extinct Doherty Ditch.

It might have recognized, too, the blue flash of a mountain bluebird, a onetime occupant of an arroyo through the middle of the next bend. But a concrete runnel has replaced the canal across the filled creek bed, making one less High Line loop and an oxbow park that no bluebird will likely visit again. Yet, beyond the mall at Chambers and Alameda, the once-again earthen channel describes a broad twin arc around an old farm decorated with a round white barn and historical farmhouse on open space destined to stay that way.

Another flood-swept wooden flume has been converted to a siphon here, this time beneath Toll Gate Creek. Some miles on, the same occurs beneath broad Sand Creek. A small animal would be lucky to survive these recurrent dowsings, but ours, used to the violent alpine snowmelt that made this water, manages to make it through intact. Prior to the Sand Creek undershot, the ditch meanders through mixed landscape of town and country. North of scabrous Colfax Avenue, a long, narrow dogleg encloses a slapdash subdivision where the size of the lot is inversely proportional to the size of the dog tied up in the backyard. They bark; toad ducks. Downslope across acres of thistle banks, Sand Creek's riparian stripe carries the essence and fragrance of the far plains, mint and quicksand and all the associated tracks and smells. But near the siphon, yet another golf course, a sand and gravel pit, and an auto graveyard have smothered the green wildness.

Beyond the KOA tower and Victory Grange, figments of the past, the ride traverses a light industrial scene where a second, rip-rapped channel parallels the first, but running counter, for drainage. Whirligig beetles spin in stranded pools as a dancing hatch of mayflies rises. The toad, hungry by now, snaps several of these with its elastic, adhesive tongue. In the remaining fields, red ants keep the perimeters of their anthills as clear of vegetation as next-door Caterpillar's warehouse grounds. Even so, ranks of cottonwoods resume across the Union Pacific tracks all the way to the fourth freeway and pick up again the other side of I-70. Trucks rumble overhead as relentlessly as the jetliners lumbering northwest toward Stapleton (and soon enough, north to DIA). A red-tailed hawk soars a leisured course halfway to a 727. Near the ground, a beehive hums in a hollow cottonwood stump, soothing rattled toad.

The ditch has shrunk to half its former size. Pink knotweed limns the flow. The forlorn hangars of the Sky Ranch lie off to the east, victims of a business park. In between runs the ever dry, high-banked trench of the Doherty Ditch in one of its few miles that no one has yet seen fit to fill. The public path has run out; the next mile, looking like the canal I knew in the fifties, is likewise posted No Trespassing. A magpie perches on the sign, impervious and, like the floating toad, ignoring the interdiction.

At the end of that mile appears a large orange wheel on a silver screw connected to a headgate. A second, working bifurcation, this is the takeout for a lateral feeding four lakes six or seven miles to the northwest. The customer, the High Line's foremost remaining rights holder, was also the largest nerve gas depot in the country. Before the government condemned twenty thousand acres for the Rocky Mountain Arsenal in 1942, this ditch and the Sand Creek Lateral both fed the High Line owners' Platte Land Company Reservoir. Water running in all three branches made a fourteen-thousand-acre island in the middle of the canal builders' empire. Now the arsenal is a national wildlife refuge, where toad might feel at home. But its lateral runs dry today, so the traveler avoids a fall into the handsome masonry intake chute and passage into this recovering Superfund site.

Before entering the heavily fenced arsenal lands, the lateral crosses a very nice piece of shortgrass prairie rich with native forbs and attendant butterflies. Evening primroses open here like wet lemon drops, and mule deer forage out from the thickets. Just beyond, a real estate sales office touts the new town of Green Valley Ranch, even as it swallows the next piece of the ditch.

The High Line sheds its cottonwood bands and shrinks to a mere four feet across, three deep. In this condition, with a fine sandy bed and still weedy margins, it approaches First Creek.

The ranch of the same name that preceded the planned city took its verdure from First Creek, where ranch boys hunted frogs and crawdads. Now small boys from the subdivision hunt whatever they can find. One of them spies what appears to be a warty frog on a floating mat of flotsam and lunges for it, but the current sweeps the prize into a shiny new metal flume, off-limits to small boys, and across the creek before he can reach it.

Vesper sparrows, horned larks, and rock wrens fly about the concrete abutments as if they were pristine canyonlands. Forget-me-nots bloom in the edge of the current, dropping blossoms that float like willowware boats on seas of deep green algae. Across the stream, the bones of a homestead lie among broken locusts. Then, beside derelict headgate 160, stands one of the largest cottonwoods on the canal, about seven feet in diameter with a small hollow for hibernating mourning cloaks or mammals. A double-trunk cottonwood and a fine big willow stand beside a second flume of wood and metal that carries the canal through a ramshackle farmyard and across the North Fork of First Creek. These flumes, this flow, those farms, will soon disappear as the High Line finds a new finish in First Creek. But for now the little ditch still swings west, north, east, and north again, crossing treeless wheatfields and dryland pasture.

The final water right feeds a holdout farm between the new town and the new Denver airport. In mere months, the water department will buy that right, and the only reason for the canal to extend past the wasteway at

First Creek in Green Valley Ranch will be gone. But the toad got here first, and now it adroitly skirts the steep drop into that old lateral's gully, avoiding a short life in a doomed alkaline farm pond.

Toad arrives at a three-way juncture where the remaining tailwater drains out east, north, and west. Ancient-looking ruins mark a broad channel into the defunct Doherty Ditch on the east. When there was extra water in the High Line, it was diverted here to thirsty places on the Antero District. On the north, extinct headgate 165 fed a small reservoir. Both functioned as the canal's endpoint at different periods. To the west, headgate 166 dumps any remaining flow into a lagoon. Surfing down into it, toad consorts with minnows, water beetles, and crayfish. Tracks of coyotes and raccoons ring the rare oasis. Henceforth, the yard-wide ditchlet inscribes one final loop west and north, past a spreading peachleaf willow, and down three drop-gates, losing altitude rapidly and giving the toad an eventful ride to the climax. Of the 170 feet the canal has dropped since the start, 60 come in this last mile. If a toad can have fun, this is the place to do it.

Our voyageur seems to have grown larger in the passage: one hop would carry it across the whole channel. A meadowlark sings from a yucca, invisible from the grassy trench. Fiery pods of Japanese lanterns and silver Bud cans rush along in the hurrying current; brass shells and rodent pellets glint in the late slanting sun. The toad rafts past the very last cottonwood.

Under Sixty-fourth Avenue, beyond a short furlong of open ditch, the floater enters a water park: two falls, a long concrete tunnel, then a two-hundred-foot, twenty-degree PVC pipe of a water slide to the end. Just as toad is getting the hang of it, the ride concludes in a splash pool over a bed of orange quartzite chunks, like the rock that roofs the source of the canal in Waterton Canyon, so very far back. From here the tailwater trickles into a small natural tributary of Second Creek.

Now our toad hops off, its waterlogged mat hung up in the weedy fringes of the brook. Upstream a short distance is a nice marsh, where it might live happily once adjusted to the altitude and heat. Or it could work its way downstream a few miles to the O'Brian Canal, thence to the wildlife sanctuary of Barr Lake, and, via more ditches, back to the South Platte River, where its crazy ride began.

Our toad will not return to the mountains in this life. But when it dies, several seasons hence after many spring night trillings of its singular tale, toad's mortal coil will release hydrogen to bond with oxygen in the pure prairie air and make water. Mixed with ditchwater, it will carry on down the river. Some drops will run to Nebraska, into the Missouri, the Mississippi, and the Gulf of Mexico. And in the natural scheme of things, some molecules, having evaporated into the atmosphere, might find their way back to the clouds above the Rockies; through the cool Colorado rain, into the headwaters of the South Platte; and perhaps, once again, through the headgates of the High Line Canal. Such is the true and full passage of a watercourse, the circuit of life.

Since that first brief flight in the Piper Tri-Pacer, I have flown in and out of Denver scores of times on many kinds of aircraft, from Constellations to 767s. Every time, if by day, I try to see the canal, how it is laid out. The conga line of cottonwoods twines 'round in the familiar pattern, thinning, but still there. I have yet to see it all, but I am glad to have finally found the mouth. For one of those times when I flew in, it would be to the new Denver airport, and the old end of the canal as I knew it would be no more.

The last time I was out there, I was thinking about the beginnings and endings of things when a great gabbling arose. The sound came nearer and grew deafening as a hundred sandhill cranes flew close by overhead, following the Platte to Nebraska. Splitting and coalescing, the flock shifted in a fluid delta of wings. Then they dropped and stretched into one long wavy line, like the canal itself, and vanished into the baked haze.

3

The Rivers of April

"That's how things are . . . You can't wear water out. No, my boy: it'll give you the go-by. Try to wear it out, and it takes its hook into vapour, it has its fingers at its nose to you. It turns into cloud and falleth as rain on the just and unjust."

— D. H. Lawrence, *The Rainbow*

I just couldn't see how a willow switch could lead a witch to water. Water witching seemed to make about as much sense as astrology. I was skeptical, then, when a dowsing rod was put in my hands around dinnertime on a hot July day in Montana. I was staying at The Nature Conservancy's Circle 8 Dude Ranch while helping to conduct an entomological survey at Pine Butte Swamp, a Conservancy preserve near Choteau. Talk had it that the manager, a genial cowboy-cum-teacher by the name of Al Haas, was a dowser of note who had witched several wells in the area. The guests, intrigued, asked for a demonstration.

Al obliged, and it looked as if it worked. Then he offered us a chance to try. Al knew where the water ran, but no one else did. He'd set you up with the wand—a copper-steel rod, not a willow twig—between your palms, blindfold you, then set you walking. Several who tried felt nothing; one or two yipped in fright or delight as the rod dipped.

My insect-collecting partner, Professor Charles Remington of Yale, had an open mind on the matter. He said he could imagine electromagnetic pulses communicating along the wand between underground streams and the upright water vessels that we are. But it didn't work for him, and he seemed disappointed. I was pretty sure nothing would happen for me, either. When the rod yanked downward, almost out of my hands, directly over the water line, I tingled, I paled, my spine shivered, and I grinned. "Perfect," said Al, removing my blindfold and showing me the spot I'd correctly witched. I felt giddy for some time, all through the chuckwagon supper.

I still don't know how or whether water witching works. But I do know that I felt the waterward tug of that wand in my hands. To have such a tool at one's command, especially in the arid West, could make a person very popular, even powerful. "To dowse" is a pleasant, wet verb for the talent, but "to witch" might be the more suitable phrase for one who can consistently produce the lubricant of life in the land of little rain. It surely must seem witchery of a high kind among thirsty settlers desperate for water on the dry western range.

Major Stephen Long, a nineteenth-century explorer and surveyor, described everything between the Mississippi and the Rockies as the Great American Desert. The tall peak bearing his name, looming over the eastern edge of the Rockies, signals the end of the arid zone. If you want to farm twenty miles east of its squared-off summit, you're still in the "desert"—the High Plains, the shortgrass prairie. The common belief at the time of homesteading was that nothing would grow without irrigation, a notion that ignored the prolific life that was adapted to the light rainfall of the plains.

Another exploring major, John Wesley Powell, underscored Long's conclusion. An expert on western rivers, famous for his navigation of the Grand Canyon, the one-armed Major Powell warned: "If you evenly distributed all the surface water flowing between the Columbia River and the Gulf of Mexico, you would *still* have a desert almost indistinguishable from the one that is there today." Like his contemporary Wolfgang von Goethe, Powell knew well that *Alles wird durch das Wasser erhalten* (everything will be sustained by water). Oblivious to this truth, settlers westered in the blind hope that water awaited. A bizarre idea sustained them, that "rain would follow the plow"—where righteous settlement went, precipitation would providentially follow.

As idiotic as this seems today, much of the westward-bound populace subscribed to this fond notion, and those who stood to profit from their arrival actively promoted it. Major Powell, commenting on the rashness of using homesteading laws to draw the masses into a water-poor land, discounted the myth. Even if it occurred, he said, it would likely be followed by cycles of extreme drought. He urged caution in settling the brown lands thickly in the hope that they might then draw rain and turn green. But the boosters told Powell, in Wallace Stegner's words, "The hell with you."

When it finally became apparent to all that there just wasn't enough water to fill the ditches or to water the fields, it was too late to turn back the wagon trains and make everyone go home. Those who promoted irrigation as the pioneers' panacea vastly overestimated the fluctuating rivers' ability to nourish and fruit the shriveled plain. They also lacked the sense of proportion that had allowed the native dwellers of the drylands to live well on little moisture. Willa Cather, in *Death Comes for the Archbishop*, described the Pueblo Indians' approach to aridity:

> *It was as if the great country were asleep, and they wished to carry on their lives without awakening it, or as if the spirits of earth and air and water were things not to antagonize and arouse . . . When they hunted, it was with the same discretion; an Indian hunt was never a slaughter. They ravaged neither the rivers nor the forests, and if they irrigated, they took as little water as would serve their needs. The land and all that it bore they treated with consideration; not attempting to improve it, they never desecrated it.*

The new settlers, in contrast, made every effort to improve what they found, and desecration followed where they went. For example, few activities disfigure the land and pollute the water as much as placer mining. Yet this was the method of choice for refining ore in the goldfields of the West. By tearing down the hills with black powder and hydraulic hoses, then running the placer (gold-bearing sands) through a sluice box, miners could separate the heavy particles of gold from the ore. Placer mining used a lot of water, and though it was only one of many draws newcomers made on the scarce supply, it nonetheless led to a new way of reckoning rights to the precious fluid.

When the colonists left behind the damp lands of Europe for similar climates in eastern America, they brought with them a set of water practices based on those of the homeland. This system came from English common law and the tradition of riparian rights—the premise that all people have equal access to the water they live beside, and each may use it for his or her purposes so long as the rights of others are respected. While imprecise, riparian rights work fairly well where water is plentiful.

In the droughty West, riparian rights worked about as well as no law at all. So a new doctrine arose, known as prior appropriation, or "first in time, first in right." It developed out of chaotic conditions among the placer mines, where, when water ran out, the sluices were left dry. As gold gave way to waves of grain, water practices cobbled together for mining took over in agriculture and were preserved as law. Christopher Meyer, a water conservation lawyer in Boulder, says that "first in time, first in right" was enforced by "a lotta guys with guns."

The laws vary among the western states, but nearly all say first come, first served. You don't have to live beside the water source to claim western water rights, nor do you have to use them in the watershed, as in the riparian tradition. In fact, it is expected that water will be diverted for "beneficial use." Western rights may also be bought and sold, with or without the land, or may pass to a new owner with the land, providing the use remains the same. First claimants receive senior rights, and they are assured their rightful amount of water (assuming adequate supply) before anyone with junior rights gets a drop.

Of course, the original users did not figure in. When the fish, the wildlife, and the streams themselves end up without rights, it is not surprising that Native Americans often find themselves waterless. Only now are various tribes negotiating to reclaim their water rights, just as conservationists are suing to secure adequate flow for wildlife. But by now the water has long been overallocated, and no one with "rights" to the basic stuff of life is going to give them up happily.

Western water law states that you have to use it or lose it. Domestic, farm, city, and industrial purposes are considered acceptable uses. To demonstrate beneficial use, you have to *divert* the water itself. So to increase the water supply, western settlers called for huge dams and diversion on a scale far greater than the local irrigation ditch. Marc Reisner wrote in *Cadillac Desert* that the very existence of the western states as we know them "is premised on epic liberties taken with water."

If the term "witching" well describes the mere finding of water, it fits much better the kinds of near-magic measures people have taken to bring water from where it is to where they believe it ought to be. Certainly the appearance of transmontane tunnels diverting the wet Western Slope's water to the parched hems of the Great American Desert would seem magical to Major Long and Major Powell, and to those who ignored their advice and followed their surveys West. But when Loren Eisley wrote, "If there is magic on this planet, it is contained in water," I don't believe this is what he had in mind.

Diversion still meant ditches when New York newspaperman Horace Greeley sent his editor Nathan Meeker to found what Marc Reisner has called "a utopian irrigation colony." The present-day college town of Greeley may not be utopian, nor can the 750,000-acre irrigation district around it properly be called a "colony." But what a district brochure calls "the indispensable commodity," applied to the arid lands around Greeley-on-the-Platte, has made a dry basin productive, as Greeley and Meeker had planned. Or, as the brochure shouts, "With enough Water . . . a better land . . . and a better life!" But "enough Water" could be had only through massive diversion.

In 1936, with the bitter dust of the Depression still on their tongues, watermen on the Platte initiated the Big Thompson Project. Big Tom, as they called it, brought water from the headwaters of the Colorado River near Granby under the Continental Divide through the Alva B. Adams Tunnel into the Big Thompson River above Estes Park, and delivered it to the Northern Colorado Water Conservancy District in Greeley. Big Tom realized, to a point, the early water boosters' dreams.

Denver was already acquiring Western Slope water rights in the twenties, with a view toward diversion. This the engineers brought about by lining the test bore for the Moffat Tunnel, a seven-mile railroad chute beneath the Continental Divide, with concrete, and running Fraser River water through it to Boulder Creek and then to Ralston Creek west of Denver.

If Moffat and Big Tom had been the only diversions, perhaps the balance would be to the good. But they were so successful that other tunnels soon followed, including the longest water tunnel in the world, the Harold D. Roberts. Built from 1946 to 1963, the Roberts runs for more than twenty-three miles from Dillon Reservoir to the North Fork of the South Platte. Eventually, the tunnel was to dump still more Blue River water into a reservoir behind the long-planned Two Forks Dam.

The era of big dams came to the West when water managers saw the need for large-scale storage to augment diversion. A megalomaniacal U.S. Commissioner of Reclamation by the name of Floyd Dominy capped his career by building Glen Canyon Dam, a concrete crescent on the Colorado that obliterated what may have been the country's most beautiful canyon beneath a deadwater reservoir most unkindly named Lake Powell. While David Brower, charge leader of the Sierra Club, lost that signal battle for what he called "the place no one knew," he helped to defeat two other dams on the Green and Colorado rivers, the former introducing the modern conservation era, the latter marking Dominy's demise at Reclamation. Dams in the Grand Canyon went just too far for even a thirsty public to buy. But to Dominy's heirs, Two Forks was one of those inevitable projects, not a matter of if, but when.

Planned as a 615-foot concrete, double-curved arc in the Platte Canyon, just below the convergence of the North and South forks of the South Platte River, Two Forks Dam was to be built by the city of Denver and a consortium of suburban water providers. The dam would create the largest lake in Colorado by backing up the South Fork twenty-nine miles and the North Fork seven and have a theoretical capacity of more than a million acre-feet. The reservoir would then inundate miles of gold-medal trout stream, a large acreage of deer and bighorn sheep range, much of the habitat for the federally threatened Pawnee montane skipper butterfly, and a hugely popular recreational canyon, while also drying out critical crane habitat downstream.

Two Forks was supposed to substantially fulfill the Denver region's water needs into the foreseeable future. But then, so was the handsome stone Cheesman Dam built in 1905. The first of Denver's dams on the Platte, Cheesman was touted as the solution to Denver's water problems for all time. Successive plugs on the Platte—Antero, Eleven Mile, Strontia Springs,

Chatfield—were built to enhance water storage and control flow. Skeptics believed the Two Forks "solution" about as much as the claim that World War I was the "war to end all wars." But the Platte Canyon site was not only the best remaining damsite in the state. Promoters wanted to build it while they still could. Writer Stu Stuller, in an issue of *Wilderness* dedicated to "Water and the Dimensions of Crisis," wondered whether Two Forks might not be the last of the West's big dams.

Along with their desire for enhanced storage capacity, the advocates of dams express a natural (if unrealistic) aversion to letting water "get away." The September–October 1983 issue of *Water News,* mailed with water bills, announced "Denver Area Loses 2-Year Water Supply." The heavy snowpack of the 1982–83 winter led to a greater than normal spring runoff. All the mountain reservoirs filled early in the summer. By mid-August, about 500,000 acre-feet—enough to meet the city's needs for nearly two years— had run on down the Platte. This was seen not as a boon for the river, for the summer cranes in Nebraska and the winter cranes on the Gulf of Mexico, in fact for the whole ecosystem, but as a great tragedy for Colorado.

Such a view considered Two Forks Dam as essential to "keep Colorado's water in Colorado." Narrows Dam was designed for the same purpose. A giant earthen structure 22,400 feet long but only 147 feet high, it was to span the broad and shallow Platte where Bijou Creek comes in, some hundred miles downstream from Denver. Narrows Reservoir would replace a rich agricultural valley, the town of Weldona, and a natural stretch of the river with a fetid, rapidly evaporating quagmire. It would inundate farms of the Weldon Valley, successfully irrigated with one of the earliest independent ditches in Colorado, while giving uphill irrigators, already prosperous from cheap Bureau of Reclamation water, a "new" source that probably wouldn't reach them because of inevitable channel losses. Downstream in Nebraska, rare sandhill and whooping cranes would lose a major migratory stop as the Platte River shrank to a dry channel most years and their key wetland habitat became unusable scrubby bottoms. Many engineers suspected the dam could not even be built on the Platte's deep alluvium without serious danger of collapse.

All this to keep Nebraska from getting a paltry portion of the Platte that Colorado considers its own. Narrows Dam was widely condemned as a bad dam, even among fervid water-project promoters. Yet even such environment-minded politicians as Senator Gary Hart and Governor Richard Lamm supported the Narrows long after it made any sense to do so, if it ever had. Two Forks wasn't much better. But in the West, it is often said, water flows uphill to money, and the water lords were used to getting their way.

In the West, after all, water is all. Or, as Thomas Hornsby Ferril put it, "Here is a Land where life is written in water." Ferril (1896–1998) was made Colorado's Poet Laureate in 1979. Inscribed in the rotunda of the state capitol building in Denver, beneath the gilded dome and among murals depicting the state's dependence on water, his poem goes on to predict:

> *And men shall fashion glaciers into greenness and harvest April rivers in*
> *the autumn.*

He little knew how profoundly true his words would prove.

Having grown up in Las Animas, in southeastern Colorado, Norma Walker knew about water. Her family valued every drop that fell on their dry scalps. When they found a rat in the cistern one day, it was a major disaster. One summer was so dry that her father, a beekeeper, had to move his hives to the West Slope to keep them from desiccating. Whenever she could, Norma played in the water of local ditches or the nearby Arkansas River.

Years later, when Norma moved with her own family to Aurora, she took her appreciation for water with her. Her son Brian, like many another lad, discovered the High Line Canal. It became his natural habitat as well as his safety net—there he would go to climb, swim, find snakes and salamanders and muskrats. Norma told me that the canal "saved his life," and I knew exactly what she meant. Sentenced to life in the drylands, we take our damp pleasures where we can. The marriage of open space and moist greenery has soothed many minds.

Norma never could take water for granted. So when she became mayor of a growing town long dependent on Denver for water and determined to provide for its own needs, she naturally took an active role in planning for her community's water future. A huge water-diversion plan called the Homestake Project was supposed to provide all the water that Aurora and

Colorado Springs, partners in its construction, might ever need. At a cost of some $60 million, it was to furnish thirteen billion gallons of water per year—water from moist West Slope basins, siphoned beneath the Rockies to storage reservoirs for the ever-thirsty cities on the plains.

As the first woman mayor of Aurora, Colorado (indeed, the first woman mayor of any sizable American city) Norma was often left out by her male colleagues in city government. Elected in 1964 by virtue of a fluke coalition, she found her mayorship frustrating. The time was prefeminist; women might sit on the City Council, but they were not supposed to be in charge. In the eyes of many, Norma, a former model, was too attractive to be a mayor. The resistance and hatred she encountered came as much from women as men—unsigned letters, night calls about her earrings, clothing, and hair style, block votes against her ideas.

Norma had her doubts about Homestake. After studying the engineering charts and receiving reports from the on-site foreman, she predicted that one of the tunnels would collapse, as it later did. Nor was she entirely happy with Aurora's plans for its water. She promoted parkways on the avenues like those in old Denver and opposed a city golf course as elitist and water wasting. When I appeared before the City Council to argue for a High Line Canal trail and open space, only Norma showed any interest. And when the golf course went in, she personally pulled the "No Trespassing" signs from the only open space her colleagues had allowed.

Norma Walker was not invited to the inaugural ceremony where the big spigot was to be tapped. But she and the only other woman on the council found out about the media show and picnic and crashed the coming-out party for Homestake. When it came time to launch the new tunnel's flow, Norma herself opened the floodgate. The newspaper photograph from June 7, 1966, shows a pretty woman in a hard hat and a polka-dot pantsuit smiling widely as she turns the big wheel, her antagonists glowering behind pinched grins.

Norma's apprehensions were borne out by the noncash costs of Aurora's first big water project for both the environment and the future livability of the city. Homestake, despite mitigation efforts, dried up four valley creeks on the West Slope, ruined fisheries, stripped vegetation and soil from eroded slopes, and substantially reduced habitat for deer, elk, and other wildlife, according to the Sierra Club. It was supposed to solve Aurora's future water needs well past 2000, furnishing water for up to two hundred thousand people. But by 1990, Aurora, predicting growth to seven hundred thousand, wanted more water.

Homestake II was proposed and begun to further develop Aurora's water rights on the tributaries of the Eagle River in the Holy Cross Wilderness Area. Colorado wilderness legislation was held up over whether the federal government had the obligation to reserve water rights within dedicated wilderness areas. The Colorado Supreme Court and the Wilderness Society said yea, the Forest Service and the Farm Bureau said nay, and Congress was divided. The U.S. Supreme Court finally nixed the plan at the end of 1995.

Another initiative, the Collegiate Range Aurora Project, proved equally unpopular. (It was quickly dubbed CRAP by the High Country Citizens' Alliance.) It called for taking water from the Taylor River, a tributary of the Gunnison; flooding the Roaring Judy Fish Hatchery for a transfer reservoir; and impounding much of the Rocky Mountain Biological Laboratory at Gothic, the oldest independent field station in the country and the site of many fundamental ecological studies. Arapahoe County's related Union Park project would have ambushed the Gunnison River country with two dams, a hydro plant, tunnels, and siphons to claim 100,000 acre-feet of West Slope water for the unslakable East Slope thirst. These capers too went down, but more arise yearly.

Today the rivers of April water the lawns of autumn from Fort Collins to Pueblo. At least sixteen greater and lesser transmontane water tunnels cross Colorado's crest, and more are planned. With 80 percent of the water on the West Slope and 80 percent of the people on the east side, this might seem appropriate, even just. But 80 percent of the residential water used in the Greater Denver region goes to green bluegrass lawns, much of the rest to flush toilets and wash cars. And until recently, eighty-six thousand Denver customers were not even metered!

Each tunnel co-opts water at the expense of West Slope irrigators, domestic users, fish and wildlife, riparian habitats, and the rivers themselves. So what happened to "first in time, first in right"? The agents of the cities have been quietly and effectively at work, dowsing the countryside for old, lapsed, or unallocated rights, buying up the plasma of the wetter districts so that their bosses might float the dams and bore the tunnels and carry on their triple-bypass river surgery, leaving the watersheds and their residents who really *were* there first high and dry, thirsty and dead: water-robbed.

Water buffalos (the diverters and dammers) maintain that the majority are served by cross-mountain detours that follow all the premises of western water law: prior appropriation, diversion, beneficial use. The wildland advocate Warren Hem countered, "There is no need to destroy the Holy Cross Wilderness in order to water lawns and wash cars in Aurora." Or, as Wallace Stegner wrote in *Beyond the Hundredth Meridian*, "If there are no technical reasons why we cannot move water from remote watersheds, there are ecological and, I might suggest, moral reasons why we shouldn't."

By the late sixties, Norma Walker felt that Aurora was becoming "a terrible place to live, sprawling beyond recognition, motivated by greed and development." The woman from Las Animas, bred to value water and green spaces, grew weary of watching water misused and green places spoiled in the process. Still hopeful of bringing about reform, she ran for a second term as mayor. But spending $600 against $10,000 by her opponent, she lost by thirty votes. Under the mayors who followed her, random growth carried on, and Aurora found itself back where it started before the floodgates were opened for Homestake.

Norma was not around to see Homestake II get bogged down in the courts, or Aurora's $6 million worth of Two Forks go down the drain when William Reilly, director of the Environmental Protection Agency, vetoed the big dam. If the floodgates had ever opened for Homestake II, she definitely would not have been invited to the party, nor would she care. Norma had long since moved to a village on the Washington coast, where she sculpted in bronze and her neighbors called her the unofficial mayor of Ocean Park. It is a green place of modest aspirations, relatively little growth, and lots of water.

My life has run tangent to the elements of this story. Growing up in Aurora, I drank water that flowed from these same dams and diversions. As apprentice city manager during our high school Student Day in Government, I looked over the shoulder of real City Manager Robert O. Wright as he signed off on blueprints and contracts for Homestake I. My family spent summer vacations in the Taylor River country, where my county would one day stake its Union Park claim. I returned as a student and later a teacher to the Rocky Mountain Biological Laboratory, where I came to know intimately the East River and Copper Creek, streams my hometown meant to impound for the Collegiate Range Aurora Project.

My brother Tom and I tubed pink granite canyons on the South Fork of the South Platte, looking up at Long Scraggy Peak as we lay supine in our soft black craft. On my thirtieth birthday we shot the dangerous Chutes near Deckers, an act of madness precipitated by too many Coors and my lost twenties. We drank more Coors and ate greasy cheeseburgers in the Sprucewood Tavern, where we signed petitions against Two Forks Dam. Tom showed me a chimerical village called Sphinx Park in a pink granite gorge—Brigadoon-like because I could never seem to find it on my own—that would vanish for real beneath dead waters of the reservoir, along with the tavern and the Chutes, if the floodgates ever closed on Two Forks.

Another summer on a Denver Audubon Grassland Institute trip, I "floated" the South Platte much farther downstream, where it becomes "a mile wide and an inch deep." Mostly dragging our rubber rafts, we passed between the very cottonwood galleries and broad banks that the Narrows Dam would have drowned in its squalid backwater. Lying back against the hot rubber raft, I felt the river that would vanish altogether downstream, and I imagined the frustration of the sandhill cranes as they arrived to survey their dried-out domain.

From that float sprang a teaching job outside Estes Park, near where the Alva Adams tunnel emerges from the Front Range. One week each summer for many years after, I led butterfly walks along the banks of the Big Thompson River, its flow swollen with water from the far Colorado. Driving westerly from there, I would pass the several ranches of my mother's forebears, the Whetstones. They had the good sense to settle on the West Slope, where the water was.

Great-uncle Jim ranched the green Yampa Valley and knew Chief Ouray. Great-grandfather Elias made a fine ranch on the Blue River, in the broad valley above Dillon. Had the Whetstones remained, they would have seen the good water they'd come for taken away to slake those imprudent ones who settled on the wrong side of the Divide. Now old Dillon lies beneath a reservoir as new Dillon sprawls close to the Whetstone ranch, and the clear water of the Blue is sucked down the tubes, bound for Denver.

I know these rivers, these ranches, these tunnel-riven mountains. But most of what I know of water comes from the High Line Canal—the first "big" irrigation project in Colorado. The High Line foretold, in Zorba the Greek's words, "the whole catastrophe": the naive optimism, the expansionism, the speculation and greed; the bad guess about flow and the bad luck of junior rights; and the downside of diversion for beneficial (if intermittent) use. Soon this big, expensive, and important project to bring Platte water to the plains became small, of marginal importance. On the fancy maps of Denver's water supply, the High Line shrinks and blushes beside the great projects of today, but it is included anyway, the first brushstroke on Denver Water's imperial portrait.

The High Line Canal anticipated all the others, setting their collective stage. One of the first Platte River dams, Antero, was built largely on behalf of High Line rights holders. Other Platte projects have all had to work with the canal, or around it. The source takes out just downstream from the proposed Two Forks damsite, while its tailwater empties not far upstream from the Narrows. A virtual link between the last two great water follies, both failed, the High Line Canal is a reminder of sensible scale, and humility.

For me, the High Line has also been a window on western water. Once of paramount importance, today almost forgotten, it spans the whole history of moving water from one place to another to keep Colorado green. When I walk its high-line loops, I look across the sunken skyline of the city to the mouths of mountain canyons and I see the delivery of the lifeblood of the land. And when the canal's own little bit of water runs, I see a seasonal transfusion. A mere capillary, the High Line throbs with the same pulse that drives the entire pulmonation of the plains. In these reflections in a ditch, I see that my own beneficial use as ditchwalker and water watcher, my very junior wading rights that no water court would ever recognize, have also flowed from water sent to where it never intended to go.

"Once in a lifetime," wrote Loren Eiseley in *The Immense Journey,* "if one is lucky, one so merges with sunlight and air and running water that whole eons . . . might pass in a single afternoon without discomfort." Eiseley, no swimmer, knew such a time when, giving in to a whim, he allowed the Platte River to carry him away. "The sight of sky and willows and the weaving net of water murmuring a little in the shallows on its way to the Gulf stirred me . . . with a new idea," he wrote. "I was going to float."

Shoving off, he had "the sensation of sliding down the vast tilted face of the continent . . . the cold needles of the alpine springs at my fingertips and the warmth of the Gulf pulling me southward . . . I *was* water and the unspeakable alchemies that gestate and take shape in water." I have known this feeling, too, not in the broad Platte but in the narrow ditch called the High Line Canal. It is, after all, the same water.

Western water practice is changing. Two Forks and Narrows dams have both been killed (although dams are always susceptible to resurrection). Aurora has abandoned the Collegiate Range project, and a water judge ruled that there wasn't enough water for the Union Park project. Water courts have begun to recognize in-stream rights for the protection of fish, wildlife, and rivers, and The Nature Conservancy has been acquiring such rights across the West. A Wyoming judge has granted jurisdiction of an entire water district to the Wind River Shoshone and Arapaho tribes. State Senator Bob Pastore launched a constitutional initiative in Colorado to require citizens of water districts to vote on any proposed transfer of water from their district. The WATER amendment (it stands for Willingness and Appropriateness in the Transfers and Exports of Rivers) would democratize diversion at last. Meanwhile, the Colorado legislature passed a bill requiring cities to form water efficiency plans, and the state Supreme Court has been petitioned to confirm that water use must consider general public interest, including protection of natural environments. With each newly proposed water grab, the opposition grows stronger, rallying behind their motto, "Not one drop over the hill."

But as river diversion becomes more difficult, the water buffalos are turning more and more to agriculture, which uses 92 percent of the state's water but accounts for 2 percent of all Coloradans, according to a special water issue of the *Denver Post*. Offered immense prices for their water, farmers find selling out almost irresistible. The *Post* also reported that Aurora offered Rocky Ford farmer Roy Moffett $200,000 for a farm and its water that were earning him only $1,500 per annum. But not everyone sells. Swink hog farmer Frank Milenski, one who resisted, said, "When they move water out . . . they absolutely destroy an economy. And for what? To grow green lawns and golf courses around Denver. I think a lot of these deals are plum stupid." In twenty years the water buyers dried up sixty thousand acres, much of it in Norma Walker's Arkansas Valley. "You watch," Olney Springs farmer Orville Tomky told the *Post*. "After Aurora's water goes, half of Ordway will close, too." Since then, Rocky Ford—famous for its cantaloupes—has lost many more acre-feet of its precious water to Aurora.

The water lobby remains immensely potent. Against its power to siphon billions of gallons of water from one side of the Great Divide to the other, to suck the very stuff of life from the green fields that support us all, the ability to divine moisture with a stick seems puny. Perhaps witching is too strong a word for the dowser's skill after all. The *real* witching goes on at a higher level, where entire rivers are found, then lost.

It makes me think of Walt Disney's rendition of Paul Dukas's "The Sorcerer's Apprentice" in *Fantasia*. Mickey Mouse, donning the absent sorcerer's cap and taking up his wand, makes the broom carry water buckets for him. But as the broom splinters and multiplies, again and again, Mickey finds his experiment in magical water transport running terribly amok. I sometimes wonder whether we inept apprentices of nature will one day find our own sorcery running away with us. And the boss will not return to put everything to rights, as at the end of Disney's animated version.

Is it in the eternal nature of things that a good witch like Norma Walker hasn't a chance against the wicked wizards of the West? There is danger in this damp magic. For when it comes to the witching of western water, we may think we know the spells; but when the sorcery goes awry, we'll have only ourselves and the water to answer to.

PART II

Landmarks

4

Lilacs and Crossflowers

When a man's house is his only castle, then he has no castle.

— Herbert Gold, "The American as Hipster"

In the West the presence of lilacs meant successful settlement. Where water could be provided, lilacs thrived in our dry climate with its cold winters. Denver grew full of bloated old lilacs wherever homes and lives took hold.

After the devastating hailstorm, my mother planted scores of irises. They multiplied, blotting out memory of battered plants with their swatches of color. She also planted lilacs, whose first blooms mirrored the pale purple irises beneath them. She patiently watered the young shrubs, coaxing their green shoots out of the dusty soil, and they grew large. Every May the entrance to our utility room was almost blocked by the lavender blooms with their vinous scent.

One summer I reared a batch of cecropia moth caterpillars. The finger-size green serpents, decorated with red and blue tubercles, had an insatiable taste for lilacs. I brought fresh leaves and cleaned out their mountains of barrel-shaped frass every morning. When I went away for several weeks, I emptied the tub with its several dozen surviving larvae directly onto the lilacs. They nearly defoliated both of our bushes. Mother was inconsolable until it was clear that her lilacs would recover.

I knew two places in particular where grand old lilacs punctuated their settlers' success. One was an old red brick house along the High Line Canal, not far from the Thunder Tree. Fronting the house on the street side and backing it on the canal stood vast monuments of lilac bushes. Here my friend Jack Jeffers and I came on spring mornings to net black swallowtails and satyr anglewings nectaring on the cloying bunches of purple florets or, in the evening, for the pink-winged sphinx moths and golden noctuids they drew in.

The other place was a spooky old stone landmark in East Denver known as Richthofen's Castle. We all talked about sneaking into it some night. After our junior prom, Jack and I climbed into my 1950 Ford with our dates and decided to do just that. The faded brown cloth upholstery gave off a dusty scent that, to a teenager with his first car, was at least as heady as the vaunted new-car smell our parents loved. The girls' perfumes were stronger still. But as we approached the castle, the scent of lilacs overpowered both.

The castle looked like something out of *Frankenstein* as we crept from the car. In the night the gray stone hulk was half hidden by elms and shadows. Spotlights illuminated grotesque forms of gargoyles and a great tower rising to a peak. Dark archways, like a shadowed cloister, probably held garden hose and garbage cans, but we imagined catacombs. Castle turrets rose black against the city glow, their chunky blocks picked out by lanterns secreted in dark recesses.

While Jack and I were daring one another to open the heavy gate in the stone wall, a light came on in one of those turrets and guard dogs started barking. The four of us ran past the castle's gatehouse, past stone hitching posts and a high round arch blocked by an iron portcullis. Then we stopped running and walked around the block toward the car, our hearts pumping. Breathing hard, we sucked in the strong scents of the night. All along the compound's wall grew lilacs, great bowers of huge old shrubs, their dusky blooms dripping scent. JoAnne and I, holding hands, wanted to sniff them all night long, but Jeffers was hot to go in case the cops came. We left, but not before JoAnne broke off a spray of lilacs. Their scent mixed with the girls' cologne, our aftershave and sweat, and the dusty smell of the old Ford as we drove off to park in a darkclump of cottonwoods out beyond the High Line.

If lilacs signified the solid roots of the old homesteads, another mauve flower with its own strong scent hinted the opposite. It grew in scruffy fields among gray-green shoots of tumbleweeds. It thrived on the waste ground where the Little League played in summer, on foreclosed farms where skinny horses curled their lips around nothing much to eat—where someone once had hopes. Even before lilac time, this little lavender weed would spring from the most abused lands, always a surprise.

When I knelt to look, I saw the four narrow petals and slender leaves on gangly green stems. Known as purple crossflower, its simple blossoms smelled of cheap perfume and cat pee, and its early spring bloom signaled the start of a new season's rambles along the canal. Crossing any battered patch of ground beside the ditch, I would smell the sweet stink of the weedy crucifer, listen to a pair of magpies clucking their courtship tussle from over by the Thunder Tree, and know that the hot days of summer freedom were coming.

Magpies and purple crossflowers love the secondhand lands that others have finished with. Content on the shaggy edges of both town and country, they get along fine in places unsuited for more refined or fastidious lives. They are resourceful organisms, as self-sufficient as any member of a community can be. And unlike the lilacs of the prosperous homesteads and towns, purple crossflowers get by on marginal moisture. Like desert wildflowers, they bloom after the spring rains, such as they are, and keep out of sight the rest of the time. But the crossflower is not native to these arid lands: it came from places where human impact on the land was an old story. Like most of our present-day weeds, from cheatgrass to Dalmatian toadflax, it coevolved with *Homo sapiens* for thousands of years. No strangers to disturbance, exotics were preadapted to life in beat-up landscapes. Tagging along with the first wave of settlers as burrs in their socks or tares in their hay, they sprang up wherever the original flora was disturbed by the cow, the plow, and the dust-storm drought. *Chorispora tenella* was one of these hitchhikers. I learned to look for it where an earlier generation of settlers had lived and then moved on.

Another European immigrant, Walter von Richthofen, sprang from Silesia in 1848. He had landed in France with the invading Prussian army as a teenager, afterward assuming the title of baron. This he held in common with a relative, Baron Ferdinand von Richthofen, a noted geographer and explorer and author of a standard work on Chinese geography. Two other relatives, Frieda and Else, were early feminists and, respectively, the wife of D. H. Lawrence and lover of Max Weber. Walter von Richthofen's nephew Manfred was to become the Red Baron of the skies of World War I.

With hopes of distinguishing himself in a new land, Walter arrived in Colorado in the early 1870s. The frontier boosterism of Denver appealed to the red-bearded baron. An entrepreneurial type, he soon built a magnificent beer garden that he named Sans Souci but everyone else called the Baron's Bower. This failed to attract the right crowd and he sold it; before long the beer hall had become a gospel mission. Richthofen then dabbled in cattle barony, mass transit, and bottled water before settling on a scheme to build an exclusive model suburb beyond the city's southeastern fringe. He called it Montclair, for its Rockies vista.

Few people had yet thought about the potential of the rattlesnake and jackrabbit empire east of Denver, but it would soon be known to all Denver, its name synonymous with that of the Prussian baron. Richthofen set about acquiring most of the section of former railroad lands that would become Montclair. He developed grand plans and advertised to attract the sort of upscale settlers he had in mind. A tuberculosis patient himself, as were many who came west, he built a milk-cure tubercularium called the Molkerei. Anticipating the future uncannily, he wrote in his 1885 prospectus: "Denver has now become so large and closely built a city that it seems impossible, within its boundaries, to fully enjoy the pure air and delightful climate." Montclair would fill what he called "a great want for a pleasant suburban town" where the moneyed could escape the noisome metropolis for the best of both worlds.

As if to peg his bare section of land to the empty map, he constructed an estimable castle in Montclair. Built of pale, rough-cut rhyolite from a quarry near Castle Rock south of Denver, the structure assumed the towered and turreted form of the eroded mesa that gave that town its name. Norman arches, castellated balconies, and machiolations all gave it a toy-box look more typical of Walter's native Germany than the frontier capital. Its most unusual feature (for other barons of cattle, silver, and gold fashioned their own Colorado castles) was a yard-high, red stone bust mounted on the northeast corner of the structure. It depicts the bearded, lion's-head-capped Frederick Barbarossa, a medieval emperor sometimes called King Arthur of the Germans, who was prophesied to arise and unite the divided people. The Richthofen arms, carved in red Lyons sandstone, hold up the main tower above the entrance: two lions crowning a just judge, symbolizing the family name, which means "House of the Just."

Having sent his first wife and children back to Germany, Richthofen then divorced her and married an Englishwoman. Louise Ferguson Davies was fair haired, round faced, with a turned-up nose and a stern but pretty mouth. Also previously married, she agreed to the match in the belief that the Montclair experiment would enable a sophisticated and comfortable existence. The castle itself was fine. But its stark and solitary position, its distance from the downtown social scene, and especially its barrenness—no trees, flowers, or anything green but tumbleweeds and prickly pear—put her off. She refused to move in until the landscape could be graced with abundant vegetation and birds.

Potential investors reacted similarly. For lack of verdure, Richthofen's extravagant lure had so far failed to attract either his baroness or the rapid development he sought. His castle, for all its glory, stood alone on the boundless bare plain. It attracted attention, all right, but few were willing to consider moving out with the prairie dogs until the noble young neighborhood came green. And, as T. J. Noel put it in *Richthofen's Montclair,* "the greening of Montclair meant ditchdigging. Water was the sparkling magic that would transform Richthofen's patch of the Great American Desert into a suburban oasis." But there was no ditch. Lacking water to irrigate his dreams, Richthofen would remain high and dry.

Denver sits in a shallow declivity a mile high on its floor, rising gently on its sides to plateaus, foothills, and mountains. The analogy of a bowl is often employed, but a bedpan might be more apt, since the concavity opens on the north into the Platte River's long, low runnel toward Nebraska. To the south the piney upland of the Black Forest rises to seven thousand feet, creating a barrier between the Platte and Arkansas watersheds known as The Divide. The western edge ascends abruptly to that greater divide, the Continental, behind the Rocky Mountain Front Range. And on the east the High Plains reach away toward Kansas.

Many of the early settlers came to rest in this basin where the westward rush of the Great Plains runs out against the Rockies. Maybe it seemed a good place to farm, to settle, to build a city, or perhaps they didn't fancy crossing the Rockies. "Right," they said, dropping their gear and turning out the oxen. "This is it."

Successive waves of silver and gold fever brought the Pikes-Peak-or-Busters, the Central City and Leadville boomers, and the hangers-on who show up wherever shiny minerals are to be won from rock. Many set their sights specifically on that attractive ramp of land abutting the foothills. A panorama of splendid mountains near enough to relieve the monotony of the plains; abundant acres of land not yet under plow or fence; Indians subdued; and an energetic town picking up steam all attracted settlers to Denver. But as they poured over the eastern rim, bounced off the western wall, and came to rest in and around Denver, they saw the grasslands running away brown in all directions. Only in the brief spring, and where Cherry Creek and the Platte River exercised their soothing sway, was much green to be found.

The new arrivals were not overly concerned with the lack of water. Irrigation was nothing new. It was only a matter of finding a source and a means of delivery to paint the brown green. Soon Denverites constructed the City Ditch to bring mountain meltwater to the elms of the early streets and parks. A multitude of water companies and districts formed to carry water from streams to people. By 1869, with nearly a million acres "under ditch," Colorado ranked second among states in irrigation development. It rose to first place ten years later, and only after forty more did California regain the title.

Pressure had been building for a "high line canal" to follow the high contour of the land from the mouth of the Platte River Canyon to the immense, potentially arable uplands beyond the city to the east. Horace Greeley had prophesied the greening of mid-America if only water could be brought to what he called the Great American Desert. In 1872 President Ulysses S. Grant visited Colorado and was impressed with the challenge of cultivating the High Plains. The next year, in an address recommending Colorado for statehood, Grant called for "a canal for the purpose of irrigating from the eastern slope of the Rocky Mountains to the Missouri river ... an arid belt of public land from 300 to 500 miles in width, perfectly valueless for occupancy of man for want of sufficient rain to secure the growth of agricultural products." (Never mind that this "arid belt" had been well occupied by the Arapaho, the Pawnee, the Paiute, the Cheyenne, the Lakota Sioux, the Kiowa, the Blackfeet, and many others. By now the Plains Indians were enfeebled, along with their staple, the plains bison, by European diseases and firepower. Besides, Grant meant "occupancy by European man.") The president said he wanted to open "reclaimed" sections to settlement under the homestead laws.

Much of the public land of which Grant spoke was rapidly becoming private. The federal government awarded vast acreages to railroads as an incentive for shoving their rails west. In 1879 rail magnate Jay Gould gained control of one hundred thousand acres of these grant lands on the High Plains east of Denver. He promptly contacted English banker Lord James Barclay, who speculated on a large chunk of the rail grants. Gould and Barclay were friends of Grant. Both the fate and rewards of irrigating the dry plateau were coming to lie firmly in private hands. But the public—not least among them Walter von Richthofen—eagerly awaited word on how and when the watering would proceed.

Lord Barclay remained in London with his banks, but his partner and agent, James Duff, came to Denver to organize their various enterprises. Their goal was to profit by lending money on land and equipment. Under Duff's management, hundreds of thousands of dollars were loaned to farmers in Larimer, Weld, and Pueblo counties, north and south of Denver. Once established on the Denver business and social scene, Duff took over plans for construction of the High Line Canal, which had gone nowhere in the hands of other promoters. Now the ditch was promptly dug.

Promptly, that is, for those days. Earth was first shifted on January 18, 1879. Local crews contracted to perform the work on various sections. All they had to work with were teams of heavy horses, hand-held scraping devices known as slips, and the occasional blasting cap when bedrock got in the way. For the first forty-six miles the canal was to be dug forty feet wide and seven feet deep with a grade of twenty-one inches to the mile; thereafter it would narrow to twenty feet by four feet, dropping thirty-two inches each mile. The results were remarkably accurate.

By 1882 the High Line Canal extended forty-four miles from its source in the Platte River Canyon to Cherry Creek and was projected to Box Elder Creek, another eighty miles. President Grant's grandiose image of an irrigation empire of thousands of square miles had been abridged to about two hundred thousand acres to be watered at an estimated cost of some $3 million. When the main branch came to a stop the following year in a tiny creek northeast of Aurora, it ran just seventy miles, had cost $650,000, and promised to irrigate just fifty to sixty thousand acres.

Not surprisingly, the English Company (as the newspapers and public called Barclay and Duff's complicated array of interlocking concerns) owned most of the land subject to irrigation. Now that the canal had come in, the English Company—having been paid handsomely to build it—was able to sell its land with glowing promises of future productivity. James Barclay, in the January 1880 *Fortnightly Review*, urged farmers to come to Colorado, "where sunshine is abundant all the year round, and where the supply of water to their crops is not dependent on the capricious clouds, but is drawn through irrigating channels from streams that never dry up." Along with the mortgages, the company loaned eager farmers money for gear, seed, teams, stock, and housing. The High Line Canal was on line, and its British developers were sitting pretty.

When completed, the High Line Canal was the largest and most expensive water project in Colorado. Local pride would have it bigger yet. As the eminent Judge W. G. M. Stone described it, "This ditch is so large and involves consequences so vast one irresistibly cranes the neck to catch a glimpse of the boats and sails which should ride its water like those of the rivers we knew in former times." Well, not quite. Far from supporting navigation, the canal could not even supply the promised water on a regular basis. Farmers dependent on the canal found, from 1889 on, that Lord Barclay had been mistaken: supply was indeed intermittent *and* inadequate. In short, the canal didn't do the promised job.

Under western water law, firstcomers acquire senior rights to any available water source they claim. Latecomers get only junior rights and must queue for leftovers. Thus water has frequently been overallocated up to and beyond what a river can provide at its best flow. Yet, as President Grant and many other easterners failed to appreciate, the flow in western rivers can be counted on for only one quality: variation.

It seems unlikely that anyone would go to the expense of building a major canal without first having secured access to the water source, but the

English Company had done just that. On January 18, 1879, the Colorado Water Court decreed an appropriation of 1,184 cubic feet per second for the new canal. When farmers bought parcels of land from the company, they were also buying into this right. It should have been plenty except in times of low water, as occurred in July 1887, when farmers were asked to waive their rights for a few days so that Denver might save its young elms in the parks and parkways. Most farmers readily agreed, but were understandably irked when in 1889 the state engineer kept the canal nearly waterless. For, as it turned out, the High Line's decree was actually junior to some seventy-four older and smaller ditches taking water from the South Platte in the same district. One thing the water courts could not do was make more water. So when they began to enforce the complex laws in earnest, some users lost out, including most of the mortgaged farmers along the High Line.

These cut-off farmers, already indignant about a royalty charged by the English Company over and above the water carriage fees, screamed. In a decision of broad consequence for the future of irrigation, Colorado's Supreme Court threw out the royalty. But the state engineer upheld his decision to close the headgates of the High Line when the Platte ran low.

Before the litigious canal game could get them into deeper water, the British investors punted. Claiming no blame for acts of God, they declared the need for a storage reservoir to ensure reliable delivery. They sold the canal and attendant holdings in 1909 to the Antero and Lost Park Reservoir Company for $600,000. Then, turning their well-watered backs on the High Line and their doomed duty to fill it, Barclay's men skipped town for the green and pleasant land whence they'd come, where water wasn't a problem.

Sometimes when Jack and I walked the canal we headed east. Passing peachleaf willows and long bank grass that bled their greens into the somnolent flow, we would come to a high check dam. Its considerable drop roiled the water and splintered wood at the base of the dam, making a muddy milkshake. A treeless stretch lined with yellow rabbitbrush led to a thicket of pungent blue sandbar willows. Coming out of the blue willows, our noses tingling with their smell of honey and rot, we could cross the Potomac Street bridge and enter the shade of the Swale.

The Swale was a broken line of deep, grass-filled hollows running parallel to the ditch. Apparently artificial, the depression resembled a broad ditch that went nowhere. Dry and grassy yet cottonwood roofed, it offered shelter when the prairie sun or wind cut too sharply. Passing our army-surplus canteen back and forth, we pondered the Swale's origins. I created my own preindustrial mythology, imagining a buffalo run, an Arapaho antelope trap, a wallow for some great prehistoric beast, or the outer defenses of a cavalry fort. Practical Jack figured that the ditch-diggers had screwed up and had to rescoop the canal.

Years later, farther onto the plains, I found traces of the ghost ditch running some distance from the main canal. Cross sections loomed like raised shaggy maws where severed by Piccadilly and Tower roads. Topographic maps showed it as an intermittent dashed blue line, but gave nothing of its origins. Finally, the Swale's identity was revealed in a musty chronicle I discovered in the bowels of the Denver Water Department archives. It was the Doherty Ditch, the relic of a grand water plan that came to nothing but briefly muddied the sporadic waters of High Line history.

With the exit of the English Company, unhappy farmers clamored for a reservoir in the mountains to ensure an even flow, and eventually the Antero Reservoir was built. Promoters subtly billed it as "the most beautiful resort in the state, the greatest natural wonder of the country, the most remarkable and notable dam in the world, and . . . good for all time," and claimed they held rights for 50 million acre-feet, or a million-acre reservoir fifty feet deep. The modest structure that was finally built, able to hold just 33,000 acre-feet, mocked the boosters' hyperbole. Nonetheless, the new lake gave hope that irrigators' needs might at last be met.

Sixty-thousand arid acres to the north and east of the High Line domain were to be irrigated with the Antero water through a new ditch funded by public money. Utilities magnate Henry L. Doherty was drafted by Denver businessmen to manage the new project. Like Duff, he seemed the right man in the right place and time. Mustached and natty, with a short trim beard and his hair parted in the middle in the style of the time, Doherty had been brought to Denver in 1899 to reorganize the shambles of the city's power and gas systems. He went on to build the richest utilities empire in the country, beginning with the Denver Gas and Electric Company. He agreed to take on the canal project, not to make money, he claimed, but to demonstrate what could be done with water in a dry land. But he stood to make a bundle nonetheless, as he was to assume control of the entire High Line network on completion of the new ditch.

Henry Doherty planned an entirely new canal, from the Platte to the Plains. That proving too expensive, he decided to carry the water in the underutilized High Line as far as its bifurcation to Sand Creek. From there he would run the new ditch parallel with the old until it reached the new Antero Irrigation District. By 1913 he had nearly finished the extension, leaving the main branch of the High Line not far east of the Thunder Tree: thus, our Swale.

Over a thousand of Denver's most prominent businessmen turned out for a gala luncheon on the magnate's behalf. The "Prophet of the New Industrial Era," as Denver's *Republican* called Doherty, told his eager listeners that Colorado had "all it takes to be a great industrial power" and that "the greatest opportunity for bringing prosperity is by the development of your dry lands by irrigation." Senator Thomas, in turn, praised Doherty's enterprise as being "of immeasurable value to a community like ours."

"Immeasurable" was perhaps the correct term—Doherty's ditch didn't work. It lacked the grade to transport water the full length. It also lacked water: Doherty had failed to obtain legal access to the vaunted Antero Reservoir. Once his ditch was on line, his company would control the High Line's flow and receive its revenues as part of the deal, but those rights were already allocated and could not be carried out to the new district. Doherty hoped to obtain further rights from Plum Creek to fill the new canal, but its flow was even less reliable than the Platte's (although it was a flood of Plum Creek that, years later, was to take out many of Doherty's flumes).

In short, when delivery day came, Doherty's Ditch was fresh out of water. Nonetheless, when the downtown party dispersed to the countryside for a look at the project, Doherty's people managed a show of flow for the occasion by breaking into wooden floodgates at Sable Road to hijack High Line water. Thus water sloshed into the head of the Doherty Ditch, for the first and only time, just days after the contract called for delivery of irrigation to the Antero District lands.

Attention was diverted from the faulty ditch by a string of contract disputes that erupted when Denver sought to take over the High Line system from the Doherty syndicate. The resulting suits were as complicated as a prairie pattern of interweaving watercourses. Not until 1920 were they settled, when the Colorado Supreme Court ruled in favor of the city after the state's most complex and voluminous trial ever: the record contains 40,000 folios of typewritten material, and the printed abstract runs 16,294 pages.

The canal has been owned and operated ever since by the Denver Board of Water Commissioners. Eventually the board negotiated release of Antero rights, bringing reservoir water to the drylands at last but through the High Line, bolstering its original river decree, not through Doherty's never-never ditch. Most of the Antero District was never irrigated, and the rights were made available to surviving High Line farmers.

Thereafter, most years, the water flowed, if irregularly. The early hopes of one thousand-plus cubic feet per second for the canal shrank to a more practical level of six hundred. Farmers became more adroit at dryland farming. They learned that life is a series of lowered expectations—not always a bad thing, for then they are more often met. Most of those who stuck it out eventually got their water—if not what they wanted, what they needed. But the majority of Lord Barclay's mortgages had been foreclosed long before the water came in reliably.

Jack had it right: the Swale was a screwup. By the time we found it, Doherty's Ditch was nothing but an on-again, off-again hole in the ground. Doherty's dust had long settled, and the High Line Canal had settled down to a half century of modest journeyman service.

Just a mile upstream from the Swale lay the fertile acres of the William Smith farm. Born in Aberdeen, Scotland, in 1860, William Smith came to

Colorado from Liverpool in 1878 with his Irish wife, Anna. Related to, and partly sponsored by, Lord Barclay, William Smith bought a quarter section of potential farmland (one hundred sixty acres) for $4,400. He adopted the pound sterling (£) as his brand, went to work, and waited for the water to come in.

When William and Anna Smith came to Colorado, their land was a patch of prairie covered with tumbleweeds, rough grass, rabbitbrush, and yucca. Prairie dogs stood sentry or scuttled below where the Smiths imagined cattle and horses grazing. The scene was treeless—just flat steppe, running as far as they could see to the east and north, and as far as Mount Evans in the west and Pikes Peak to the south. But the Smith spread was situated at one of the prime locations on the whole canal: smack-dab on the Great Bifurcation. Tucked between the main branch and its Sand Creek Lateral, Smith's farm had access to both. No doubt banker Barclay, recognizing the dodgy nature of his enterprise, steered his kinsman Smith to one of the least risky bets on the scheme.

William Smith ran a fine and diverse farm, growing fruits and vegetables and grains and practicing dryland grazing where the water from well or ditch wouldn't reach. He landscaped the area, planting the dozens of lilacs I later came to know and cottonwoods, including the Thunder Tree, along the ditches. And he built the red house. Beginning in 1910 and finishing the following year, Scotsman Smith spared little expense in making a fine home, although he did practice thrift by paneling the public areas in oak, the family rooms in pines. But such pines! The joists were Oregon, the flooring Texas, and the porch Mexican pine. Walls were built of ten- and twelve-dollar red press brick, three courses for the first floor, two above. Fine-cut Hathaway del Norte lava and Bedford limestone dressed foundations, lintels, pillars, and corners.

My great-great-uncle Amos Whetstone operated a renowned brickworks about then, just one ridge away from the canal's source at Waterton. The brick kiln still stands at the entrance of the spectacular red-rock canyon of Roxborough State Park. I've often wondered whether William Smith's bricks came from Amos Whetstone's brickworks. They would not have been shipped down the canal itself, which was never used for commercial barge transport; but even coming overland by wagon, the bricks would have traveled from the start of the ditch to near its finish, from one of my rooted connections with the Colorado landscape to another.

Smith installed a carbide generator for gas, and he had hot and cold running water and flush toilets served by an artesian well. You would never have known from his verdant spread that water was the limiting factor here. He surrounded the house with orchards, shade trees, flowers, and shrubs to create, if not a little patch of Scotland, at least one of the greener corners of early-day Denver's environs.

An avid supporter of education, Smith donated land for the first school in Fletcher, as Aurora was then called. Later, the first high school was to bear his name. When he died in 1946, Smith had held elective office longer than any other official in state history, serving as secretary of the school district for half a century. His daughter, Margaret Robina, born in 1889, was also a benefactor. Retiring from a career in teaching and nursing to care for her father, she occupied the red house, keeping its lawns and lilacs, for almost forty years. She died a day before her ninety-fourth birthday.

Baron von Richthofen, too, finally realized his green hopes thanks to the High Line Canal, if only briefly. He and other developers convinced the Denver aldermen to buy 40 million gallons of water for $600 per year to irrigate the parts of Capitol Hill that lay above the City Ditch. The lateral ditch they built branched off from the High Line Canal at Windsor Lake, a few miles west of William Smith's ranch. As it passed Montclair, the patient baron got his water. He even got a moat for his castle, for so he insisted on calling the homely ditch that partly circled the manor grounds.

Able at last to water them, Richthofen planted elms, box elders, spruces, and other trees all over Montclair, plus hundreds of lilacs. He created a deer and antelope park reminiscent of a European estate, and introduced hardy canaries (but not hardy enough). He brought prospective lot buyers to the new town site in a coach-and-four. The baron escorted the coach from the Tabor Grand Opera House, blowing the tallyho on a hunting horn as his Russian wolf hounds loped alongside.

Some of the prospects bought, and the community was under way, soon to have its own newspapers and trolley line. Montclair was to be free of liquor, improper language, and bird persecution—the baron's model community. But according to T. J. Noel, "Only after the Baron's roses bloomed a year later did the Baroness move out of the Albany Hotel and pick Montclair roses for their first evening at the castle."

As Montclair real estate took off, so did the noble couple. They traveled abroad in high style, visiting a succession of fashionable spas in Europe, Mexico, and elsewhere. Following the Crash of 1893, they returned with big ideas for a "Colorado Carlsbad"—a fabulous health spa, lung-disorder treatment center, and hotel to be built on the European model. Montclair lacking mineral springs, Richthofen must have thought that High Line water would do until he could pipe in springwater.

The Colorado Carlsbad, like his failed art museum, was not to be. But its promotion, and that of his many other schemes, kept the baron downtown in Denver much of the time. And like his German contemporary, "mad" King Ludwig of Bavaria, who slept only nine nights in his fairy-tale castle of Neuschwanstein before drowning, Richthofen was not destined to enjoy his castle for long. In 1898, at the age of forty-nine, he died of appendicitis in Denver's Hotel L'Impériale.

Baroness von Richthofen, freed to desert her vast moated castle, decamped to the city with some relief. There she took up residence in the Brown Palace, still the grand dame of Denver hotels. The lovely sandstone Brown, triangular in form, received its renowned produce from Windsor Farm. Begun by the ditch-digging English Company, this 480-acre compound had become the finest farm on the High Line Canal. Not surprisingly, it always seemed to get enough water to support its splendid array of grain, fruits and vegetables, hay and feed for hogs and steers, honey, and milk from the largest herd of Holstein-Friesians in the United States. The farm existed to provision Barclay and Duff's Hotel Windsor in Denver, whose board groaned beneath the farm's fresh largess. By 1900 Windsor Farm also furnished food for the Hotel Metropole and the Brown Palace. I picture the Baroness von Richthofen in her elegant mourning garb, in self-chosen exile from Montclair, fed by the fruits of the farm whose riches drew from the same ditch that watered her husband's megalithic dreams.

Now surrounded by hundreds of modern homes, William Smith's red house stands out from its neighbors almost as much as it did in the open farmland eighty years ago. It is like a fine old enameled box stuck among a shelf of saltine packages. Having grown up in one of the look-alike tract houses nearby, I still feel that the red house is the only one in all Aurora I would really like to live in. A dentist named Randy Sanders felt the same way. He found the old place sulking in the suburbs, recognized its unique beauty among the boxes all around, bought and restored it. I visited the Sanders family for a look around the house I'd so admired while poaching butterflies from its lilacs. On the broad veranda we spoke quietly of William Smith and his vision of the desert. The moist breath of the canal reminded me of the only reason the red house was there at all.

Westerly a few miles from the red house along the High Line Canal you come to Fairmount Cemetery. The big burial ground arose next to, then atop, the old Windsor Farm. Richthofen and other civic leaders developed Fairmount as a place for the patrician dead, thus raising the tone of nearby East Denver and Montclair. The baron himself did not remain to enhance the ground, returning instead to the family vaults in Silesia. But Squire Smith, the bourgeois farmer whose modest plans worked out rather better than the German nobleman's grand schemes, remained behind in Fairmount, where he lies beside Anna and Margaret Robina. There, to this day, the High Line Canal waters the green hackberries, the blue spruces, and the broad lawns.

The canal makes a deep loop through the graveyard, on the inner edge of which my own people lie. When I visit them, or walk the canal's graceful swoop among the goldenrods, I think of its flow running down the line to William Smith's place, or shooting off here to water Lord Barclay's company farm and fill Baron von Richthofen's castle moat.

I also think of all the settlers along the ditch who didn't get the promised water and moved on. Because for every big brick house or speculator's mansion with its lush lilacs, there were a hundred shacks and cabins beside a headgate too often closed. Theirs was a water saga also, one that left dreams parched and dusty far more often than green and satisfied. They, too, planted lilacs lovingly, then watched them thirst into brown sticks. You can tell the failed farms easily enough—just look for the places where the purple crossflower grows.

Not long ago I visited an abandoned pioneer house. The structure was much more modest than that of the red house on the High Line or the castle on the lateral. This was in a different western landscape, where the concern was too much water, not too little, and shortage of greenery was not a problem. Yet the effect was the same as I'd often felt when prowling the last of the ghost houses along the High Line before the suburbs subsumed them: one of rot and decay, of ambition defeated and possessions resorted by wood rats, of premature foreclosure on dreams.

In an old notebook left in this moldering ruin, someone before me had written: "I suppose these people had hopes. Maybe feeble ones—or maybe not."

5

Magpie Days

Magpies sing of bubbling, sloshing, and gurgling waters, horned owls and hawk whistles, and, sometimes, the mystery of the coyote's bark and call.

— Tony Angell, *Ravens, Crows, Magpies and Jays*

It was bird night at Cub Scouts. The wooden floor of the Peoria Elementary auditorium gleamed back at the faces of a hundred scuffling Cubs. The pack master called the monthly meeting to order. We filed onto the folding chairs beside our respective den mothers like the young of some large-brooded animal, still in our immature pelage of blue and gold.

First came the flag and our mumbled allegiance, then the Cub Scout Promise "to obey the law of the pack." Badges and awards were dispensed, den reports rendered, and then it was time for the main business of the evening, the ornithological competition. Our artwork lay fully displayed on cafeteria tables, ready to be judged. The art event would be followed by a bird quiz before refreshments. I sat forward on my chair, flushed and ready to receive my prize for the best drawing of the Colorado state bird.

I'd joined Scouts in the belief that they had something to do with the out-of-doors. The promise of woodcraft appealed to me, but all the other Cubs seemed to want to do was horse around, talk sports, or play war—not my idea of woodlore. Our den mothers came up with games and crafts like making key fobs from bright plastic braids or pictures in punched tin or burned wood. I managed to make a crude hat rack that my dad reluctantly approved for points toward my Wolf badge. But where was all the nature study the handbook promised?

My brother Tom was a consummate Scout who moved quickly through the badges from Wolf to Bear, Lion, and on to Webelos and Boy Scouts. I barely managed to mount the points required for the Wolf badge. And when I finally did, my award failed to come, meeting after meeting, even when our dad was pack master. So I failed to move up the hierarchy of predators, remaining a mere Bobcat.

My interest was on the wane when Bird Month arrived. We were to observe the theme by studying birds and drawing the official state bird during the regular den meeting. When the day came, our den mother handed out crayons and paper and pictures and asked us to do our best to depict the subject in our own way. Finally it was time to pay attention to nature for a change.

This was more like it! Birds grabbed me much more than baseball cards. I'd spent time with birds in my backyard, as squawking house sparrows and wheedling house finches came to investigate the greening neighborhood. During my walks on the High Line Canal I'd come to know a handful of wild birds: bright Bullock's orioles the color of my orange-yellow crayon, whose scrotal nests dangled in the cottonwoods over the ditch; crested and ruby-studded cedar waxwings prying pasty berries from the Russian olives; and a great horned owl erupting from a hollow snag. Eventually I learned who left behind the red feathers I sometimes found among dried cottonwood leaves in the fall, and the red-shafted flicker's piercing complaint became as familiar as its molted primaries. But the bird I noticed most was the black-billed magpie. With its striking black and white plumage, raucous repertory of calls, and dramatic swooping flights over field and ditch, who could miss it?

I watched magpies often and long, so I was ready when my den mother asked us to draw magpies for the pack-wide artistic competition. Scarcely referring to the pictures she provided, I drew them from memory with all the brilliance Crayola could devise. That long sickle tail, the wings like doors of a Black and White taxicab, the bright eye and sharp bill flowed onto my construction paper in several poses. None of the others even attempted to capture the bird's stunning iridescence. Their magpies looked like scraps of black and white newsprint.

At the pack meeting the master explained for the parents that each den had submitted entries depicting the state bird. Then he conferred with the judges and prepared to announce the several winners. I jittered with anticipation. At last my parents would be proud of something *I'd* done in

Scouts, my brother Tom, too. The pack master, clearing his throat from his constant Camels, read off the names of the winning artists. Mine was not among them. I was dumbfounded, and near tears.

Our den mother asked the master why no one in our den had won a prize. That was when she learned that the state bird is the lark bunting—*not* the magpie. All the other dens had drawn lark buntings. No birder, she'd assumed the picture of a black and white bird on the entry form was a magpie. Our drawings were duly disqualified. The others laughed it off, but I was righteously disappointed. Magpies mattered to me.

Magpies, with ravens, crows, and jays, belong to the family Corvidae. Throughout much of western North America they announce their presence with their strident cries, conspicuous colors, size, and abundance. Short rounded wings and a long graduated tail mark the magpie in its slow and graceful flight. That amazing tail shimmers with tinges of green, bronze, purple, and blue. Stretching to some twenty inches, the bird makes an impressive sight. John James Audubon's classic *Birds of America* portrait not only conveys the spectacle of a magpie in flight, but hints at the bird's grace and intelligence.

Magpies, like other corvids, really *are* smart. They make their living by their wits, feeding on insects, crayfish, birds and eggs, small mammals, lizards, carrion, green leaves, grain, and whatever else they can get. A mixed rural habitat like the High Line Canal makes perfect magpie country. The bird occurs across the prairies and steppes of much of the American West and north to Alaska, but not in the eastern states. Until Lewis and Clark's expedition it was thought to be solely an Old World resident. Audubon, giving William priority over Meriwether for perhaps the last time ever, reported that

> to CLARKE and LEWIS . . . is due the first introduction of this bird into the Fauna of the United States. Those intrepid travellers first observed the Magpie near the great bend of the Missouri, although it was known to have been obtained at the fur-trading factories of the Hudson's Bay Company.

So this familiar bird joined the American checklist of birds during that April of 1804.

The black-billed magpie has been known by hundreds of vernacular names, such as "side-wheeler" and "creek-crow." It has been called an "unscrupulous roysterer," a "symbol of loquacity and mischief," and a "handsome, knowing, resourceful fellow." Yet all over the English-speaking portion of its range, it is called magpie.

In *Ravens, Crows, Magpies and Jays,* Tony Angell suggests that magpie might be a contraction of the Middle English term "maggot pie," growing out of the birds' habit of harvesting botfly maggots from the backs of beasts. Another version allows that "Magot Pie" came from the French Margot, a diminutive of the name Marguerite, referring to its chattering habit as "resembling a talkative woman." Or might it have come from the querulous call, which Roger Tory Peterson characterizes as "maaag, maaag"?

The "pie" part refers to the animal's pied (black and white) condition. The early Romans called the bird *pica,* which meant "pied" or "piebald" in Latin, and Linnaeus echoed this in giving the bird its Latinate binomial, *Corvus pica.* When it was differentiated from crows, the magpie's name became *Pica pica.* The American black-billed magpie, once thought to be a separate species, is now considered a subspecies of the Eurasian bird. It is known as *P. p. hudsonia,* for the region where the fur traders first observed it in North America. As the first-named subspecies, the Old World variety, in a sublime stroke of superfluity for such a thoroughly unmistakable creature, is called *Pica pica pica.*

P. pica's pied image projects as strikingly as that of any orca, avocet, or panda. A magpie's overall black plumage contrasts with snow white in the webbing of its primary wing feathers, its lower breast and belly, and the shoulder patches almost meeting over its back like a priest's cope. The eyes are black beads, the bill a blackish scythe. A simple pattern, but just black and white it is not. For the feathers blacked with the pigment melanin also have ridges and furrows that diffract sunlight, scattering it rainbowlike into prismatic colors. Like the special scales that create blue in a butterfly's wings, these feathers produce intense iridescent hues known as structural colors, as opposed to the plainer tints reflected by pigments.

And such iridescence! If you combined the green of the speculum of a teal, the purple of a Colorado hairstreak butterfly, and the blue of a 1955 Chevy, you would scarcely have the range and depth of the magpie's metallic sheen as it swings through a sunbeam. These gleaming colors mate with the black and white to give the magpie a truly dramatic presence. "In flight," says Roger Tory Peterson, "the iridescent greenish black tail streams behind and large white patches flash in the wings." Audubon called the magpie "splendent." But these feathered fireworks do not exist merely to delight painters, birders, and writers. They have a profound purpose for the bird.

Edward Armstrong, the ethologist who coined the term "displacement activity," pointed out that in birds, "deficiency in song tends to be counterbalanced by conspicuousness in flight." Though capable of endearing whistles and gentle gabbling as well as its famous harsh scolds, the magpie with its chattering vocabulary can hardly be called a songster. Conspicuous in flight, however, it is. Armstrong suggests that this dazzling display flight might serve to stimulate the female and perhaps to intimidate intruding males. Armstrong describes this in *Bird Display and Behavior*:

> Early in the year when I have noticed three birds together the males utter a rapid clinking cry—a higher-pitched version of their usual chuckle, which it sometimes immediately follows. After perching on some lofty point for a time uttering a medley of these calls the male will set out on a high direct flight, the female accompanying him some distance away. Every two or three seconds as he flies he gives a double or treble rapid beat of his wings, a curious intermittent flutter . . . over what will become the breeding territory.

Should the sexual display prove successful, the magpies mate for as long as they both live. Together they build a remarkable nest, consisting of hundreds of sticks arrayed in a rough sphere so as to point outward from the hollow interior. The floor is cemented in place with mud, the roof arched overhead. An entrance in the side gives way to a cozy bowl of finely woven grass, rootlets, sometimes hair, fully protected by the outer walls. Small as a basketball or big as a barrel but usually about a bushel, the nest is built anywhere from six to sixty feet up in anything from a sagebrush to a cottonwood, with a preference for thorn trees. Audubon called the nest "a formidable fortress—difficult to penetrate, even by a human hand."

Within the fortress, in the nest proper, the female places five to ten eggs in April. Bluish or olive, spattered with muddy marks, the inch-long oval eggs vary greatly. The mother incubates them for a fortnight and a half until the naked helpless chicks hatch, then her mate joins her in the pursuit of baby food. The returning parents face a phalanx of deep pink gapes, the offspring advertising their hunger and beginning a life of ravenous preoccupation with food. Helpless, the young lie safe within their soft basket, protected from owls and other predators by the solid dome of twigs overhead. There they remain, frequently fed by the harried parents, for several weeks. Then one day in May, clumsily, they crawl through the door, clutch the nearest branch, blink, and flutter to the ground.

Pacing the bank of the ditch one day, we heard laughter. Crazy laughter, like the perpetual shrill hoots and giggles of the dummy fat lady perched above the entrance to the Fun House at Lakeside Amusement Park in West Denver. Tom and I exchanged puzzled looks. We walked on, quietly, searching for the source, half expecting to find a maniac among the brush.

Then four black and white lumps tumbled out of the hem of a low willow's skirt. Almost tailless, they bore only the remotest resemblance to their graceful parents, who now swept down beside them in an amethyst flash. The maniacal laughter came again, issuing from the throats of the four baby magpies. Bobtailed, big billed, awkward, not shiny like their parents, they seemed a different species. But the elegant adults, a mixture of shyness and boldness in Audubon's eyes, remained close by, to let us know who they were and to amplify their babies' din.

We wanted a magpie of our own. Another boy told us that if you split its tongue, a magpie could learn to talk like a parrot. Indeed, the big checkered birds, like the related jays and crows, can make great pets, learning to imitate a remarkable array of sounds. But the hilarious fledglings looked like too much of a handful to us. Even if we managed to catch one, we figured its assassin's bill would section us before we got it home, let alone split its tongue. So we gave it up, promising to have a go the following year.

When the next spring came, we saw the parent magpies adding to their big stickball nests. Tom decided it would work best to try to get eggs and incubate them, as we'd done with Easter chicks and ducklings. We figured we could feed them grasshoppers and rear several, keeping one and selling the rest. So we went out to a stretch of the Sand Creek Lateral behind Peoria Elementary, where we'd seen several occupied nests. As we approached one of them, a pair of adult magpies lifted off. Outraged, they scolded us harshly before flying away to a safe distance where they could watch and continue screaming their protest. As always when I watched their graceful but labored flight, I wasn't sure whether their long trailing tails helped or hindered them in the air.

We climbed up a locust tree to the low crotch where the nest was jammed. Tom, far braver than I, found the opening and thrust his hand inside the great, sloppy basket. I expected him to lose a finger, at least. But instead of grimacing in pain, he smiled with triumph as he withdrew his brown hand and held up an egg. Blue and speckled, like the sky in a dust storm, it was not much bigger than a shooter marble. Tom handed it down and went back for more. The soft cup in the nest embraced eight eggs in all. Tom decided to take four. "And four for them," he said. Seemed fair to me. He shinnied down past me, the eggs safe in his cap.

As he reached the ground, a big kid emerged from the willows and demanded our prize. "Gimme 'em now," he said, "or I'll pound both you and your shrimp brother." He and Tom fought and the bully ran off, leaving Tom with a shiner showing all the colors of a magpie. The parents had returned and were shrieking from the top of the tree. Up close and angry, they seemed as threatening as the bully. Locust thorns scratched as I dropped hard from the lowest branch. Thudding to the ground, I cried out and collapsed in a heap. The eggs, oozing yolk into the ditch dust, lay broken beside me. I'd sprained my ankle. Weeks later, when the adhesive tape came off, four screeching fluff balls decorated that tree.

Magpies and their kin—the crows, jays, rooks, jackdaws, and ravens—have long been persecuted by gamekeepers and vermin hunters. I remember coming upon the "keeper's larder" on an English country estate as recently as 1977, where dozens of corvids were strung up from a bough. The keeper intended the macabre sight as a warning to any "bloody vermin" that might consider preying on his master's precious pheasants. It made me think of a boutique for widows' weeds.

As the great magpie authority Jean Myron Linsdale wrote, "Man encroaches on the territory of the magpie in nearly every part of the range of the bird." He explained that this was so because "the requirements of these two kinds of animals overlap so much that they come to occupy common ground." Certainly this is so in purely geographical terms, but there the "common ground" between our species and *Pica pica* ends. Seldom has such an attractive animal been so hated by so many. Among other accusations, magpies answer to charges of robbing the nests and young of songbirds, gamebirds, and poultry; stealing grain; and springing traps for fur bearers, predators, and small mammals while filching the bait.

John James Audubon, in *Birds of America*, quotes Colonel Zebulon Montgomery Pike, writing of an experience when he was a lieutenant exploring the Red River in Louisiana:

> *Our horses were obliged to scrape the snow away to obtain their miserable*
> *pittance; and to increase their misfortune, the poor animals were attacked*
> *by the Magpies, who, attracted by the scent of their sore backs, alighted*
> *on them, and, in defiance of their wincing and kicking, picked many places*
> *quite raw; the difficulty of procuring food rendering those birds so bold as to*
> *alight on our men's arms, and eat meat out of their hands.*

A Mr. Suckley wrote to Audubon in 1860 that frontier traders and mountain men disliked magpies for this very habit of feeding on the raw exposed flesh of broken-down horses and mules, and evidently they have been known to do the same to cattle and sheep.

But magpies also prey on ground squirrels, voles, and injurious insects, especially grasshoppers. Their benefits as control agents probably far exceed the damage they do by getting into the grain. On balance, magpies are the farmer's friend. As elegantly adapted native creatures, magpies contribute profoundly to their ecosystem as well. If they invade the nests of birds from time to time, their own towering structures provide shelter for many others. Several species of owls, hawks, ducks, herons, and songbirds have been known to use old magpie homes as nests, day or night roosts, and shelter from rain, snow, wind, and hail. Magpies often build near hawks and eagles (occasionally in a common structure!) in order to be on hand to clean up the raptors' leavings.

If they pester the festering sores of stock, the practice began by searching for external parasites on the animals' hides. This habit came from long association with deer, elk, and bighorns, whom the birds service by ticking their backs and heads. Too, magpies followed the great buffalo herds, feasting on parasites in the vast expanse of their hides and the insects in their monumental leavings of dung. When the bison nearly all became carrion within a few short years, the magpies were there to cleanse the lonely boneyard.

Yet, as Linsdale wrote, "Improvement of the habitat by magpies . . . is usually not noticed at all by people. However, if the magpies remove, or interfere with, any article claimed by people, this is likely to be noticed immediately and to be followed by some kind of retaliation." In 1931, a newspaper-sponsored magpie destruction derby in British Columbia saw 1,033 birds killed. In order to keep them out of poison-bait traps set for coyotes, agents nearly eliminated the birds from whole counties in Colorado, Oregon, and California during the harsh winters of 1921–23. Some five thousand magpies were shot or poisoned in Umatilla County, Oregon, alone.

A wildlife biologist reviewing these campaigns in 1927 concluded that the magpie seldom presents a serious menace, "and there are times when its influence may even be decidedly beneficial." This realization failed to take hold, for such practices have continued over much of the West until recent years. So it was that in 1956, in Aurora, Colorado, the county agent still offered a twenty-five-cent bounty on magpies.

When Tom and I became "Bill" and "Joe"—I was Bill—we might be miners stuck in a shaft; marshals on the track of outlaws, or vice versa; mountain men pursuing the wily beaver; or stranded pilots of a downed plane in the Alaskan (or African) bush. The High Line Canal's service road stretched off to unknown parts, giving free rein to our plots. Wandering like the magpies from cottonwood to cottonwood as a couple of guys on adventure, we acted out whatever parts and plots suggested themselves. The amplitude of our imagination and the length of the day were our only limits, and we often ignored the latter, arriving home late for dinner.

Not infrequently we would spoil our dinner by stopping off at the Dolly Madison for an ice cream sandwich. This and other "supplies" took money, so Bill and Joe were ever alert for ways to augment their allowances of a quarter a week. We dug dandelions for a nickel a full peach can, clipped edges, or picked up the yard for a dime. Joe relieved neighborhood kids of their spare change by auctioning bits of colored fishbowl gravel as pirates' jewels from the briny deep. Bill sold seashells by the curbside. Inspired by our father, a dedicated salesman, we both peddled White Cloverine Salve, Christmas cards, and Burpee seeds, door to door. But these yielded dumb prizes instead of cold cash. We were always on the lookout for more lucrative enterprises.

When we heard that we could get two bits apiece for bringing them in dead, we turned our financial attention to magpies. After all, we often played at being hunters. We clipped the ads in the back of *Boys' Life:* "Become a government bounty hunter—have a rewarding career of adventure bagging marauding mountain lions, wolves, and coyotes for the U.S. Government." Fortunately, such benighted thinking was waning even then, but we knew no better, and bounty hunting certainly seemed more exciting than dandelions and salve. We could start with magpies and maybe move on to mountain lions later.

I had never shot a living thing in my young life. When we visited Cousin Alta's farm with GrandPop, out east of Aurora near Byers on Bijou Creek, Tom joined Cousin Eddie in popping off rabbits with a .22. A devoted fan of the Thornton Burgess *Bedtime Stories* and a confirmed bunny lover, I demurred. I liked magpies as much as cottontails, and it seemed that might be a problem. But I managed to catch and poison my beloved butterflies, and I read Jim Bridger and Kit Carson as well as Thornton Burgess. So I obscured my scruples with a romantic vision of Bill and Joe as buckskin-clad trappers and mountain men, with magpies for quarry instead of beavers and bison. I decided I could probably plug the pretty birds after all.

We went out to the ditch to have a look. The magpies were common, but how easy would they be to shoot? Grammy's Audubon called the magpie "wary," and went on: "When one pursues it openly, it flits along the walls and hedges, shifts from tree to tree, and at length flies off to a distance." Here there were no walls or hedges, but trees there were and flit away they did. Sweeping their incredibly long glossy tails behind them, asking soft questions of the day, they swooped and lit, swooped and lit. I could think of uses for those tailfeathers—maybe a headdress.

Their wariness would give them a sporting chance and make the chase more fun. We agreed to wait until the chicks were grown, as it didn't seem fair to hunt the adults while they were on the nest, or the clumsy tailless young. Besides, we hadn't any guns. Then GrandPop drove us back east in his long black Packard to visit more cousins in Ohio and Indiana, and the project went on hold.

We walked softly on the oak woodland path. An Indiana Pyle kid led the way, Tom followed, then me. His farm chores completed, our cousin was taking us into the woods for target practice. He was looking for anything on which to "train in" his sights, in preparation for dove season. He carried a double-barreled shotgun; Tom had a twelve-gauge. The cousin had placed a little four-ten shotgun in my virgin hands, saying, "Shoot what moves."

I felt every bit the deer stalker. This was Bill and Joe, but with real guns. My safety was off, my trigger finger ready. We approached a pond, gray beneath afternoon thunderclouds, deep in the forest. Bittersweet and poison ivy trailed around the margin. The thick scent of rank vegetation filled the clearing. I watched the water for any sign of life, a habit I'd acquired on the High Line Canal. A ripple appeared and slowly became a shape. A painted turtle emerged from the pondweed. It swam toward me, just beneath the surface, only its snout breaking the water. It was six or seven inches long.

The only turtles I'd ever seen were the little dime-store variety that made decent pets for a while, then died. Fascinated and thrilled by my first wild turtle, I forgot about my gun and watched, rapt.

"Shoot, Bobby!" my cousin yelled. "Before it gets away!" I hesitated a moment longer, then pulled the trigger.

"*Blam!*" The shot shattered the surface of the pond like the windshield of the wreck we'd seen on the highway the day before, and stained it red, just the same. Bloody bits of turtle shell spackled the water and the shore. There seemed to be turtle all over the world. I was horrified; I loved turtles. I cried, and was disgraced.

That did it. I never shot a magpie, or anything else, after that turtle. Neither did Tom. Instead of the BB gun I'd wanted for Christmas I received a popgun that made a big noise but killed nothing. Tom actually got a shotgun. But Dad was an angler, not a hunter, and when he and Tom went shooting they killed only bottles and tumbleweeds. Tom sold the gun before long. Our bounty hunting days were over before they began.

Back on the canal I became the magpie's ardent watcher. When the male spread his glistening wings in butterfly fashion in display to the female, I was watching. I watched those cackling young take their first clumsy gliding flights, directionless without their tails. And whenever a magpie made its long sickleswoop from one cottonwood to another, I stopped what I was doing and watched. Magpies became the very signature of the countryside, scrawled across the summer sky in opalescent ink. I was relieved one day to learn that the bounty had been abolished.

After the judging of the state bird portraits at that long-ago pack meeting, there came the quiz on bird facts. I expected to excel in that at least, being the only birdwatcher around. I owned a set of little bird books—red, yellow, blue, green—each containing a number of species one was likely to see. I slept outdoors in order to be up with the birds, although I usually came in to my bed well before dawn and remained till long after.

Those books had been with us on the trip back east, enlivening the miles with the absurd portrait of the neckless bittern like a beaked schmoo, sending us into paroxysms of giggles that irritated GrandPop. Magpies followed us all the way to Joplin. We spotted orchard orioles among Osage orange in the Ozarks. And on an old family homestead in Kentucky where we caught hell for throwing ripe peaches at the pigs, I beheld my first cardinal, the same scarlet as the little book in which I found its likeness. Back home, I was ready for the ornithological quiz.

I awaited my first question in the single elimination round. "Identify the bird named in this popular song," commanded the pack master, who proceeded to whistle "Mockingbird Hill" with a wheeze. I couldn't believe my ears; why in the world should I know *that*? I hadn't a clue, and I was out. Well, that was ornithology a la Cub Scouts—no bitterns, flickers, or orioles, no cardinals, no magpies—just a bum steer and a dumb ditty.

After the fiasco of Bird Night, I stuck with scouting a little longer because it held out the promise of camp in the Rocky Mountains. Tom, by now a fully fledged Boy Scout, went to Camp Tahosa and regaled me with tales of frog-filled marshes and flowery meadows brimming with butterflies, snakes, and such. But when we visited on open day, I could tell it wasn't for me. The Scouts' busy schedule left little time for exploring the meadows on your own, and the boys' macho banter excluded a shy kid like me.

I never made it to camp. Instead, I stuck with my ditch on the plains. No Eagle Scout material I—that much was clear. More, I would say, a magpie scout.

6

Mile Roads

The land lives in its people. It is more alive because they worked it, because
they left this hillside and that creek bottom marked by their shovels and
axes. The meaning of this place lies in the rough weight of their hands, in
the imprint of their gum-booted travel.

— John Haines, *The Stars, the Snow, the Fire*

My childhood territory east of Denver was bounded by mile roads. Starting
from the center of the known universe, the Thunder Tree, the mile roads
stretched away in all directions. To the south lay Alameda Avenue, Mississippi
Avenue, then terra incognita. To the north, Sixth Avenue, Colfax Avenue,
and t.i. Heading westerly, I'd come to Havana Street, Yosemite Street, then
the built world of Denver, of little interest; easterly, to Peoria Street, Potomac
Street, Chambers Road, and the edge of the world. Del Mar Circle made
a bull's-eye in the middle, and the Union Pacific shot across like a straight-
line function on a graph.

Thanks to Thomas Jefferson, the West is marked off with mile roads. If
you look at a map of any city west and north of the Ohio River, on the
edges where the solid streets run out into the blankness of the undeveloped
country, you'll see this grid. Following the monumental Louisiana
Purchase, Congress commissioned the survey of the West through the Land
Ordinance of 1785. James Monroe's doctrine of Manifest Destiny required
a ground plan. Jefferson envisioned an orderly system for dividing the land,
unlike the random jigsaw of the East.

First the Midwest felt the imprint of the mapmakers. Next, not long
after his advance men, Lewis and Clark, returned from their journey of
discovery, President Jefferson dispatched an army of surveyors to draw their
lines across a western land the explorers had found virtually unmarked.

The unit of the Jeffersonian system was the square mile, known as the
section. Thirty-six sections made up a township. All legal descriptions of

property boundaries have since been designated in terms of sections and townships. Early land claims often consisted of single sections, blocks of 640 acres, a mile on a side. When roads began to appear on the open range they frequently followed the section lines, to simplify rights-of-way. Therefore the distance from one main country road to the next would be an even mile.

My brother Tom and I had a potential home range of sixteen square miles, as defined by the mile roads. Our actual meanderings used only portions of this empire, but sometimes we ventured a little beyond, especially when we rode our bikes. On foot, we noted the mile roads but didn't stick to them. For overlaid across the grid, minding no straight lines but strewn in lazy parabolic arcs, ran the High Line Canal.

Since it looped so, the canal squeezed much more than a mile into the passage from one mile road to another. A mere three miles along Sixth Avenue, Havana to Chambers, became more like five miles as the magpie flew, cottonwood to cottonwood, loop by loop. The lateral ditches, the creeks crossed, the other obligatory diversions made a High Line journey still longer. As a short-legged and easily sidetracked wanderer, I seldom pushed the frontiers. And when I came to the edges, I felt both the suck of wanderlust and the fragility of the city walls.

One summer day the heat hit early, and I was up and out by eight. Tom was away at Camp Tahosa, so I was on my own. Heading east, I passed Potomac, continued beyond the shale beds at Sable (a half-mile road), and kept going even beyond Chambers Road. There the canal described a wide sweep easterly, crossing Toll Gate Creek in an old redwood flume. Then it swung around toward the north, enclosing the cottonwood bottoms of an abandoned farm pond. A round white barn with a green ball on top squatted across the creek from the pond. A flight of rock doves erupted from the barn, circled, and returned to the green shingled roof. Beyond there, the High Line struck off northeasterly for Colfax and (for all I knew) Kansas. I'd never been this far.

I looked up Toll Gate's gully from the flume. Heavy rains of the previous summer had carved its sand canyon deeper than ever. The sun was hitting hard, and the cottonwoods were on the wrong side for shade. Toll Gate's deep gorge, with its cool, shaded stream in the bottom, drew me off my ditchside route. I skidded down the crumbly bank where horses had done the same. Pulling off my sneakers, lacing them through my belt, and rolling up my jeans, I stepped into the shallow flow. My hot feet, itchy from cheatgrass, dust, and sweat, loved it. The current lured me on. Now after noon, the sun broke across the top of the gully without quite reaching within. The air was still and hot, the creek almost cold. I put up a cloud of sulphur butterflies that had been puddling at the damp sand of an outside curve. I walked a little faster, splashing, to see where they would settle, and alarmed a brilliant ruddy copper. My feet stuck in the loose sand, then sucked out again.

Many times I'd listened to GrandPop's stories of quicksand in the streams east of Denver. Out near the cousins' place at Byers, he'd tell me, a Union Pacific steam locomotive had once jumped the trestle over Bijou Creek and plunged into the creek bed's quicksand. All over the Platte drainage on the High Plains, underground streams and aquifers underlie saturated layers of loose sand. Where this occurs, anything heavy stepping or falling on the sand can become stuck in the soft, runny substance, or even disappear altogether.

"Well, that old locomotive," GrandPop would say, "they never did find 'er. They poked around with hundred-foot-long poles and never felt a darned thing. Not a darned thing."

I knew just when GrandPop would launch the story as we approached Bijou Creek, how he would gesture in the general direction of the catastrophe, shake his head, tsk, and frown as he repeated "not a darned thing." And it would make me shiver, to think of sinking into that cold, breathless sand.

But I did not sink into the sands of Toll Gate. My feet shed the stream bed, popping out with a squish. Quicksand doesn't so much suck you down as part to let you in, and that's what the afternoon did, as I splashed around each swirling curve. Willow boughs trailed in the current. Their sharp vegetable tang mixed in my nostrils with drops of cold water and the smells of crawdad rot and mud.

When I clambered out of the canyon I didn't even know where I was. I'd passed the borders of known territory. The grid seemed to stretch, the world came wider at its seams, and I saw that borders, like mile roads, are no more than lines on a map.

We all follow lines on the land. How else to sort out the infinite array of points that make up the globe's skin? We choose routes. We make tracks. We go our way. We may imagine that we lead, but almost always we follow.

Lewis and Clark followed rivers and the knowledge and intuition of a Native American named Sacagawea. We still follow rivers and canals. We mark the ways of water and mimic its progress. We find our ways where we can: a gully, a narrow gorge, a green-brown stripe of winter wheat furrow; a sequence of steps from some foregone illusion, a deer trail, a rabbit path; an imaginary line to the horizon or a crease in an old map, more alluring than any highways, blue or red: something, anyway, that draws the eye and points the foot. Seldom do we track the traceless waste, for there is none. Even the deserts and the ice have seen the passage of the wind, which makes its own way.

The ways that lead our feet can be as old as the hills. In England, one hears of ley lines: often invisible vectors across the landscape along which ancient holy sites and structures are arrayed. The intersections of leys are thought to be nodes of power, and the lines themselves are supposed by some to indicate paths of power in the earth's surface. Others believe they are aligned with stellar paths. The leys were first discerned in modern times by Alfred Watkins, who described them in his book *The Old Straight Track*. Many of these tracks radiate from Avebury Stone Circle, seat of northern European civil-ization in the Bronze Age. Other systems center on Neolithic monuments such as Stonehenge, Silbury Hill, or Glastonbury Tor. They link beacon hills, mounds, earthworks, moats, and old churches built on pagan sites. Watkins's observations convinced him that Britain was webbed by a great many such tracks. Yet there were no surveyors in the days described. Or were there? Somehow, the makers of the leys found their way.

The English also preserve their green roads: ancient routes of travel between wool town and cinque port, thatching region and brewing district, cattle pasture and market square, countryside and cathedral. Perhaps it should not be surprising that they often overlap with the leys. Reinforced down the ages, some of these venerable ways of merchant, drover, and pilgrim have survived unpaved to become today's long-distance footpaths. When a green road has been designated by official maps and route signs, it is said to be *way-marked*.

This way-marking extends to the waterside. J. H. B. Peel, author of *Along the Green Roads of Britain,* counts the towpaths of England's canals among the historic green roads. The barge canals themselves, built to link eighteenth-century centers of commerce, mining, and industry across broad bands of countryside, now provide a pleasing network of public waterways and pathways over a thousand miles in extent.

I was once married to an Englishwoman named Sally Hughes, who grew up near the Kennet and Avon Canal where it runs through her cheddar-colored hometown of Bath. She frequently walked its towpath in her youth, just as I walked the High Line. After we were married, we exchanged canals as a kind of wedding gift. First she took me walking from Bath to Bradford along the Kennet and Avon. We watched fingerling pike, children netting for tiddlers, yellow flag irises, and reed buntings nesting in the cattails. We finished the ramble at a massive tithe barn from the fifteenth century.

A few weeks later, in reciprocity, I led Sally beneath the overarching cottonwoods of the High Line Canal. We picnicked in their shade, flowed with the current as mourning cloaks floated overhead, and watched Canada geese, killdeer, and crescentspots. Again our destination was a barn, the round white one dating only from 1895, but old here.

I felt the same sense of fresh connection along both canals, as different as they were. Half a millennium separated "our" barns, and Sally's barge canal was twice as old as my irrigation ditch. Yet lilting magpies and cattails forged a common currency between the watercourses, and today they both serve as green umbilici linking the countryside with the people of the towns, offering them a way back, if only for a day.

Whether straight like a ley line or mile road or curvy like a canal, the ways we follow have one thing in common. What makes a way work is its landmarks—places visited again and again or often sighted across the summer fields. They might be trees, hollows, rises, or old barns, the trestle where the train fell in the quicksand, or the flume that the big flood of 1965 took out. Places that lend the land its distinctiveness, familiarity, and warmth—its stories. It was out near the round white barn where I first gained a sense of this, and a word for it.

The round barn stood on an old, overgrazed horse ranch near the redwood flume on Toll Gate Creek. Across Chambers Road from the original ranch house, beside the canal, two modern "ranch-style" houses had been built of brick in the late fifties. They were the only new homes for miles around, scouts for the suburb that was preparing to pounce. One belonged to the rancher, whose hired hands lived across the road in the old place. In the other new house lived Mr. Korman, one of my high school teachers.

Julius Korman taught an aerospace course. My friends and I all took his class as a more interesting alternative to Basic Business. It was known as an easy B and almost as much fun as Driver's Ed, not so much for the field trips to the airport and the flight simulator as for Mr. Korman's jovial gullibility. He was a short, roundish man with big smiling lips, a sallow complexion, and a relaxed, slightly raffish manner that we admired yet mocked mercilessly. He was the target of more abuse than anyone but the band teacher. Too ingenuous and good hearted to see our game, he ignored us half the time, laughed along with us the rest. Once I delivered a fictitious and puerile report on "the use of light aircraft to transport beavers for soil and water conservation" that convulsed my buddies and embarrassed the girls, but Mr. Korman gave me an A. I always felt a little bad about the deception.

Mr. Korman often said things that sounded unbelievably square to us, then winked conspiratorially. For example, one of his favorite phrases was "feature this." As in, "Now, feature this, you guys. You're flying in a thick fog, and all of a sudden your zero-altitude alarm starts screaming. What do you do?" We'd shout, "Bail out!" and he would shake his head sadly. Outside of a forties movie, we had never heard anyone say "feature this."

Even so, he was a good teacher, and I liked him. I also liked where he lived, out on the High Line. On one walk I found him there, mowing his lawn. He told me to visit, and I took him up on it, partly out of guilt over our cruelty in class but also because I enjoyed his stories, advice, and wit.

I took to driving out to Mr. Korman's on my metallic blue Vespa motor scooter on summer evenings. In later years, partly at my instigation, the canal path was declared off limits to motors. But all through that summer of 1964, I would speed down the vale to the ford of Toll Gate Creek beneath the flume, up the other side, and into a faceful of cool evening air hung with the scent of ripe barley on a thunderstorm's breath. That was magic! When I reached Mr. Korman's I would allow the engine to putt for a minute to announce my arrival, then turn it off. "Reminds me of a little taildragger Piper Cub I once had," Mr. Korman would say, opening his screen door. "Its engine wasn't much bigger than that, and it'd cut out just about as fast, and whenever it felt like it. Feature that!"

Invigorated by sailing along the bumpy path at forty-five, I stood on Mr. Korman's porch with him and snorted the smells of some of the last alfalfa hay cuttings that country would ever see. I was surprised to see him dressed in a madras shirt that my friends and I might well wear. In school he wore mud-colored, short-sleeved dress shirts with bolo ties. His Bermuda shorts vitiated the madras and restored the Mr. Korman effect. He popped Dr. Peppers for us, and we sat back in his aluminum lawn chairs, facing the sunset and the partial view of Mount Evans, and drank them slowly. I mostly let him talk, and he obliged with aeronautical anecdotes.

In the golden light before dusk, sweet air rose off the alfalfa he somehow coaxed from a farmed-out field. Mr. Korman wiped his mouth with the back of his hand and laughed slowly and deeply, reminiscing about the fun we'd all had in class. He still didn't realize that he'd been the butt of it, or maybe he did and never let on.

On one of those visits, as we were finishing our second Dr. Peppers, Mr. Korman's mood changed. We'd been quietly sharing our mutual affection for the old ditch that bubbled nearby. "Feature this, Robert," he said. He paused and looked alert. Then again: "Feature this: in a few short years this entire area will be obliterated by one gigantic development." His stubby hand swept around in a gesture indicating the cottonwoods, the ranches, the old barn—everything. "Solid housing tracts as far as you can see," he continued. I just shook my head. He took his last sip, stood up to go in, and said, "I never would have imagined it when I bought this place. Good night, Robert." I featured it all the way home.

Mr. Korman was right. The fields are about all built up now. Near what was his land, the canal has been diverted into a concrete runnel to cut off a loop and clear the builders' path of an awkward obstacle. Mr. Korman's house is still there, thronged by condos on almost all sides. It stands out for its relaxed dimensions and period style almost as much as William Smith's old red farmhouse upstream a few miles. The lot on which it sits seems large for the suburbs, but not for the country. A sign calls it God's Little Acre. Too little for Mr. Korman, who has long since moved on to other prospects.

The round barn, the ranch house, and the quarter section of weedy fields and gullies across Chambers Road remain. When I go back, I still wade the current of Toll Gate Creek, my sandals looped through my belt, on July butterfly counts. Down inside the deep gully, with sulphurs and coppers sucking salts from the damp sand, I might as well be back in 1964, or 1954. But when I emerge and see the round barn moated by the ditch and surrounded by subdivisions, it reminds me of a castle keep under siege.

Mr. Jefferson's surveyors waffled the West with section squares. Mile by mile, they stepped off the states and tied down the territories with townships and ranges. Their successors installed brass benchmarks, blazed witness trees, and inscribed boulders that designate meridians—something solid to anchor the system, since places pegged by nothing more than grid lines on a map have a way of flapping free in the wind and the rain.

But benchmarks can disappear, and witness trees fall down. When the gusts of growth arrive on the scene, lines once drawn can cease to mean much. They might establish what we call ownership, but can they tell us where we are going? Where we've been? Even the solid mile roads let us down as the spaces between fill in. They lose their way, going nowhere, gridlocked in the traffic jam of time. And we, attempting to follow, become lost as well.

To find our way, like Lewis and Clark, we need our landmarks. Losing them, we lose our bearings. When I asked directions of a young clerk recently, she could describe the route only in terms of a succession of 7-Elevens. Are the new mileposts to be standard issue? Shall we clone the landscape? In a culture where more of the same is the name of the game, we relinquish diversity at the risk of inheriting a featureless domain.

To keep the canals, the barns, the weedy fields between the mile roads is to maintain the landmarks—and a good thing, for these are the holdfasts of the land in the hurricane of change.

PART III

City Limits

7

Snodgrass, Tatum, and Beasley

"Now what about the farm?"
"What about it? It exists."

— John Updike, *Of the Farm*

Fragrant cottonwood flickers into fire. A large can of Van Camp's Pork and Beans stands propped by a smoking log. Tom gathers more firewood as I watch the small blaze and block it from the breeze.

My father squats across the fire from me, stripping willow switches for weenie sticks with his fishing knife. His closed lips are drawn bowlike into a broad smile; he hasn't shaved. He wears a gray sweatshirt, brown slacks, old boots whose heels sink deeply into the sandy dust. No hat hides his black wavy hair, combed back and smoothed down with Wildroot. Looking across the fire, he catches my eye and chuckles wordlessly. The smoke shifts into his face and he moves around to my side, putting his arm around my shoulders. He smells of Wildroot oil and the mixed smokes of Lucky Strike and plains cottonwood.

For now there are no sharp words, no jobs, no homework. Just the dry ditch, the fire, our hunger, ourselves. Overhead, the trees and the sky the color of starling's eggshell, underfoot the sweet brown cottonwood leaves. A magpie calls some way off: "Maaag! maaag! merk?" Knobby twigs snap and crinkle into coals. I can already taste the warm bean gravy and the lump of pork fat that Tom and I will fight over. We will eat directly from the scorched can with our army-surplus mess-kit spoons. Weenies and marshmallows crinkle black, the way we like them. On this autumn Saturday on the Colorado plains we are only a mile or two from home, but we might as well be high in the Rockies.

Actual trips to the mountains with Dad were too infrequent. More often, "going to the country" for Tom and me meant a walk to the High

Line Canal. Neither ditchriders nor farmers had any use for us around the ditch. The water company men told us to scram, while the landowners slung barbed wire across the canal on wicked, branchy poles to snag our inner tubes. More than once we looked down their double barrels. The shotguns were just for show, but we didn't know that and skittered away like pink water striders. Once out of sight, we climbed a slat ladder nailed up the gnarly trunk of a cottonwood until the ditchrider passed or the farmer went back to work. The slat ladders and swinging ropes, the diving branches and tree houses, likely as not were first put up by those same farmers and ditchriders in their youth.

The canal snaked its way through farm country. Hungry in our wanderings, we swiped sweet corn from ripe stalks on DeLaney's farm and gnawed the raw ears among the rows, followed by tart apples from Robina Smith's orchard for dessert. Somehow the mere act of feeding ourselves beneath an open sky imparted a sense of self-sufficiency. Sometimes when I went by myself I stopped off at the drugstore to buy a jug of Pep-so, the syrup for a cherry cola drink served at Mr. Prico's pharmacy fountain. Once at the canal, when the day got hot, I settled into a leafy green glade beside the headgate of a feeder ditch. Then I mixed the Pep-so with the cool water in my canvas-covered canteen and drank it in the shade. The simple fact of mixing my own made it "camping."

When we were lucky, we could get Dad to go with us. He preferred fishing in the Front Range streams and lakes or staying home and working in the yard and listening to the ball game, but sometimes we could lure him into a weenie roast along the canal. Showing Dad our summer haunts was our way of repaying him for the times he took us to his favorite trout spots in the hills. We never camped overnight, but these day trips at least meant time out from digging dandelions.

Our father was happy to have "arrived," as he put it, in the comfy suburbs. Just a long generation before, his folks had been country dwellers seeking to distance themselves from the land. Though obscure branches of the family kept on farming here and there in the Midwest, my grandparents had already left the tobacco fields of Kentucky by 1910. GrandPop and Neni were soon divorced—why, we never knew—and they both found city jobs. She became a Toledo beautician; he worked in the wood shop of the Packard Motor Car Company in Detroit.

My father, born in the backwoods on a western Kentucky farm, first saw the West on a summer vacation with his father. They drove one of the last of the Model Ts out to Colorado, where they were both smitten by their first look at Big Thompson Canyon. Back in Ohio, Dad convinced Neni to bring him west on the Union Pacific to settle in Denver. There he met my mother at East High School in 1932. Her Whetstone and Phelps forebears, having given up Pennsylvania Dutch farms for Colorado cattle ranches, finally came down to the city. After he retired in the fifties, GrandPop too came to Denver, this time driving one of the last of the Packards.

So while my family always liked visiting the country, the town was the only place to live. When I admired the lives of kids who lived out along the canal, Dad asked, "What do you want to do, go back to the *farm?*" Or he'd say, "Believe me, you wouldn't want to go back to the *farm!*" He pronounced the word as if it were anathema.

At the time I couldn't understand Dad's antipathy. Had I known the sheer drudgery, poverty, and boredom that my farming ancestors had endured, it might have made more sense. As Betty McDonald put it in *The Egg and I,* "Their days slipped down like junket, leaving no taste on the tongue." My people came off the pre-REA outback and made comfortable homes in the suburbs with great effort and sacrifice. No wonder the farm, to them, represented a backward past.

During the summer of my fifth birthday we drove from Denver to Kamas, Utah, in our hand-me-down Packard. We went to see our cousins who lived on the edge of the Wasatch Mountains and had horses, which we rode over mountain meadows bleeding with Indian paintbrush, the state flower. That satisfied two of three big expectations I'd brought with me: that I would ride a horse and see Indian paintbrush. The third was to bounce on an aspen tree. I'd heard my mother say that we would see aspens and that the supple trunks of the saplings made fine teeter-totters. I'd taken it for a promise. We saw aspens all right, but the chance to play on them was somehow omitted from the program. On the way home, I fussed until, just before leaving the mountains, Dad managed to find a scraggly little aspen, bend it over, and plant my fanny on it. Looking back, I'm surprised he didn't let go.

That trip—the horses, the wildflowers, the trees—opened my eyes to the mountains and made me long to live beyond the city. The turquoise-trimmed flagstone houses up in Boulder Canyon became my model of the perfect abode.

In 1953 we did leave Denver, but in the other direction. Dad said we were moving way out into the country. I pictured pastures and paintbrush, whereas Dad had more bedrooms in mind. When we visited the house site with only the foundation in place, Colorado brown spreading for miles in the March rain, I couldn't see how anyone could live there, much less like it. The land resembled the bombed-out French countryside we saw on newsreels from the recent war. Dad said it would improve with time, and Mom, imagining the gardens she would make, did her best to look cheerful.

Those who came before us had rolled in from the East, run up against the Rockies, and come to a stop. We were bouncing back toward the plains, part of the wave of latter-day settlers who speckled the open spaces with their postwar settlements. We were all seeking to regain the spaciousness our forebears had left behind, without giving up the convenience of the town. In doing so, we changed the countryside into a suburb.

Indeed, this new place had been country until our family and a few thousand others arrived. So when we moved that June, we landed in a drab crosshatch of brick houses on bare lots stretching away for blocks and blocks, without a horse in sight. And I found myself farther from the mountains than I'd been in Denver itself, where at least the city limits lay at my doorstep.

My mother said we'd have trees in Hoffman Heights. I'd expected them to be in place already when we moved in, like the house. But the lot, even if its mud was now summer-warm instead of gelid, was still empty. The British distinguish yards from gardens. "Garden" means a planted space, if only a plain lawn, whereas a "yard" is a bare place, paved or earthen. Our new yard was certainly that.

Mother, and the town, rapidly planted hundreds of trees: hackberries, ashes, birches, spruces, crabapples, American elms, and lots of fast-growing Chinese elms. I asked for parrot tulips and a cherry tree for my birthday, and got them. The bluegrass left behind in Kentucky soon followed, blanketing the new town in a quilt of sprinkled green. But in the beginning, there was mud.

Besides the bleak scene, another disappointment awaited me on Revere Street. We had taken the four-bedroom option instead of the garage. Mom and Dad occupied one bedroom, Susan had another, and the third was a nursery for newborn Bud. Tom and I had the largest room. In compensation for having to share, Dad promised that our room would have a checkerboard floor. And so it did—Dad laid the asphalt tiles onto the concrete slab, in alternating colors, himself. But as with the aspens in Utah, I took the promise literally. I'd envisioned giant checkers games played on red and black. When the squares turned out to be brown and green, I was crushed. How could you play checkers on that?

Eventually I got used to the floor. The Chinese elms grew into high perches for boys and their pet anoles. Garden beds colored the spring, and lilacs swabbed sweet scents all over the month of May. But even when Hoffman Heights greened up, it was still a suburb. I'd thought we were going to live in the country, like our cousins in Kamas, and this was not it.

Countryside means a place of brown uncertainty and green chance, where life is not all spelled out like the squares on our bedroom floor, where surprise still lives. In the grid of greater Aurora, there was nothing more surprising than the sudden appearance of a building where yesterday there had been a vacant lot. So Tom and I, tiring of checkers, took to the High Line Canal and played at living in the country. And Dad asked incredulously, "What do you want to do, go back to the *farm?*"

When I was nine my parents were having bitter problems. During the worst of it, my grandfather took Tom and me back to Kentucky. We traveled in his second black Packard, the one in which he'd driven off into retirement when the company folded. We crossed torrid Kansas with our feet out the window, cooled off at the Big Spring in Missouri. South of Paducah we searched for the ruins of my father's birthplace, but the cabin had been swallowed by the hardwood jungle. In the humid evenings fireflies came out, like irresolute lanterns seen at a distance. GrandPop showed us a big frame house where he had lived as a boy; the farm was still there, though the barn he'd built had burned. So we did go back to the farm, if only for a few days, and I liked it. GrandPop, like Dad, said I wouldn't like it if I had to work on it. He was probably right, but when we got back to Aurora and my parents told us they were going to split up, I wished we'd never left the farm.

At school there were a few kids who really lived in the country. They came in from small spreads fronting one or another of the mile roads out along the High Line. In particular, three Mikes brought the soft scent of the barn to school on their flannel shirts. They looked to me as I thought farm kids should. Tall, skinny Mike Snodgrass had buck teeth, a yellow cowlick, and a quick temper. Short, skinny Mike Beasley★ had a pleasing grin, a quick wit, and a brown cowlick. Big, husky Mike Tatum's gravelly voice came from the sturdy frame of a regulation dirt-farm lad, and his left hand easily filled his big baseball glove, the same color as his black cowlick. All three spoke a little differently from the rest of us, not quite Okie or Arkie, but maybe leaning in that direction.

★ After a reading I gave at Black Oak Books in Berkeley, California, soon after this book was published, two almost-familiar faces approached me. They turned out to belong to old school chums, Bill Bannister and the above-mentioned Beasley. They had only kind words to say about the book, and later, when Beasley sent me a thoughtful, delightful letter about old and new times and the ditch we had shared, including a wonderful snapshot of our Cub Scout den (see "Magpie Days"), he signed it, simply, "Beas."

Two years later, at the picnic for our thirtieth high school reunion, I was talking with my good old friends Jack Jeffers and Bill Sampson. Bill asked me diplomatically, "Isn't Beasley's name *Gary?*" "Sure, Gary Beasley," I said; and then, "Oh, jeez!" as the penny dropped: I had made him into a Mike, for a better fit among his farm neighbors Mike Tatum and Mike Snodgrass. In meeting and writing to me, Gary had been too kind to bring the error to my attention. Well, it was an honest alias I gave him, insofar as it was done subconsciously and ingenuously, not for intentional effect. So Gary you are, Beas, but in this essay Mike you shall remain.

The three Mikes, being neighbors and outsiders, hung out together. Normally I didn't have that much truck with them, but we were all in the same Cub Scouts den. When Mrs. Tatum did her stint as den mother, and we met in her farmhouse kitchen, I just wanted to wander the back forty. But the Mikes looked to town for entertainment, and one spring they convinced me to turn out for Little League baseball with them. I didn't collect baseball cards like a lot of guys, nor did I know the names of many players, except for Marv Throneberry and a few other Denver Bears we sometimes watched with Dad at Bears Stadium. But I enjoyed playing Five Hundred with Dad and Tom; I thought it would be like that.

The first practice came on a brilliant early June morning. On a dirt ball field near the High Line Canal, I stood in center field, half asleep, squinting against a low sun I would not normally have been up to see. I was wondering whether there might be butterflies in a nearby field when the first fly ball came my way. I missed it by a mile. Mike Tatum's big, gruff dad was the coach. "Whatsa matter, Pyle?" he shouted. "Sun in your eyes?"

Big Mike Tatum, pounding his huge black mitt, yelled, "Try using your butterfly net next time!" Snodgrass and Beasley just shook their heads.

I envied Snodgrass, Tatum, and Beasley. They were competent, confident kids off the land. They could come into town and play good baseball, then go home and master a dozen farm chores. But my envy had little to do with their athletic or agricultural talents. I didn't much like the idea of farm chores, from what I had seen at Cousin Alta's place out at Byers. And after I struck out in the first lousy game, I abandoned Little League for painted ladies and swallowtails. My incompetence on the diamond was trivial. I didn't want the three Mikes' lives, just their habitats.

One late spring day there was to be a Cubs meeting at Mike Beasley's house. The four of us rode our bikes out the canal. Past Peoria, we stopped to survey the flotsam in the roiling pool behind the check dam. "There's our raft," said Mike Tatum. "Water'll hafta get higher than that before we can float it over the dam." He knew when that was likely to be—his father the coach had water rights, and Mike knew when the ditchrider was due to open their headgate, and when the canal would likely be shut off.

A little farther on, around a bend by Sable Road, we stopped again. Mike Snodgrass leaped to grab the lowest rung on a slat ladder nailed up the side of a cottonwood. He scrambled up, hand over hand, till he reached the highest slat, maybe thirty feet up. Then he took a hammer and nails from his dungarees. Mike Beasley tossed him up a broken hunk of two-by-four, which he caught on the third try. He nailed it to the largest branch; then he caught and nailed another slab and another, until he had supports in place well out over the canal. "Ditchrider keeps taking down our rope," Snodgrass panted as he scrambled down. "Now we can dive in without it."

By the time we got to the den meeting I felt like a foreigner on my own turf. I'd known the butterflies and some of the birds of the canal, but nothing about how it worked. The water came, the water went. I had no real connection with it. The price of the Mikes' school shoes came from crops and livestock and land bank payments; they depended on the canal. Money for mine came from downtown. Tom and I would ride a raft for a way, or scramble up the tree ladders. The Mikes made the rafts and ladders, like their dads before them. This was the big difference: Snodgrass, Tatum, and Beasley *lived* the ditch life; we merely played at it.

While we ventured into the country for weenie roasts, they lived there day and night. While Tom and I talked about it, these guys really did shoot magpies, rabbits, ground squirrels, and prairie dogs, and they didn't worry about it as I would. I imagined them cooking the meat on spits over an open fire with pork and beans. These Mikes really were different from the rest of us suburban latecomers, if only in living apart from the herd, out of the grid. I wished it could be Snodgrass, Tatum, Beasley, and Pyle. But Mike was only my middle name.

When the town traveled east, the Snodgrass, Tatum, and Beasley farmsteads were there to greet it and be eaten. The interstate would become their front yard, condos would bump their backsides. Now you can walk miles beyond those vanished farms and still be deep in the tracts. The new city center looms across the canal from where their barns once stood, their fields once lay.

In town for a high school reunion a few years ago, I strolled a shaggy street of holdout houses across from the vast Aurora Mall. A rural mailbox caught my eye: "Tatum," it said. Snodgrass and Beasley were nowhere to be seen. At the reunion, in a rec center by the canal, only Mike Beasley turned up. His grin was intact, if not his cowlick, and he was taller. He had long since moved into town to pursue a suburban livelihood that had nothing to do with farms.

One man who grew up along the ditch and then stayed put was George Swan. Intimately connected with the Denver Water Company and the High Line Canal all his life, George Swan came to represent the ditch itself in many people's minds. He rode ditch, fixed flumes, cleared brush, and otherwise kept the water moving for so long that his admirers could be forgiven for thinking of the High Line route as "Swan's Way."

It would have been George who bounced us boys from the swimming hole more than once. Our relationship with him and the other ditchriders was not so much adversarial as worshipful: we attempted to avoid them whenever possible, while admiring them from afar. Sure, they were a pain and a fear, for they held the power to throw us out of our wild playground and spoil our fun. But on the other hand, these were the men who were actually paid to wander the canal day in and day out. From the vantage of free kids in the summertime, Dad's world of going off to a job in the city every day did not much appeal. Yet, if you could grow up and stay on the ditch, even if it involved a bit of work—that seemed more plausible.

If I had known how much and what kinds of work were really involved in the job, I would not have romanticized it so. But to me it looked like a lifetime's lark—chasing kids, dozing in the cottonwood shade, prowling the service road in an old pickup, and getting to know every inch of the ditch. Surely there would be time to chase butterflies along the way. For years I thought I had a vocation as a ditchrider. Maybe I could earn a life on the High Line after all, though I wasn't born to it like my three friends named Mike.

George Swan was born at the Kassler Filter Plant in Waterton Canyon, hard by the source of the High Line. His father, a foreman for the water company, raised George in a brick house beside the reservoir that came to be known locally as Swan Lake. George went to high school in Littleton, driving a Model T and carrying other students for fares. Each school day he cranked the engine up at four A.M. for a six-forty-five departure. George sometimes encountered blizzards in the open car, or his axles would crystallize and break in the frigid dawn. He made it through school but remained on the canal. For the next forty-one years he worked a variety of jobs, from laborer to foreman. Most of those years were spent riding ditch. In reality, there was little snoozing in the shade. The job meant everything from clearing dead horses and wind-piled tumbleweeds out of the canal and dealing with beaver dams and skunks to rebuilding flood-damaged structures and chasing errant kids away from the attractive nuisance of the ditch.

Such dynasties as that of the Swans were not uncommon among the early canal families. The first ditchrider, Charles Bryant, was also the first High Line superintendent. Bryant drove the ditch in a buggy, paid his workers in gold, and carried a deputy's badge and a revolver. He switched to an early Dodge and found the black car equal to the terrain. Charles's son Harley followed him as superintendent, riding the ditch himself on a horse, then a series of motorcycles—Excelsior, Indian, and, of course, Harley-Davidson—and finally in an automobile. His son Kerker sometimes rode with him as a child and later had a thirty-eight-year career of his own with the Denver Water Board. The Bryants, it was said, put in "a century of service to water."

Ray Livingston rode ditch for over forty years, Edwin Stout almost as long. The last ditchman to have held such a tenure was Bob Rosendale, who grew up along the canal and knew the value of "a cool crick on a hot day," as he once told me. "When we saw the water coming, we'd run down to the canal, strip, and hop in—even during harvest." After forty-two years on the canal, where he was also born and bred, he retired as superintendent. Longtime ditchriders find it hard to sit still, and he thought he would work again. "But when I retire," he told me, "I'd like to find a job with no responsibilities, scheduling, appointments, discipline—to relax my mind." He thought he might take occasional walks along the canal to help him do so.

George Swan, too, sometimes went back for a look at the old ditch he'd kept flowing for so long. He deplored the changeover to recreation and the visitors' failure to realize that the real purpose of the canal was still water conveyance. But he stopped coming the day he was arrested and ticketed for motorized trespass on the recreational trail, finding himself—like the very kids he had ejected over the years—on the ditchrider's bad side for the first time in half a century.

I met some of the new generation of ditchriders, young men like Pete Reinhart, who viewed the trail a little differently. They welcomed the recreationists, if not the new problems they bring, as inevitable. Pete himself jogged along the canal path after work and ice-skated portions of it in winter. In his section from Waterton to Plum Creek, Pete had just one inactive headgate, a huge ranch-cum-subdivision, and one active, a horse boarder with a pond and a polo field. Yet the water had to get through his stretch in order to reach the rest on down the line. So Pete still had to ride every inch of ditch in his section every day—the *sine qua non* of all ditchriders.

Pete Reinhart has gone on to other work. The High Line workers of today might not spawn ditchrider dynasties or give thirty or forty years to the ditch. But they stand in the grand tradition of the men who make sure the water flows where it is supposed to go, keeping the farmers and walkers happy, the fields and cottonwoods green, and kids like Snodgrass, Tatum, Beasley, and me out of the ditch—at least until they drove on.

As ditches everywhere drop out of the suburban picture, their flow going to gutters and pipes and water mains, ditchriders may be an endangered species. A later superintendent, Gil Martinez, knows that the skills of the ditchmen will remain important, even as recreation takes over more and more. "The canal represents the biggest park in the state, given its length," Gil told me. "We try to anticipate the changes and to adapt." But the number of High Line riders had been cut from five to four, and Gil wonders how long his loyal corps would be seen as relevant by the higher-ups.

The day that George Swan was tossed off the canal by an Aurora cop perhaps forecast the end of one very long view of the land. Had I remained fixed on being a ditchrider when I grew up, in my ignorance of the heavy labors involved, maybe I would actually have become one. Then, like Snodgrass, Tatum, and Beasley before me, I might have found myself wedded to a way of life whose certain passing was written in ripples in the bottom of a silting ditch.

Decades after the last High Line weenie roast, and far away, I bought part of an old farm. Once, on a fishing trip, my father came to visit. Of course, he knew it wouldn't really be farm life as he had lived it. We have a farmhouse, a garden, and some big trees planted by the homesteaders, but our few acres are covered mostly with brambles and alders, maples and spruce. Someone else does what farming is left in the valley. Except for television, which is no great loss, we have just about everything we had in town. And more: mergansers nesting in an oak tree by the house; unburdened air and good water; a night sky free from streetlight haze; and the quiet to hear ourselves think. There are also steelhead trout and chinook salmon in the river at the bottom of the pasture, and that, at least, Dad could appreciate. Even so, he was clearly amazed that I would prefer the country to the comfortable suburbs where he reared me.

Like so many of his generation, my father spent his life getting away from the land. Like so many of mine, I've spent my time finding a way back. The High Line Canal runs a muddy route between those two desires and the landscapes each has left behind. In my eyes, the old ditch stands for a century that belongs to the suburbs, for a landscape that once was country.

8

Of Grass and Growth

Sandy, the Aurora is rising behind us.

— Bruce Springsteen

When Henry Crow Dog sang "Wolakota," a Lakota Sioux peace song, he was singing to grass. As his voice rose and fell like the prairie wind, it flowed into the Grass Song called "Omaha." Stemming from a ceremony of the sacred Heyoka clown dancers, the song is the Northern Plains Indian equivalent to the Southern Plains war dance of the Oklahoma. Traditionally, Grass Song dancers array tufts of grass in their hair and belts. As the people danced, undulating like the rippling waves of prairie green, Henry Crow Dog sang the sacredness of grass to steppe-dwellers everywhere.

The territory of the Sioux and the rest of the Prairie Americans once supported a wide array of grazing ungulates, including native horses, camels, and antelope. Only the elk, deer, pronghorn, and bison survived the late Pleistocene. The entire sustenance and culture of the Plains Indians depended on the American bison, or buffalo. The system to which they all belonged was based wholly on grass.

Grasses are the most successful plants in the world in terms of area covered. Only orchids and asters are more diverse. They survive where many other plants cannot because, with both shallow and deep roots, they can use ephemeral rainwater as well as groundwater. Grasses can also resprout from the base once they've been cut, burned, or grazed. Thanks to these traits, grasses dominate the steppes, prairies, and tundras of the world.

The shortgrass prairie on the High Plains of eastern Colorado consisted of a vast and stable ecosystem for millennia. Buffalo grass and blue grama dominated the bunchgrass communities, but there were also big and little bluestem, sand dropseed, blowout grass and Indian grass, June-grass, needle-

and-thread, and foxtail, squirreltail, switchgrass, and red three-awn grass. The first grasslands I knew had none of this euphonious diversity: they were lawns of Kentucky bluegrass, as if my people, coming from Kentucky, had brought their blue-green carpets with them. But such a sward was my habitat, and I got to know it much as a Lakota youth might become familiar with a buffalo grass patch.

A lawn need not be a biological desert. Little managed but for occasional mowing, it can support a variety of herbs and insects. Once noticed, these often provoke more intensive "lawn care," since reactionary householders don't seem to appreciate a rich and interesting lawn. Ours had tailed blue butterflies in the clover, caterpillars in the crabgrass, crab spiders in the dandelions. Though it was my job to dig dandelions, I valued them highly—their pungent scent so evocative of spring, their abundant nectar for butterflies and bees, their fluffy seedheads; fortunately, I never made a dent.

Since Dad didn't mow too closely, we had lots of tawny-edged skippers. These did no harm and made lawn work more interesting. I took a particular fascination in skippers and satyrs, butterflies whose larvae feed on grasses. Like the prairie ungulates, these insects depended on the grasslands for their very existence. When I began wandering along the High Line Canal I found myself in shortgrass prairie, albeit degraded by overgrazing. Cheatgrass and other aliens dominated in place of blue grama, filling my socks with their stickery pink awns. Most of the skippers and satyrs that I might have found on the original prairies were long since locally extinct. But some remained in remnant patches of native grass: a colony of gray-and-tan Riding's satyrs with Grateful Dead lightning streaks across their wings, out beyond Tower Road; a coterie of golden grass skippers on the ditchbanks. Where grasses grew, grazers followed.

The satyr that most caught my imagination dwelled on the high alpine rockslides. It was entirely black and bore the name *Erebia magdalena;* I called it Maggie. Another dark-winged satyr flew close to home. The common wood nymph haunted the long grasses overhanging the banks of the High Line Canal. From its scientific name, *Cercyonis pegala,* I called it Peggy. If Maggie remained mostly aloof in her high-country habitat, Peggy was readily available. And while neither as black nor as rare as the rockslide resident, she had much to teach me.

All through junior high school I carried around a paperback copy of *The Origin of Species*. Over the three years I actually read a good deal of it, constantly looking for evidence of natural selection around me. As I discovered one summer, the wings of wood nymphs were perfect canvases of evolution. Or, as Darwin's contemporary Henry Bates put it, "On these expanded membranes Nature writes, as on a tablet, the story of the modification of species." Alexander B. Klots, in his Peterson field guide, wrote that "a terrific amount of work is needed" to sort out the blue-eyed graylings, or wood nymphs. I'd already spent hours watching the chocolate brown butterflies as they flicked through the bank grass. I'd written everything I knew or could find out about them in a ninth-grade science paper and raised a lot more questions than I answered.

Inspired by Professor Klots, I obtained a small grant from the Colorado–Wyoming Academy of Science and tried to resolve some of those questions. As soon as the butterflies began to break out in the summer of 1964, I was out on the canal with the wood nymphs. One green glen in particular, near where the canal crossed Sand Creek in a big wooden flume, drew me again and again for its great numbers of *C. pegala*. I soon saw that in this one colony I could find butterflies resembling many variations of the large wood nymph—each once described as separate species or subspecies. I reared larvae from as many distinct types as I could find around Colorado, hoping to get a handle on the heritability of this variation.

One day as I picked my way through the Sand Creek glade, watching out for the poison ivy whose leaves were as shiny as the cottonwoods', I spotted a pale female wood nymph and gave chase. She took cover in a clump of willow and disappeared on a trunk of her own color. Large and perfect, she was invisible with her wings tucked down. Then, disturbed by a fly, her forewings spread, revealing the big, cowlike eyespots that gave her subspecies the name *bo-opis*, or the ox-eyed wood nymph. She wasn't perfect after all. One of the forewings, directly between its two eyespots, had a big chip out of it in the shape of a bird's bill.

I sat against a cottonwood trunk, hot and sweaty, shaded by its quivering leaves. The image of that beautiful cocoa-brown wood nymph peered out from the willow thicket with her black and blue ocelli. Of all the traits that varied so in wood nymphs, those eyespots were paramount. In some forms they were small, others had big ones, and in certain races they were surrounded by prominent yellow patches. But all the wood nymphs, and most other species of satyrs, had eyespots. The textbooks labeled them fright devices, supposed to protect against small predators. But the little false eyes didn't look very scary to me, and birds would fly right up and take a nip out of a wood nymph's wings, so they weren't too intimidated. What if the eyespots served an entirely different function? Maybe they were *targets*—so that if the butterfly's camouflage failed and it were spotted, the bird would attack it away from the body, toward the expendable wing margins. I began to watch carefully for chips and tears that indicated such attacks. It turned out that of the hundreds of wood nymphs I netted that summer, almost a quarter of them bore clear bird strikes near the prominent eyespots on their forewings or among the row of smaller ocelli along the hindwing borders.

I concluded that all of these Peggies belonged to one big plastic species with a lot of latitude for expression, a theory later confirmed by better scientists than I. And I showed, to my satisfaction, that wood nymphs escape predation by flashing their big blue eyes. This, too, was shown experimentally by others.

I was enormously impressed by the power of natural selection to furnish these insects with such effective defenses; even more, by their ability to survive at all, given the thin halo of their requisite grasses lining the loops of the ditch. Maggie and Peggy, using the grasses suited to their respective environs, showed me the meanings of habitat, adaptation, and natural selection more clearly than anything else had. No Lakota was better fitted to the High Plains, no Arapaho to the peaks, than these brown butterflies. Darwin came alive for me through the eyes of the wood nymphs, and I felt just a bit of the thrill he knew among the tortoises and finches of the Galapagos.

Jicarilla Apache and Pawnee traded the grassland empire between the Arkansas and the Platte rivers back and forth. Their arrowheads occasionally turn up in the annual shifting of sands in prairie streambeds or in the sifted soils of prairie dog workings. The sharp points were no match for bullets.

The Arapaho and the Cheyenne, having mastered rifles and the horses brought by the Spanish, moved south and took over much of the territory.

Government explorers like Lieutenant Zebulon Pike and Major Stephen Long found the High Plains hostile and unpromising and recommended against settlement. But furs, gold and silver, and finally free land brought droves to the dusty basin that became early Denver. The ruts of their wagons following the Smoky Hill Trail would later become U.S. 40 and Colfax Avenue. Way stations along the trail grew into ephemeral settlements existing at the whim of the wagon masters and the pleasure of Arapaho warriors.

Indian resistance ceased briefly when Black Kettle and other chiefs surrendered at Fort Lyon. Their band of Arapaho and Cheyenne set up an encampment some forty miles away. At dawn on November 29, 1864, Colonel John M. Chivington and 750 cavalrymen attacked the peaceful native encampment on Sand Creek in Kiowa County, killing several hundred men, women, and children in what became known and reviled as the Sand Creek Massacre. This led to the last of the Indian wars in Colorado, with the Arapaho, Cheyenne, and Sioux fighting the territorials for the next four years. The surviving Indians were shipped to Oklahoma reservations in 1869, the same year the railroad arrived. Now eastern Colorado was prepared for the century of evolution that would culminate in modern Aurora.

Donald Fletcher came to Denver in 1879 in the wake of the silver rush. A Canadian, a sometime preacher in Chicago, and a natural promoter, Fletcher became president of the Denver Chamber of Commerce. Correctly guessing that growth would follow Colfax Avenue to the east, Donald Fletcher and his partners, Thomas Hayden and Samuel Perry, speculated on land lining the road. In 1889 they platted the Aurora Subdivision, and by 1890 they were already advertising it as "the most popular subdivision ever placed on the market." As the plats sold, the Colfax investors began to profit from their four square miles bisected by the avenue. In 1891 the state of Colorado certified the embryonic suburb as the Town of Fletcher, "a hamlet of 202 people."

Then the silver crash and the Panic of 1893 struck. Along with acute and chronic problems with the provision of water, these crises stifled the investors and slowed growth. Donald Fletcher vanished in a cloud of bad debts and dust. His name survived him locally by a decade. Fletcher officially became Aurora in 1907, when it was a knot of people about five hundred strong.

Growth proceeded in spits and spurts over the next decades. Most of the business had to do with servicing the farms east of town. Water continued to circumscribe Aurora's proportions. One of Donald Fletcher's speculative schemes had burdened the town with onerous water bonds for a system that didn't work.

These bonds became the major monkey on Aurora's back for the next half century. Not until 1956 was the original debt of $150,000 retired, at a vastly higher cost. Denver controlled Aurora's water until past the half-century mark, accounting for the modest and pleasant proportions of the place when my family arrived in 1953.

Meanwhile, a series of military developments propelled Aurora beyond the population of one thousand it reached sometime around 1917. After World War I, the Guthiel Nursery was appropriated as the site for a major army recuperation camp for victims of mustard gas and other lung disorders, largely on the strength of its High Line Canal water rights. The Art Deco edifice of Fitzsimons Army Hospital became Aurora's outstanding landmark and its only tall building for decades. "Fitz," as we called it, was named for Lieutenant William T. Fitzsimons, an Army medic who was designated the first U.S. military fatality in World War I.

In 1937 Congress approved the construction of Lowry Field, a U.S. Army Air Corps base on the southern edge of Aurora. This had an economic impact similar to that of Fitz on the north, for the first time taking growth southward along Havana Street, almost to the canal. Lowry's legacy was to be many years of shrieking trainer jets overhead, a Superfund site, and, out east of town, a bombing range and eighteen Titan intercontinental ballistic missile silos.

By 1940, some three thousand people occupied Aurora—two of whom were black. Buckley Field, a naval and then national guard air base, bolstered growth on the east side of Aurora as its jets joined in the aerial cacophony. Buckley littered the landscape with big radar domes looking like giant golf balls chipped onto the edge of the town from one of the many nearby links.

The final military "boon" for Aurora came in 1942 in the form of the Rocky Mountain Arsenal. The government selected a huge area of prairie on the city's northwest flank to house the premier depot for production and storage of nerve gas and other chemical weapons. Then came World War II, and after that, the baby boom.

In the forties, Aurora claimed the world's largest chicken, mink, and rabbit farms. By 1953, these made way for about thirty thousand humans. In 1960 it was fifty thousand. Further prospects were clouded by Denver's resistance. For three quarters of a century Denver had doled out Aurora's water, but with its tax base shrinking as residents fled to the suburbs, Denver attempted to slow suburban growth by blue-lining areas beyond which new taps would not be approved.

Frustrated and tired of Denver's control, Aurora fought back by diverting water from the West Slope, as described in "The Rivers of April." The future solvency of the city depended on ever more people to use the increased water supply and to pay off the construction bonds, but at last Aurora was independent of Denver. It had enough water for at least 100,000 people, and when that wasn't enough, they knew what to do. With plenty of water and no blue line, Aurora saw no further limits.

Boosters in business and government got together to ensure that Aurora would continue to expand. AID (Aurora Industrial Development) successfully brought railroad and other industrial warehousing to the rural High Line corridor in the northeast. ECO (Explore Commercial Opportunities) began in 1976 to seduce high-tech industry to Aurora. ECO was described as an "umbrella for encouraging growth." At this it succeeded. But for animals and plants in dire need of an open-space umbrella and ecological aid, these would prove ironic acronyms.

In 1970 the city called for a comprehensive plan. Growth restrictions were even discussed, but if growth was indeed limited, it was only in the existential sense: the universe presumably has limits, too. Subdivisions leapfrogged in all directions. Blocked at the Denver line, new housing skipped to the edges and beyond. Denver's suburbs on all sides did the same. By 1978 Aurora, on behalf of its 150,000 residents, had sucked up 63 square miles, nearly 1,600 percent more prairie than it began with.

Most of the miles we'd once known as open had been filled by 1984, and Aurora rankled under its borders like a fat man in too-tight trousers. Boosters lobbied to annex a new region of potential growth that would double Aurora's size. After the annexation took place, the September 30, 1987, *Aurora Sentinel* asked, "Who's the biggest?" Then it answered itself: "Aurora is." In April, Aurora had reached 126.81 square miles in area, compared with Denver's 115. Urban analysts projected that Aurora's population, as well as its size, would leap ahead of Denver's by the millennium.

I watched Aurora inflate from twenty thousand to two hundred thousand people from the vantage of a tract on its edge, now deep in the middle of town. It was easy to find the countryside when we moved to Hoffman Heights—we were practically there. Of a summer evening we often drove east to see pronghorn antelope, usually catching up to the tawny herds within five miles of home. Along the High Line Canal, we could reach rural surroundings in minutes. But change galloped faster than the pronghorns. When we finally learned that the canal didn't really go to Kansas, we joked that we could get there anyway just by standing still, and we wouldn't even have to click our heels, because at the rate Aurora was growing around us, our town would soon annex Kansas outright.

The chancre around us began in 1954 with the Hoffman Heights Shopping Center. While far smaller than any modern mall, the twenty-eight-store HHSC was ambitious for a neighborhood "shoppette" of its day. The thirty-acre pond on the site, fed by the High Line Canal, disappeared beneath twenty-two feet of fill, so it's not surprising that the asphalt has always ponded and slumped: I suspect this will always be the crappiest parking lot in Christendom. Houses, parks, and schools arose around the shopping center, consuming the cornfields and pastures. The conventional wisdom of the time was that Aurora would never spread south of the High Line. By the late sixties, an ersatz English mall called Buckingham Square sprang up near the canal on Havana, dragging a slew of car dealerships and fast-food depots behind it like cans and shoes strung behind a honeymooners' car. The moat breached, Aurora charged south of the High Line after all.

Growth advanced southeasterly from Denver's hinterland toward the Cherry Creek Reservoir, northeast along Sand Creek, due east on Colfax Avenue. All obstacles fell, all proportion fell away. With the advent of the town house and condominium, a powerful new tool of growth came on line. Colonies of cloned domiciles stormed the remaining countryside. Every vacant field bore signs offering it for sale. One of the most active speculators was named Field, and signs with his name in large black letters seemed like interpretive panels for city slickers: "Whoa! So *that's* a field!" A subtext gave away the actual field's future in smaller print, reading "Offered by" and "Will develop to suit."

As one measure of my town's immoderate expansion, I watched its public libraries migrate eastward. The first one I knew was a low building of maroon bricks with a flat roof and fashionable fifties turquoise trim like the city hall next door. It was a split-level with fiction downstairs and nonfiction above. Among those serried stacks, searching for Thornton Burgess titles or books on seashells or otters that I'd not yet read repeatedly, I was situated in the approximate geographic center of town: a mile from Denver, about a mile from the town frontier in any direction.

By the early sixties, a new, bigger library arose beside a High Line lateral on Peoria Street. Haunting the expanded stacks for butterfly books, I stood a full two miles from Denver, but still in the middle of town. The city hall was as far from the center of things as its turquoise trim was out of style.

Twenty years further on, still another library arose like a giant puffball popping up on the plain. A great white block, huge compared to its predecessors, it is part of a city hub called Town Center. The municipal complex also includes courts and a jail, a fire station, and a post office, all devoid of turquoise or any other trim. The newest library, three miles from Denver, still lies just about in the middle of the built-up town. That means Aurora experienced about 900 percent of solid growth in thirty years. By then the annexed area due for development had become thirty times the size of that first Aurora I'd known, and Town Center was rapidly becoming off center itself as the builders charged eastward once again.

As the years and bulldozers rolled by, our outpost house became more and more deeply immured in the 'burbs. If we wanted to see antelope, we had to drive miles and miles, way out by Strasburg. Even then we'd be lucky to find them.

In the early sixties, my friend Greg Pierce and I would ride our motor scooters all the way out to prairie hamlets such as Parker, Franktown, Elizabeth, and Last Chance, looking for what we were losing close at hand. By the time we traded our Vespas for Fords, Parker and Franktown had fallen into the commuters' web. Soon Elizabeth went as well, lending Last Chance a new perspective on its name. I left Colorado in 1965. Each time I returned, approximately every six months, I witnessed a later stage in the metastasis of an American town. Nor was there any end in sight: city planners predicted a population of 700,000 by 2035, a hundredfold growth in a hundred years.

Denver's other suburbs indulged similar growth frenzies. So did Aurora's Homestake water partner, Colorado Springs, where my brother Tom and his family settled. Though far from the middle of town, his home is closer to Kansas than we ever got on the canal. What really characterizes these places is the sheer rapidity with which they have grown from small towns to big cities, and the kind of cities they seem bent on becoming: massive, yet faceless.

The brown cloud that envelops the Denver basin and leaks out northward along the Front Range is only the most obvious cost of great growth. People now derogate Denver for something they used to praise: its air. Many days, it is simply bad; others, unsafe. The traffic that wrecks the air means wretched congestion, from the infamous Mousetrap on the Valley Highway to the frontiers of settlement in all directions. Along with bad air and crowding come all the usual handmaidens—crime, drugs, homelessness, and decay of many kinds. Nowhere are these ills more conspicuous than along the "miracle mile" of East Colfax Avenue.

A faded archway used to regale travelers from the east on U.S. 40 with the message "Welcome to Aurora—Gateway to the Rockies." Once the proud doorstep to the "Queen City of the Plains," the tinsel strip of Highway 40 (aka Colfax Avenue) is now "a vast wasteland of sleazy bars, porno shops, and cheap motels—an area of acute urban blight . . . a grim litany of crime and squalor . . . a visual nightmare . . . a virtual abyss," according to the city's historians.

Just west of the arch, a ganglion of activity formed, in the thirties, at Colfax and Peoria. On the northeast corner was the gate to Fitzsimons Army Hospital, a busy bus stop. A Powerine gas station occupied the southwest corner next to the Boleana Motel and Drug and the train-shaped Zephyr Bar. Across Colfax stood a miniature windmill that underwent many incarnations. Throughout my boyhood it was a one-chair barber shop where GrandPop took me for haircuts. And kittycorner from the windmill stood the elegant Town House Supper Club. Colfax and Peoria was a visually and socially diverse corner, full of energy and early ambitions.

Today the foundation of the Town House lies beneath a dead supermarket, a blank barn of a building with discount tenants constantly revolving through an ocean of asphalt. The windmill, the Zephyr, and the Boleana all went in favor of various commercial ephemera. Never mind that an enormous medical city has arisen all around the old Fitzsimons Hospital; that whole corner still presents a scene as bleak as any in the postindustrial wasteland of Springsteen's Jersey shore. A couple of miles down the drag to the west, the old downtown lies forsaken and largely forgotten, like so many city centers in the age of malls. Aurora seems to have left its heart as far behind as the turquoise trim of its old city hall.

The price of overgrowth goes beyond bad air, crowded roads, and a changing cityscape. The September 30, 1987, issue of the *Aurora Sentinel* carried this headline: "Budget Cuts May Close Pool. Council Meets Thursday in Search of Money for Police." An article about cuts in libraries, senior and disabled programs, fire and police, and recreation faced a column headlined "Aurora Public Schools Hone Ax for Deep Budget Cuts; District Will Ask State to Raise Property Tax." Many related articles on fiscal problems, crime, and social ills followed, bracketing ads and sports news. Neighborhood notes, a staple of the older, slimmer Aurora papers I knew, seem no longer relevant in a city nearing a quarter million population. But the really dramatic section began on page 68 and continued without a break to page 94: twenty-six solid pages of home foreclosure notices. When I looked around, I saw that most of the old businesses we had known on Del Mar Circle were empty and dead.

Examining Aurora's growing pains, the *Sentinel* stated with spectacular irony that "Aurora's role in the big picture" is "nothing special, really. Aurora is just a recent ally on the side of growth." In reality, the Aurora syndrome goes all the way back. Apparently it represented nirvana to some. James Griesemer, Aurora city manager from 1984 to 1990, told the *Denver Post* that the old city models were obsolete, that cities of the future will be based around strip centers and regional malls and that downtowns will be irrelevant. Griesemer, who saw Aurora as the model city, celebrated the car as the tool liberating people from the core city. "Much of the so-called sprawl people complain about—the geographic dispersion, I call it—is driven by the car." I, for one, prefer to drive my car rather than let it do the driving. To my ears and eyes, "geographic dispersion" is just a bald-faced euphemism for a hell of a mess.

Mayor Dennis Champine said Aurora would continue to attract developers since other towns were "incapable of providing services, especially water." Speaking of controversial Two Forks Dam, of which Aurora was a 15 percent partner, city utilities director Tom Griswold truculently stated, "It will be built." The *Sentinel*'s Ron Dawson adopted a similar tone:

> *At a time when the state is worried about its economic health and politicians from the governor on down are talking about prodding economic growth, the environmentalist–rural–West Slope interests seem bound to lose the war. Their weapons—underfinanced public relations efforts, nit-picking over environmental impact statements, obscure legal challenges—seem puny compared to the heavy economic artillery arrayed on the other side.*

But Dawson and Griswold turned out to be wrong. Two Forks Dam was canceled, Aurora's other big water projects came under serious challenge in court, and the city found itself reevaluating its water policies. Water conservation, efficiency, xericulture (the use of drought-adapted plants), and growth limitations were all discussed more and more. Even the Aurora City Council, long devoted to aggressive water development, began to question its approach toward environmentally sensitive projects. But Dawson's military metaphor and Griswold's bellicosity had been entirely apt, in view of Aurora's historical reliance on the armed forces to bankroll its expansion habit.

"Sometimes it is hard to tell the boosters from the suckers," wrote Wallace Stegner about the overgrown cities of the arid West. "They may be the same people."

I saw the apotheosis of the Aurora model one day in the early nineties when I was exploring the eastern reaches of the High Line Canal, out north of East Colfax along Tower Road. The last time I'd seen Green Valley Ranch, years ago, it was just that—a willowy, grassy crease across the yellow plain, with a whitewashed ranch in the middle. Now, as I neared First Creek, a shock awaited me.

A last little holdout farmhouse clung to the southwest corner of the section. Beyond, platted, 'dozed, and built land stretched away for hundreds of acres. A massive wood and stone sign greeted prospective home buyers and befuddled butterfly collectors, advising that you had indeed arrived at Green Valley Ranch—just in case you couldn't tell.

The old Green Valley Ranch was homesteaded by pioneers Frederick and Ferdinand Ebert and several other families. The Eberts became major ranchers and public figures, bringing irrigation (the High Line Canal) and a rail line close to Green Valley. Like those before them on that land, they knew the worth of good grass. When Ferdinand died in 1900, the Ebert spread supported twenty-two ranch hands, valuable beef and dairy stock, and a diverse streamshed of many hundreds of acres of shortgrass prairie.

The new Green Valley Ranch will cover twenty-four hundred acres when complete. A consortium of builders and developers plans a mixed-use community with over twenty-two thousand homes in four distinct neighborhoods with covenants covering "entry monumentation" (such as the sign I'd seen) and other visual elements. Many design and cost options will be offered, schools will be built, ethnic diversity will be actively sought (this, at least, would be an improvement over early Aurora).

It all sounded pretty good, and it didn't look bad, either, except for the builders' scraps and trash slung for miles along the sides of nearby Piccadilly Road and the tacky materials used in most houses these days—instead of the bricks of Hoffman Heights, these houses have green two-by-fours and walls of composition board that can be breached by a good swift kick. I could scarcely imagine their lasting many winters of fierce prairie winds out on the high plateau, above the shallow little valley.

Across Piccadilly, a skinny red Hereford scratched his head on an orange natural gas pipe as an alfalfa butterfly flicked the steer's horn. The ditch entered a different precinct here, a shaded place of cows, concrete silos, windmills, wooden sheds, old tractors, a collection of rusted little Studebakers, and a nickel Coke machine. The place seemed uninhabited. Entering the yard, where house finches whistled among the cattle, I saw that the unpainted clapboard farmhouse had been vacant for some time. But a little white shack next to it showed signs of life.

John Petty and his sister, Mrs. Merry, were loading trash bags into a decrepit pickup to take them to the landfill. The local roads had been made into linear dumps by developers and residents too cheap or lazy to take the stuff to the county landfill, yet these dirt farmers, clearly poor, living among the detritus of a life long past, were packing up their refuse for the five-mile, five-dollar trip. The illegal roadside dumping scandalized them.

John was a rail of a split-lipped old farmer in overalls and a blue chambray shirt buttoned at the collar with an old felt hat on his head. Mrs. Merry, in a calico blouse and jeans, was heavier. Lady and Teddy Bear, the farm curs, barked at my butterfly net. Teddy had chased coyotes for seventeen years and never been touched, not even by the cyanide coyote traps that claim a lot of dogs around here. John had been a shepherd at the next place up the hill for eighteen years; now the owner had gone to cattle, which were foraging for a blade of palatable grass among the cheatgrass and prickly pear.

The main house (the Big House, they called it, though it was big only relative to their tiny cabin) had been dwelled in until the flood of 1965. It sits hard by the creekside, on the west bank. The High Line runs a few yards away, and the old Doherty Ditch (Petty called it the Old Ditch) looped just uphill across the stream. "They got it from all three," he said. "The crick, the canal, the Old Ditch—they was all in flood and they all came down on the Big House." Bursting in, the water flooded well up the walls, ruining the contents and nearly drowning the occupants. The house had been empty ever after.

John Petty's leathern face crinkled with the recollection. Chickens crowded around an old red pump. A bed frame made a fence in front of us, across which three old pickups chewed their cud. Less than a quarter mile away, Bill Pulte's Master Builder homes arose and Richmond America built its version of America. A huge flag fluttered over all. The nation's second flag, orange Day-Glo surveyor's tape, showed where houses would soon be built right up to the creek and the canal, which will presumably never flood again.

The original Green Valley ranch house, the home forty, and the riparian fringes of First Creek had so far survived. But they were slated for a golf course, clubhouse, multifamily and luxury clusters of homes, a landscaped park, civic center, and shopping center. Then some sixty thousand people will occupy about four square miles, the same size as all Aurora eighty years back, where fewer than five hundred people lived. After that, fourteen thousand more homes, worth $300 million, will appear in the projected "Green Valley Ranch East." John Petty, Mrs. Merry, and the Studebakers do not figure in.

According to the promotional brochure, "A new home in Green Valley Ranch means more than a secure and inviting lifestyle for your family. It also represents a piece of Colorado history, of the heritage of pioneers who came in search of their dream." Of course, it means the obliteration of that history, too, that dream, as the old homesteads and grasslands go beneath the bulldozer's blade.

Were these people coming to Green Valley Ranch in 1993 any different from my family landing in Hoffman Heights forty years earlier? We, too, were simply seeking the nicest place we could afford, as far from town as possible. In terms of durability, we had the better deal. Sam Hoffman's brick village was named a historic district less than forty years after groundbreaking; would these new subdivisions even last that long? In other respects, the "ranch" might prove still more desirable. While my old neighborhood has become much more ethnically diverse in recent years (the Southern Baptist church is now Vietnamese Baptist), it was unbroken Anglo when I lived there. Green Valley kids will know more human variety. They will even be able to explore the High Line as I did. It runs narrow and treeless through the new town, but not far away the arsenal lateral winds away, off limits and wooded, much like the ditch we knew.

The children of the latter-day Green Valley Ranch will play around the *Danger: Keep Off!* signs on the First Creek flume, cut their feet on broken pop bottles in the mud, chase monarchs among the ditchbank milkweeds. Their brothers and sisters will trade their vulnerable virginities in the grass-bottomed honey locust thicket on the site of an old homestead across the flume. They'll dodge among the Chinese elms and Russian olives, straddle cottonwood logs, and chase in and out of the creekbed before settling into the locust grove to practice their clumsy night moves.

They'll do these things. But they'd better hurry: the old homestead and its locust grove are labeled "Single Family Clusters" on the Green Valley Ranch development map. And before long, when those kids are driving, they'll have to go farther and farther east just to find a place to park at night. Even as the great make-out spot we called Antelope Hill first lost its pronghorns, then its darkness, finally its very summit to a mall, so theirs, too, will vanish "in the wink of a young girl's eye."

For they are the same as we were in this respect, too: it won't stop there. Green Valley residents might feel as if they live in the country—they're up out of the brown cloud, for now. They can drive out east and see pronghorns on the High Plains within a few miles. But it won't last. Just as Hoffman Heights found itself absorbed in the aging inner city within a scant generation, Green Valley Ranch will be sucked in before anyone knows it. As the new Denver airport was built nearby with its flight paths overhead, as its periphery develops, as the world turns, this new colony on the edge of the country will become midtown, too, with all its charms.

As I drove away from Green Valley Ranch I realized another feature shared by our two new towns. All the people here were busy putting in or caring for their juvenile lawns, as we had done before them. Even the designated "open space" for the community will be sown not in native blue grama but in the ubiquitous Kentucky bluegrass, just like our own Hoffman Heights Park.

Yet there was a difference. When our young lawns went in during the summers of the mid-fifties, the smell on the air was that of manure. Now the odor is the chemical stink of Weed and Feed, and the ChemLawn truck arrives even as the contractors depart. The new artificial lawns have about as much chance of hosting butterflies as bison. Of course, they will look more perfect. When we buy into the Trugreen view of the world, we justify the widespread belief in the lawn as a biological wasteland. Our parks and lawns of sprayed Kentucky bluegrass might as well be Astroturf, except that Astroturf would be safer for the groundwater—and use a lot less of it.

By the 1880s, according to Alvin Steinel's agricultural history, Colorado had already been ditched "out of all proportion to the actual acreage watered," thanks to the speculative attitude of developers intent on "squeezing unfair profits out of both land and water." By that early date, much public opinion had already "given way to the feeling that the limit of development had been reached." Had natural supplies of water been the deciding factor, that opinion might very well have held. But the developers, recognizing no such limit, found ways of bringing in more water. In fact, the development had just begun.

The problem with making water available on demand is that it enables us to ignore our natural limits. The result is unsupportable growth of cities and suburbs in places little suited by nature to sustain them. All populations of organisms in nature have limits that they must ultimately obey. In all of evolutionary history there have been no exceptions. Plants and animals either exist in relative stability, balancing gains with losses in their numbers, or they collapse—from starvation, predation, parasites and diseases, or dead-end emigration (like lemmings and locusts)—when their limits are exceeded.

The natural limit to human population growth in the arid West is, or should be, water. If the available water were used sensibly where it occurs, our numbers would remain modest, our cities livable. But humans have seldom behaved with modesty, at least not since industry enabled us to avoid reason and to wildly neglect our natural limits.

Wendell Berry, the essayist, poet, and novelist of the Kentucky soil, maintains that for "the human economy . . . to be fitted into the natural economy in such a way that both may thrive, human economy must be built to proper scale." He feels that "ignorance of when to stop is a modern epidemic, the most obvious result of which is a critical disproportion between the scale of human enterprises and their sources in nature."

We ignore the natural limits to growth at our peril. Nothing can grow forever without exhausting its resources and collapsing inward—no organism, no population, no economy. Released from their profound natural restraints, our arid-land cities have become bloated with the lifeblood of other places, vampirelike. I fear for the future of these frayed hems of Denver, no longer prairie. With limits dismissed, can any sense of proper scale survive?

The Plains Woodland Indians lived within limits keenly defined by the American bison, which relied in turn on the broad American steppe. Knowing this, their hunters perpetuated the prairies with fire. The United States government, seeking to cripple the ferociously defensive tribes, went for the buffalo. What bovine diseases had already begun, the rifle completed. Once the plow broke the prairie sod and barbed wire arose, a system that had lasted since the glaciers' retreat collapsed in a decade.

The bison were nearly extinct, the Native Americans subjugated, and the new people dependent on new kinds of grasslands by 1896, when Nebraska's William Jennings Bryan issued a stark warning to the Democratic national convention about the cities claiming the plains:

> You come to us and tell us that the greatest cities rest upon our broad and fertile prairies. Burn down your cities and leave our farms and your cities will spring up again as if by magic; but destroy our farms and the grass will grow in the streets of every city in the country.

Bryan's apocalyptic view comes true as we destroy the farms by draining off their water, just as we destroyed the grasslands before them to make the farms—and now our own system looks shaky.

Ironically, Aurora now finds itself in the business of sowing and irrigating native grasses in arid Otero County. Near the town of Rocky Ford, famous for its sweet cantaloupes, this new rangeland is meant to mitigate the loss of productive cropland when the water rights of distant Rocky Ford Ditch head toward Aurora. Almost fifty years ago, before its Homestake undermountain tunnel had come on line, Aurora drew water off the plains through the Last Chance Ditch. Now one can only wonder if the growth will go on forever, if there will always be another source to tap. Or will

Aurora awake one morning to find its last-ditch chance at sensible scale gone forever?

There was a colony of prairie dogs and burrowing owls living in Aurora on a fallow corner of William Smith's old homestead. A miniature golf course with artificial grass took its place, followed by flimsy apartments and asphalt. The new succession calls for a slum to come next. But even if the owls are gone, the prairie dogs are waiting. Was Bryan right? Will the climax see a return to rank grasses and rodents as the cities crumble and a new savanna reclaims the land at last?

There is an alternative. We could invite the grasses back with all their blessings. It is the grasses, and the grazers with which they have coevolved, that know how to live well on the dry High Plains. We would do well to pay attention to them. We could, for example, fashion our lawns and parks from blue grama and big bluestem. We could bring back buffalo grass, if not the bison.

Lois Webster kept such a lawn in the middle of old Aurora. She didn't water it, and it rewarded her with wildlife and beauty in season. The time Lois saved by not working on her lawn she spent in her favorite places—the Pawnee and Comanche National Grasslands—where she studied the birds, the plants, the plains, and their ways. Recognizing limits, Lois lived with grass, not against it.

An early promotional folder called on settlers to cleanse the High Plains of "sage, sand, cactus, prairie dogs, and owls" in favor of the lawns and shade trees of civilization. They did the job well. Now an enlightened few are seeing these signs of the savage land in a new light, as symbols of proper proportion. This is good. For, as the definitive High Plains photographer Robert Adams says, "Developers destroy places where we become and continue to become ourselves."

The citizens of Arapahoe County will never be Arapaho. We can't get back to Black Kettle's day. But if we were to watch the wood nymphs, ponder the pronghorns, and seek to adapt accordingly, perhaps we could still share in the grace of the grasses. We do have limits after all. It is the gamble of our growth that says we have no further need for the Grass Dance.

9

The Extinction of Experience

We need not marvel at extinction; if we must marvel, let it be at our own presumption in imagining for a moment that we understand the many complex contingencies on which the existence of each species depends.

— Charles Darwin, *The Origin of Species*

I became a nonbeliever and a conservationist in one fell swoop. All it took was the Lutherans paving their parking lot.

One central, unavoidable fact of my childhood was the public school system of Aurora, Colorado. My path to school for ten out of twelve years followed the same route: down Revere Street, left at the fire hall, along Hoffman Park to Del Mar Circle, then around the Circle to Peoria Street, and on to whichever school was currently claiming my time. Detours occurred frequently.

The intersection of Hoffman Boulevard and Peoria Street was two corners sacred, two profane. On the southeast squatted the white brick Baptist church. Across Del Mar lay a vacant lot full of pigweed, where Tom and I cached brown bananas and other castoffs foraged from behind Busley's Supermarket in case we needed provisions on some future expedition. Then came the Phillips 66 gas station and the Kwik Shake, a nineteen-cent hamburger stand whose jukebox played "Peggy Sue" if you so much as tossed a nickel in its direction. On the northeast corner lay Saint Mark's, the red brick lair of the Lutherans, marginally modern, with a stained glass cross in the wall. I spent quite a lot of time dawdling in the vacant lot among the pigweed and haunting the Kwik Shake after school, but I seldom loitered in the precincts of the pious.

Lukewarm Methodists at best, my parents flipped a coin and took us to Saint Mark's for the Easter service. The next Christmas I was roped into being a wise man, and I felt both silly and cold in my terry cloth robe.

Later, when my great-grandmother came to live with us, she hauled me off Sundays to the Southern Baptists. Gemma desperately wanted me to go down the aisle and be saved. A shy boy, I wasn't about to prostrate myself in public before a bunch of people with big smiles and bad grammar. Besides, I couldn't see the sense in confessing to sins I didn't feel I had properly enjoyed as yet. Had I been compelled to choose among them, I'd have taken the cool, impersonal approach of the Lutherans over the Baptists' warm-hearted but embarrassing bear hug of a welcome. But Gemma passed on, and my parents pushed in neither direction, so I opted for the corporeal pleasures of "Peggy Sue" and pigweed and put the soul on hold.

Behind the Lutheran church lay another, smaller vacant lot, where the congregation parked in the mud. The new community of Hoffman Heights had been built partly on a filled-in lake. The water poked up here and there, making marshy spots full of plants that grew nowhere else around, like cattails and curly dock. The far corner of the Lutherans' lot held one of the last of these.

One September day, coming home from school, I cut across the boggy corner, almost dried out with late summer and tall with weeds. Pink knotweed daubed the broken mud and scented the afternoon air. Then I noticed, fully spread on the knotweed bloom, a butterfly. It was more than an inch across, richly brown like last year's pennies, with a purple sheen when the sun caught it just right. I knelt and watched it for a long time. There were others flitting around, some of them orange, some brown, but this one stayed put, basking. Then a car drove by, disturbing it. The last thing I noticed before it flew was a broad, bright zigzag of fiery orange across its hind wings.

A couple of years later, when I became an ardent collector, I remembered the butterfly in the Del Mar marshlet clearly. My Peterson field guide showed me that it was, without question, a bronze copper. The orangey ones had been females. Professor Alexander Klots wrote in his *Peterson Field Guide to the Butterflies East of the Great Plains* that it is "the largest of our coppery Coppers" and "not uncommon, but quite local. Seek a colony," he wrote, "in open, wet meadows." Dr. F. Martin Brown, in my bible, *Colorado Butterflies,* explained that the species extended no farther west than the plains of eastern Colorado and called it *very* local (which I translated as "rare"). He went on to say that "the best places to seek *[Lycaena] thoe* in Colorado are the weedy borders of well-established reservoirs on the plains," which the Hoffman Heights lake had certainly been. I eagerly prepared to return to the spot at the right time and obtain *Lycaena thoe* for my collection.

Then, in early summer, the Lutherans paved their parking lot. They dumped loads of broken concrete and earthfill into the little marsh, then covered it with thick black asphalt. Gone were the curly docks, the knotweeds; gone were the coppers. Searching all around Aurora over the next few years I failed to find another colony, or even a single bronze copper. Concluding that a good and loving god would never permit his faithful servants to do such a thing, I gave up on the Lutherans and their like for the long run.

Biologists agree that the rate of species extinction has risen sharply since the introduction of agriculture and industry to the human landscape. The decline mirrors ancient mass extinction episodes that were caused by atmospheric or astronomic events. In response, we compile red data books and lists of endangered species and seek to manage conditions in their favor. This is good, if only occasionally successful.

Our concern over the extinction of species is appropriate. As our partners in earth's enterprise drop out, we find ourselves lonelier, less sure of our ability to hold together the tattered business of life. Every effort to prevent further losses is worthwhile, no matter how disruptive, for diversity is its own reward. But outright extinction isn't the only problem. By concentrating on the truly rare and endangered plants and animals, conservationists often neglect another form of loss that can have striking consequences: the local extinction.

Protection almost always focuses on rarity as the criterion for attention. Conservation ecologists employ a whole lexicon of categories to define scarceness. In ascending order of jeopardy, the hierarchy usually includes the terms "species of concern" (= "monitor"), "candidate," "sensitive," "threatened" (= "vulnerable"), and "endangered." All plants and animals so listed might fairly be called "rare," but people employ that term when some other word might be more precise.

Most endangered species are rare in the absolute sense: their range is highly restricted and their total number never high. Biologists recognize a fuzzy threshold below which the populations of these organisms should not drop, lest their extinction likely follow. That level is a kind of critical mass, the minimum number necessary to maintain mating and other essential functions. A creature is profoundly rare when its members are so few as to approach this perilous line.

Perceived rarity is often a matter of the distribution of a species over time and space. The monarch butterfly, for example, is virtually absent from the Maritime Northwest owing to the lack of milkweed, while across most of North America it is considered a commonplace creature. Patchy and fluctuating from year to year when dispersed in the summertime, in a good year monarchs can become incredibly abundant in their Mexican and Californian winter roosts. Yet the migration of the North American monarch is listed as a threatened phenomenon because of the extreme vulnerability of winter clusters and growing threats in the summer range.

Another orange and black butterfly, the painted lady, appears in northern latitudes by the millions from time to time. In certain springs, such as those of 1991, 1992, and 2002, these butterflies can block entire highways with their very numbers. In drier or colder years, when their southern habitat produces little nectar or conditions do not favor mass movement, nary a lady might be seen in the temperate regions come summertime. Nevertheless, this thistle-loving immigrant is so widespread globally that its alternate name is the cosmopolite. Are these insects common or rare? Evidently they can be either. Painted ladies and monarchs stretch our sense of rarity.

The concept becomes a little less slippery when we speak of sedentary or specialized animals and plants such as the bronze copper. But are such creatures actually rare, or merely "local," as Professor Klots described the copper in 1951? The fact is that as the countryside condenses under human influence, that which was only local has a way of becoming genuinely scarce. Somewhere along the continuum from abundance to extinction, a passenger pigeon goes from plenitude to few to nothing at all.

In light of the relativity of rarity, it is not surprising that scarce wildlife preservation resources go almost entirely to the truly rare kinds. But, as with

Ronald Reagan's decision to restrict federal aid to the "truly needy," this practice leaves vulnerable populations subject to extinction at the local level.

Local extinctions matter for at least three major reasons. First, evolutionary biologists believe that natural selection operates intensely on "edge" populations. This means that the cutting edge of evolution can be the extremities of a species' range rather than the center, where it is more numerous. The protection of marginal populations therefore becomes crucial. Local extinctions commonly occur on the edges, depriving species of this important opportunity for adaptive change.

Second, little losses add up to big losses. A colony goes extinct here, a population drops out there, and before you know it you have an endangered species. Attrition, once under way, is progressive. "Between German chickens and Irish hogs," wrote San Francisco entomologist H. H. Behr to his friend Herman Strecker of Pennsylvania in 1875, "no insect can exist besides louse and flea." Behr was lamenting the diminution of native insects on the San Francisco Peninsula. Already at that early date, butterflies such as the Xerces blue were getting difficult to find as colony after colony disappeared before the expanding city. In the early 1940s the Xerces blue became absolutely extinct. Thus local losses accumulate, undermining the overall flora and fauna.

The third consequence amounts to a different kind of depletion. I call it the *extinction of experience*. Simply stated, the loss of neighborhood species endangers our experience of nature. If a species becomes extinct within our own radius of reach (smaller for the very old, very young, disabled, and poor), it might as well be gone altogether, in one important sense. To those whose access suffers by it, local extinction has much the same result as global eradication.

Of course, we are all diminished by the extirpation of animals and plants wherever they occur. Many people take deep satisfaction in wilderness and wildlife they will never see. But direct, personal contact with other living things affects us in vital ways that vicarious experience can never replace.

I believe that one of the greatest causes of the ecological crisis is the state of personal alienation from nature in which many people live. As a culture, we lack a widespread sense of intimacy with the living world. Natural history has never been more popular in some ways, yet few people organize their lives around nature or even allow it to affect them profoundly. Our depth of contact is too often wanting. Two distinctive birds, by the ways in which they fish, furnish a model for what I mean.

Brown pelicans fish by slamming directly into the sea, great bills agape, making sure of solid contact with the resource they seek. Black skimmers, graceful tern-like birds with longer lower mandibles than upper, fly over the surface with just the lower halves of their bills in the water. They catch fish, too, but avoid bodily immersion by merely skimming the surface.

In my view, most people who consider themselves nature lovers behave more like skimmers than pelicans. They buy the right outfits at L. L. Bean and Eddie Bauer, carry field guides, and take walks on nature trails, reading all the interpretive signs. They watch the nature programs on television, shop at the Nature Company, and pay their dues to the National Wildlife Federation or the National Audubon Society. These activities are admirable, but they do not ensure truly intimate contact with nature. Many such "naturalists" merely skim, reaping a shallow reward. Yet the great majority of the people associate with nature even less.

When the natural world becomes chiefly an entertainment or an obligation, it loses its ability to arouse our deeper instincts. Professor E. O. Wilson of Harvard University, who has won two Pulitzer prizes for his penetrating looks at both humans and insects, believes we all possess what he calls "biophilia." To Wilson, this means that humans have an innate desire to connect with other life forms, and that to do so is highly salutary. Nature is therapeutic. As short-story writer Valerie Martin tells us in "The Consolation of Nature," only nature can restore a sense of safety in the end. But clearly, too few people ever realize their potential love of nature. So where does the courtship fail? How can we engage our biophilia?

Everyone has at least a chance of realizing a pleasurable and collegial wholeness with nature. But to get there, intimate association is necessary. A face-to-face encounter with a banana slug means much more than a Komodo dragon seen on television. With rhinos mating in the living room, who will care about the creatures next door? At least the skimmers are aware of nature. As for the others, whose lives hold little place for nature, how can they even care?

The extinction of experience is not just about losing the personal benefits of the natural high. It also implies a cycle of disaffection that can have disastrous consequences. As cities and metastasizing suburbs forsake their natural diversity, and their citizens grow more removed from personal contact with nature, awareness and appreciation retreat. This breeds apathy toward environmental concerns and, inevitably, further degradation of the common habitat.

So it goes, on and on, the extinction of experience sucking the life from the land, the intimacy from our connections. This is how the passing of otherwise common species from our immediate vicinities can be as significant as the total loss of rarities. People who care conserve; people who don't know don't care. What is the extinction of the condor to a child who has never known a wren?

In teaching about butterflies, I frequently place a living butterfly on a child's nose. Noses seem to make perfectly good perches or basking spots, and the insect often remains for some time. Almost everyone is delighted by this, the light tickle, the close-up colors, the thread of a tongue probing for droplets of perspiration. But somewhere beyond delight lies enlightenment. I have been astonished at the small epiphanies I see in the eyes of a child in truly close contact with nature, perhaps for the first time. This can happen to grown-ups, too, reminding them of something they never knew they had forgotten.

We are finally discovering the link between our biophilia and our future. With new eyes, planners are leaving nature in the suburbs and inviting it back into the cities as never before. For many species the effort comes too late; once gone, they can be desperately difficult to reestablish. But at least the adaptable types can be fostered with care and forethought.

The initiatives of urban ecologists are making themselves felt in many cities. In Portland, Oregon, Urban Naturalist Mike Houck worked to have the great blue heron designated the official city bird, to have a local microbrewery fashion an ale to commemorate it, and to fill in the green leaks in a forty-mile-loop greenway envisioned decades ago. Now known as the 140-Mile Loop, it ties in with a massive urban greenspaces program on both sides of the Columbia River. An international conference entitled "Country in the City" takes place annually in Portland, pushing urban diversity. These kinds of efforts arise from a recognition of the extinction of experience and a fervid desire to avoid its consequences.

A Green Man for our time, Houck has launched an effort to involve the arts community in refreshing the cities and devoted himself to urban stream restoration. As streams are rescued from the storm drains, they are said (delightfully) to be "daylighted." And when every city has someone like Mike Houck working to daylight its streams, save its woods, and educate its planners, the sources of our experience will be safer.

But nature reserves and formal greenways are not enough to ensure connection. Such places, important as they are, invite a measured, restricted kind of contact. When children come along with an embryonic interest in natural history, they need free places for pottering, netting, catching, and watching. Insects, crawdads, and tadpoles can stand to be nabbed a good deal. Bug collecting has always been the standard route to a serious interest in biology. The insect net is still the best wedge to get kids out. To expect a strictly appreciative first response from a child is quixotic. Young naturalists need the "trophy," hands-on stage before leapfrogging to mere looking. There need to be places that are not kid-proofed, where children can do some damage and come back the following year to see the results.

Likewise, we all need spots near home where we can wander off a trail, lift a stone, poke about, and merely wonder: places where no interpretive signs intrude their message to rob our spontaneous response. Along with the nature centers, the parks, and the preserves, we would do well to maintain a modicum of open space with no rule but common courtesy, no sign besides animal tracks.

For these purposes, nothing serves better than the hand-me-down habitats that lie somewhere between formal protection and development. Throwaway landscapes like this used to occur on the edges of settlement everywhere. The British writer and naturalist Richard Mabey calls them "unofficial countryside." He uses the term for those ignominious, degraded, forgotten places that we have discarded, which serve nonetheless as habitats for a broad array of adaptable plants and animals: derelict industrial lands or railway yards, ditches and gravel pits, abandoned farms and bankrupt building sites, brownfields, embankments, margins of landfills, and the like. These are secondhand lands, as opposed to the parks, forests, preserves, and dedicated rural farmland that constitute the "official countryside."

Organisms inhabiting such Cinderella sites are surprisingly varied, interesting, and numerous. They are the survivors, the colonizers, the generalists—the so-called weedy species. Or, in secreted corners and remnants of older habitat types—like the Lutherans' parking lot—specialists and rarities might survive as holdouts, waiting to be discovered by the watchful. Developers, realtors, and the common parlance refer to such weedy enclaves as "vacant lots" and "waste ground." But these are two of my favorite oxymorons. What, to a curious kid, is less vacant than a vacant lot? Less wasted than waste ground?

I grew up in a landscape lavishly scattered with unofficial countryside—vacant lots aplenty, a neglected so-called park where weeds had their way, yesterday's farms, and the endless open ground of the High Line Canal looping off east and west. These were the leftovers of the early suburban leap. They were rich with possibility. I could catch a bug, grab a crawdad, run screaming from a giant garden spider; intimacy abounded.

But Aurora slathered itself across the High Plains, its so-called city limits becoming broader than those of Denver itself. In reality it knew no limits, neither the limit of available water nor that of livability. Of course the lots filled in, losing the legacy of their vacancy. The park actually became one, and almost all of its fascination fled before the spade and the blade of the landscaper's art. By the time the canal became an official pathway, part of the National Trail System, most of the little nodes of habitat embraced within its curves and loops were long gone. As butterflies fled before bulldozers, the experience I'd known was buried in the 'burbs.

In a decade I recorded seventy-five kinds of butterflies—nearly a tenth of all the North American species—along the canal. In doing so, I learned perhaps the most important thing the High Line had to teach, which was also the saddest. It had to do with the very basis of ecology, that organisms ask their own specific needs of the landscape, and when these cease to be met, they vanish unless adaptation happens fast enough to accommodate change and allow species to survive.

The admiral butterflies flitting along the High Line Canal were survivors. Butterflies related to both red and white admirals lived in central Colorado approximately thirty-five million years ago, as shown by Oligocene fossils from the shale beds of Ancient Lake Florissant. Sharing many characteristics with today's relatives, they kept up with changing landscapes and climates and prospered. They will change further, just as wood nymphs change their spots over time, refining their protection. But because few butterflies can adapt fast enough to outpace a Caterpillar tractor, they must depart or die out when development comes. Altered habitats along the High Line have provided all too many examples.

At first, faunal changes on the canal were largely additive. Itself a product of human intrusion, the old irrigation ditch came to provide habitats for many opportunistic animals and plants. When I began studying its butterflies in the late fifties, the High Line was probably at the peak of its diversity. Habitats had matured and gained complexity for the better part of a century. New species were still coming in, riding the long pipeline of life downstream from the Rockies or up from the prairie.

One season, my mother and I found a large colony of painted crescentspots in a field beside Toll Gate Creek. This southern butterfly had never been recorded in Colorado outside the Arkansas River drainage. Here it was, deep within the basin of the Platte. How it had crossed the Divide, the piney plateau that serves as a biogeographical barrier between watersheds, we hadn't a clue. But once beyond, it began spreading rapidly. The Platte River flood of 1965 took out most of the original colony, but it came back from remnants. Then the painted crescent, more adaptable to disturbance of canalside habitats, began to replace the formerly common pearl and field crescentspots. Painted and gorgone crescentspots, feeding on bindweed and sunflower, respectively, became the common species on much of the eastern High Line, while the pearl and field crescents, dependent on asters, retreated to a few less disturbed sites. With change, something was lost and something else gained. But still more years on, all four species of *Phyciodes* were gone.

As change intensified with the growing population of Aurora, losses began to outnumber additions. Many of the habitats I'd known were erased by rampant development of housing tracts and malls. Places where black swallowtails, purplish coppers, and silvery blues once flew became other kinds of places, where they didn't. The only colony of Olympia marblewings was sacrificed, along with their crucifer hosts, mourned by no one but my butterflying buddy, Jack Jeffers, and me. A bluegrass playing field for a new school appeared in their place—the very field where I would throw the discus all through ninth grade. Even as the platter flew high above the new green turf, I thought of the mustards and marbles that would not be back. Dreams of illusive Olympics replaced the actual Olympias I'd once had.

None of these butterflies became extinct in the strict sense, for they survived elsewhere, in places still wild and rural. Still, through these local losses, I learned about extinction. Like spelling or multiplication tables, it was a lesson learned by rote, for it was repeated again and again. My work with the butterflies of the High Line Canal has gone on for fifty years. For thirty-five years, a group of friends has gathered each July to hold a butterfly count centered at the site of the Thunder Tree. These ongoing censuses have revealed that since 1960 some 40 percent of the butterfly species on my High Line Canal study sites have become extinct or endangered. This is a greater rate of loss than Los Angeles, San Francisco, or Staten Island has experienced. The decline corresponded with the growth of Aurora's population from about forty thousand to more than a quarter of a million human beings.

On a recent visit, I saw many more kids walking along the canal than in my day, and in many more colors, but none of them were catching bugs, trapping crawdads, or running from spiders. Merely putting people and nature together does not ensure intimacy; to these kids, the canal path might have meant little more than a loopy sidewalk, a shortcut home from school. But I wondered how much was left to find, if these youngsters had actually wanted to look.

The next day I followed the High Line Canal out onto the plains. A few dozen tall cottonwoods marked off an unspoiled mile strung between a freeway and a new town. Where the ditch dove into a culvert beneath a road, an old marshy margin survived. Monarchs sailed from milkweed to goldenrod.

Then I spotted a smaller brilliancy among the fall flowers. Netting it, I found it was a bronze copper—the first I'd seen in more than thirty years, since the Lutherans paved the parking lot. It was a male, and a female flew nearby. Maybe, I thought, releasing the copper near her, some kid with a Peterson field guide will happen across this little colony before the end of it.

Had it not been for the High Line Canal, the vacant lots I knew, the scruffy park, I'm not at all certain I would have been a biologist. I might have become a lawyer, or even a Lutheran. The total immersion in nature that I found in my special spots baptized me in a faith that never wavered, but it was a matter of happenstance, too. It was the place that made me.

How many people grow up with such windows on the world? Fewer and fewer, I fear, as metropolitan habitats disappear and rural ones blend into the urban fringe. The number of people living with little hint of nature in their lives is very large and growing. This isn't good for us. If the penalty of an ecological education is to live in a world of wounds, as Aldo Leopold said, then green spaces like these are the bandages and the balm. And if the penalty of ecological ignorance is still more wounds, then the unschooled need them even more. To gain the solace of nature, we all must connect deeply. Few ever do.

In the long run, this mass estrangement from things natural bodes ill for the care of the earth. If we are to forge new links to the land, we must resist the extinction of experience. We must save not only the wilderness but the vacant lots, the ditches as well as the canyonlands, and the woodlots along with the old growth. We must become believers in the world.

PART IV

Still Life

10

Butterflies in Winter

In a world made smaller by human dominance, the butterflies of spring
keep me in touch with the planet's abiding distances.

— John Hay, *The Bird of Light*

My father was a fisherman, not a naturalist. Sometimes they're the same
thing. In Dad's case, if he went outdoors without a golf club or a lawn
tool, it was usually to fish for trout with flies. Not that he didn't care for
the scenery of the canyons and lakes where the browns and rainbows and
brookies lived, or for the general pleasures of the countryside. But he never
took a field guide afield.

I've known naturalists whose parents were biologists, and I always felt that
they had a head start on their hobby. I have also known children fascinated
by nature whose parents abhorred it and actively discouraged them. I was
somewhere in between. Dad never opposed my enthusiasm—except once,
after I read a *Life* magazine article on Charles Darwin and announced that
I planned to turn my bedroom into a laboratory. "Oh no, you're not!" my
father boomed. When I did, in a modest way, he ignored it.

The best thing my father did for me, besides the fishing trips to the
mountains, was to take me to the Denver Museum of Natural History.
Close and free, a frequent destination for family outings, the museum sat
on top of a hill in City Park. Facing the Front Range across the duck lake,
it loomed like a tan and blocky outcrop. Inside its cool and cavernous
galleries I stood in silent awe by the dinosaurs while my father shook his
head, my grandfather "tsked," and my brother Tom vanished.

In particular, I liked the artful habitat dioramas of the High Plains, the
Front Range, the Continental Divide, Pikes Peak. Next door were the
Arctic, the tropics, the desert. On my way in I would make a courtesy
visit to shiver with the harp seals, swelter with the tropic birds. But always

I would hurry on to the Mead Ecology Hall with its Colorado places and its pumas, mule deer, wild turkeys, and yellow-headed blackbirds. There I lurked for hours, searching for butterflies secreted among magically real columbines, aspen leaves, and blades of mountain grass, all made of wax and paper. Where else could you find butterflies in the winter? Especially then, I longed to disappear into the dioramas. Those green seasons, swamps, and meadows were months away, but in the meantime the dioramas would do.

Down the hall, in a small room, was the Mason collection of butterflies and moths. They were the real thing, though I almost preferred the immortal fakes to these pinned and faded specimens taken from their habitats. Even so, I stood in awe of the giant birdwings and Atlas moths, the shimmering blue morphos, the Indian Kallimas that looked just like leaves.

On one of my many visits, I thought I noticed telltale piles of dust beneath some of the butterflies, signifying carpet beetle damage. These dermestid beetles can devastate an insect collection if not arrested. I asked a guard if he knew who took care of the butterfly exhibit. He showed me a door marked "Staff Only" and said it would be all right to go in to inquire. I picked my way among varnished skulls and fossils, stacks of herbarium sheets, and waxen leaves in the making, until I came to an open door marked "Curator of Spiders and Insects."

Both arachnophobic and shy to a fault, I almost ran back out. But I knocked instead, and a soft, deep voice bid me enter. Mr. Walker Van Riper was near the age of my grandfather. His hair was a thin white fuzz, his spectacled expression proper but not severe. He welcomed my interest as a diversion from the usual run of questions from the public about insect pests in the garden and "spider bites." "Yes," he admitted, "the butterflies could use some care. They probably haven't been fumigated since they were installed." Butterflies were not his specialty. I avoided asking him about spiders. "And we have a great many specimens for the research collection, waiting to be spread. I'm afraid we haven't the staff to do it."

Walker Van Riper had come to Colorado in 1914 in search of respite from tuberculosis. He became a respected investment banker and financial adviser in Denver. A relapse of TB forced a long vacation that launched his lifelong involvement with nature study. He became an arachnologist of note, a herpetologist, and a pioneer in high-speed strobe photography. Later, on retirement, he joined the museum staff as curator. His position was honorary, yet it allowed him to pursue his studies in the company of such great naturalists as Robert Niedrach and the museum director, Alfred M. Bailey. Had I known that black widows were one of his primary areas of expertise I might not have been so eager to work with him; and had I been aware of his fame, I surely would have been intimidated. But Van Riper was quiet and shy, much like myself, and he obviously shared my fascination for nature. I couldn't wait to sit at his knees, spreading butterflies for hours.

Jack and I wrote the museum, formally proposing that we assist in curating the butterfly collection. Mr. Van Riper responded, inviting us to telephone to make a date to visit and discuss the arrangement. "I will be interested in seeing examples of your work," he wrote on December 3, 1959, "your list of butterflies collected, your school marks, and the names of the books you use." We complied, then arranged a return trip to the museum with samples from our collection. The Curator of Spiders and Insects praised our work more than it deserved and said he would work it out with the administration and get back to us. I left the museum that day buoyant, feeling more important than in my usual role as mobile exhibit in the Mead Ecology Hall.

Before I became a butterfly collector I used to roam the High Line Canal with no particular purpose. The summer I turned nine, a vision arose from one of those walks. Three-fingered leaves of ragweed arched above my head like a ceiling of green gloves. Higher, the canopy of cottonwoods dappled the light as their leaves wagged in the breeze. A small, fleet shade passed, and I followed it with my eyes. The shadowcaster lingered just long enough for me to get a glimpse before vanishing downwind. Broad, supple wings of black, spangled with bright colors, lifted a yellow-spotted body dangling long legs. I watched long after it disappeared, pretty sure it had been real.

The ragweed went to pollen and then to seed. I came in from daily trips to the ditch and went back to school. One afternoon, in the library of Peoria Elementary, a booklet caught my eye. *National Audubon Society Nature Program,* it said: *Butterflies.* On the cover, and again on a stamp inside, appeared the creature from the ragweed canebrake: a black swallowtail. I could see every detail of the butterfly: double bands of yellow spots crossing the silky black wings, and on the hind wings a field of blue speckles running in rays out toward sharp tails punctuated by fiery orange spots with black pupils like fierce eyes. What an animal! I was amazed that there could be such things right here on the High Line Canal, in my own small corner of the world.

My first great passion was for seashells. I'd been hooked on their fabulous colors and forms and the lives of the creatures that made them ever since I could say their names. When GrandPop visited aunts in Florida and sent home boxes of kumquats, their citrus tang carried the Atlantic air and the expectation of shells. Inside I might find pink-blotched strawberry scallops, heart cockles still crusty with their black mantles, and strangely glyphed alphabet cones, all nestled among the pungent orange ovals and their crinkly leaves.

I took to blowing my small allowance on Triton's trumpets and corals in the museum gift shop, or on scorpion shells and sea fans from dealers. Before she left home, Mother built a pine shelf for my collection, which quickly filled it. I lusted for ever more shells, but Colorado was a crummy place for conchology. The only shells I could collect myself were dull little pond snails from the slime at the muddy margins of prairie creeks.

As my discontent with mail-order shelling grew, I began to notice butterflies. First there was the swallowtail. Then, across the street in a weedy patch of Hoffman Park, I noticed a bluish buzz that never seemed to alight. I watched one until it finally did. A tiny butterfly, its wings were triangular and checkered gray and white, not blue. The fuzz covering its thick body shimmered blue in the sunshine. I began to see these (and others that were just as small but slower and coal black with white speckles) everywhere that cheeseweed grew. I knew it was cheeseweed because GrandPop made a poultice from it whenever White Linament—an obnoxious, turpentine-based substance he favored for burns, cuts, or sore muscles—failed to do the job. Eventually, among the white clover in the newly seeded park, butterflies appeared that really were blue.

One day, ambling through the park, I passed the local ball diamond. In the pulverized dust of the pitcher's mound lay a dead butterfly. Its saffron-colored wings were spread almost as if by a collector. These black-veined membranes felt thin and dry when I rubbed their color between my fingers. But as I handled this husk of a viceroy butterfly, it gave me a sense of pleasure my shells seldom could, for I had found it myself.

My father had remarried in 1958, bringing me a stepbrother named Bruce Campbell. That first summer he was with us, Bruce decided to collect insects and asked if I wanted to go along. "Sure!" I said. "I'll do the butterflies." We set out with two makeshift nets and not a clue as to how we were supposed to keep our prey. On the way to the canal we stopped off at the brand-new supermarket in the young shopping center. As a promotion for ready-made dinner rolls that came in a cardboard tube, they were giving away empty tubes with a slot at one end to serve as coin banks. We nabbed a few of these as specimen containers.

All I caught that first time out were a few rather faded painted ladies. I deposited them like bright coins in my bank, where they quickly beat themselves to bits. As much as I loved their coral oranges and blacks and whites and blues, they looked more like last year's confetti than butterflies by the time I got them out. But it didn't matter. I had found a new love.

Childlike obsession can trigger a learning curve seldom seen in school. Parents of young dinosaur enthusiasts know this. For me, smaller quarry called. Over the next few months I learned the early lessons necessary to the young lepidopterist: how to build and use a proper net; how to handle insects with forceps and gentle fingers so as not to damage them; how to squeeze harder to stun them, and how to make killing bottles with carbon tetrachloride to finish the job. I learned how to make paper triangles in which to transport or store specimens—much better than cardboard banks—how to mount them with balsa wood boards, insect pins, and paper strips, and how to keep my spread treasures safe from carpet beetles with naphthalene or paradichlorobenzene. (I learned nothing about keeping myself safe from carbon tet, naphtha, and PDB, whose sharp stinks filled my room for years.)

My shell books had to move over to make room for volumes on butterflies. W. J. Holland's classic *The Butterfly Book* pictured most of the North American fauna in fine early color lithographs between its heavy green buckram covers and the author's delightful old-fashioned asides. F. Martin Brown's *Colorado Butterflies,* with its brilliant purple Colorado hairstreak on the slipcover, became my gospel. Dad gave me the Brown for Christmas of 1958, Mom the Holland when I saw her for the first time in three years at Christmastime 1959. Then I made my first-ever solo book purchase in a bookshop on East Colfax Avenue: Alexander B. Klots's splendid *Peterson Field Guide to Butterflies East of the Great Plains.* Klots told where to find butterflies, how best to study them, and what they did in the ecological scheme of things. "When you are ready to do so," he wrote, "go out and collect."

After years of wishing I could do so with shells, I was ready, all right. But I felt the need for a companion. Entomology proved not to be Bruce's metier, and he made that first expedition his last. My brother Tom wasn't to be seen much anymore, as he and his redheaded friend, big Billy Rose, spent their days riding around on their Schwinns. So I asked Jack Jeffers to join me. Jack's family and mine had moved into Hoffman Heights the same summer, and we had played together off and on for half our lives. Now we were turning twelve. Jack was slender, with dark straight hair. He had an ironic laugh, a reticent and frowning smile, and a smooth, considered way of moving. We shared an interest in girls, but he could see that butterflies were more accessible. So he came along, and found he liked it.

Butterflies gave Jack and me the kind of bond that would make us, for a while, like brothers. Besides, through Jack's backyard, past his mother's red and yellow cockscombs, lay the park and the shortest route to the canal. Each time we went out we recorded our finds in a brown spiral pocket field book, as Professor Klots had instructed us to do in his *Peterson Guide*:

Rhopalocera Notes (Book I). April 4, 1959. *Polygonia satyrus,* JJ, not common, flying in association with *N. antiopa; Pieris protodice; Nymphalis antiopa, N. milberti* common. J.J. & B.P., High Line Canal, S.E. of Aurora, Colo.

Jack and I walked east into the early spring green, along a brushy bank. The pungency of the sandbar willows laced the brisk morning air as the day began to warm. Jack lunged at something I didn't see and brought his net *smack!* down onto the ground, raising dust. A satyr anglewing struggled in his net. Golden tawny above, warm speckled and striated tan beneath, it was our first. "Good going," I called, batting at something stirring from last year's leaves. A Milbert's tortoiseshell flashed its orange-and-yellow-banded wings right past me. Lanky Jack, quicker and more graceful, stalked it, struck, and had it safely in his net. When I tweezed it from the folds of his net I was disappointed to find it pale and chipped, not at all the brilliant, banded creature of fiery orange and yellow the books pictured. But the books also said that these anglewings and tortoiseshells spend the winter as adults. That's why they were out so early, and why they were faded and ragged. No matter; they made great sport, and we would find their fresh offspring in the fullness of summer.

May 17, 1959. *Papilio polyxenes asterias, Phyciodes tharos, Microtia gorgone carlota, N. milberti, N. antiopa, P. satyrus, Colias eurytheme, C. eriphyle, Strymon melinus, Pholisora catullus.* B.P. & J.J., Aurora, Colo.

The ninth outing of the spring. Each time, as the season cooked and coaxed butterflies from their chrysalides and hiding places, we found new species on the wing. This morning, bright crescentspots, sulphurs, skippers, and gray hairstreaks were emerging. We prowled among the ragweed, watching the water so recently let into the ditch. I kept thinking of something I had seen here, years ago—or did I dream it? But no, I had recognized that vision in the Audubon stamp book and knew it was real enough. And now here it was, dallying above a clump of bursting spring vegetation: the black swallowtail. Ebony wings spread broad, its yellow spots like so many suns in the night sky, the scales of blue clouding its hind wings like a galaxy of sapphire stars. Wide-eyed admiration didn't save the beast. Vladimir Nabokov wrote of such a moment, "I stoop with a grunt of delight to snuff out its life." I did the same.

May 30, 1959. *Euchloe olympia rosa,* High Line Canal.

I left the canal near a check dam and dropped down into a field full of purple crossflower and other pungent, weedy mustards and spurge. Diminishing returns had begun to set in, and I wondered if I could still find anything new. Halfheartedly I swung at what I thought must surely be a small cabbage white. In the bottom of my net I found a delicate stranger. The size of four thumbnails, the color of cottage cheese sprinkled with pepper, it was unremarkable above. But the underside was marbled with pure chartreuse set in a creamy field blushing with rosy light. I netted a dozen or so, leaving many behind, and took them home to spread them before they lost an iota of their fresh loveliness. Consulting Brown's *Colorado Butterflies,* I glowed to read that this was the Olympia marblewing, subspecies *rosa,* "a good catch in any year." Each year we would make a good catch of rosy Olympia marblewings between the weeks of late April and late May.

In June, the big, bright species coursed the canal—fresh, second-generation mourning cloaks; western tiger swallowtails, bigger and faster than the blacks; and broad, white-banded black Weidemeyer's admirals. All three species glided among the waterside willows, claimed sunny spots as territorial perches, then darted out at one another as well as at any swallow, dragonfly, or anything else that deigned to pass their positions.

Mid-July brought the large wood nymphs flitting through the long grass skirts overhanging the banks. Rich chocolate brown when fresh, the males seemed to peek through the grass blades with rows of small eyespots. The larger, paler cocoa females glared with their imposing ocelli. Russet skipperlings and golden skippers occupied the banks, too, shooting through the grass thatch of the ditchside like living brass projectiles.

Butterflies signaled the seasons. Just as one month's fauna dropped out, a new assemblage of mint-fresh butterflies would take the place of the tatty remnants of the earlier generations. These might be the second brood of a type we'd encountered earlier or late-emerging, single-brooded novelties. Bright salmon painted ladies basked beneath a certain cottonwood before sunset, offspring of the immigrants in April meadows buttered with dandelions. This time we got them home in good condition. In August and into fall, the milkweeds crowded the sides of Toll Gate Creek with dripping blossoms and swelling pods. They were in turn thronged with great gray coppers and monarch-mimicking viceroys. Before the frost, the monarchs themselves, having fed on the milkweed as larvae, fueled on milkweed nectar for their long flight south to Mexico.

With the monarchs went the summer. The mourning cloaks and Milbert's tortoiseshells bedded down in hollow trees, and Jack and I went back to school. We took part of our embryonic collection for show-and-tell, and the other kids regarded our black swallowtail and white-lined sphinx moth with both amusement and astonishment that such creatures actually lived in Aurora.

On the one hand, Jack and I wanted to keep our hobby to ourselves. On the other, Dr. Klots advised group study. The more generous inclination took sway. Jack and I launched the Monarch Lepidoptera Society of Aurora, and brazenly asked Dr. Brown himself to join. From the safe distance of Colorado Springs, he accepted. Mr. Van Riper was also invited to join our club; citing poor health, he politely declined, but wished us well. A handful of kids came to the first meeting. They were impressed by the letters from famous entomologists, but not with the tasks I had in mind for them, and soon drifted away.

The Monarch Society defunct, Jack and I would go it on our own, if spring ever came back. Our impatience to take down our nets again grew like ragweed. Crazy butterfly dreams came on in midwinter, placing exotic species in familiar haunts, but the early butterflies took their time coming out. I could hardly wait for the rapture of "going afield," as the old books put it, with my friend. Every winter since, I have known that ache.

In the meantime, we hoped for the museum job to help pass the months. Then one evening my father was scanning the *Denver Post* when he came home from work. I sat on the floor reading the funnies. Dad's glasses were low on the bridge of his nose, his tie undone, as he turned the pages. "Well," he said, "that's a fine how-do-you-do."

"What's that, Dad?"

He called me over, and put his arm on my shoulders. The comfortable aroma of his hair oil and tobacco mixed with that of newsprint. "Bobby," he said, "that nice Mr. Van Riper you used to go see at the museum—I'm afraid he's passed away."

"What?" I couldn't believe it—Jack and I had seen him just a few weeks before. I took the paper to read it myself. Dad did not resist. It said that Van Riper, despondent over his illness at seventy-two, had apparently killed

himself on January 15, 1960. He was found in Washington Park, shot through the mouth with a .38 revolver. Shocked, I felt a cold shade fall, like winter.

The following spring the butterflies came out as usual, and I still cared. But the museum forgot about butterflies for decades. Mr. Van Riper was not replaced, and the insect drawers were stowed away with plenty of PDB to await some future curator. The Mason collection lost ground to the carpet beetles and was eventually replaced by a new exhibit. Only in the dioramas could butterflies be seen, if you looked closely among the waxen wildflowers.

> May 26, 1961. High Line Canal. 4 *E. olympia* (2 JJ, 2 BP), *Strymon melinus,* 1 *Vanessa atalanta,* 1 *Pyrgus communis,* 1 *Anaea andria* (farm west on canal, JJ).

The telegraphic notes scarcely tell the tale, but the names give a whiff of the third summer's great venture: to catch the goatweed butterfly. One of the rarest butterflies in Colorado, this member of the tropical genus *Anaea,* the leafwings, closely resembles a dead dried leaf when its wings are closed. Wings open, however, the male glows with a deep and fiery orange, the color of a ripe persimmon sprinkled with cinnamon. Another collector had caught a tawny female nearby. Jack and I were determined to crown our collection with this fabulous insect.

From time to time we thought we had spotted one, a spurt of flame glimpsed from the corners of our eyes; but it always vanished so soon that we couldn't be sure. The butterfly's caterpillar fed on goatweed, we knew, but we didn't know enough botany to identify *Croton.* Had we known to bait the butterfly with rotten bananas, we might have succeeded sooner. Our anticipation grew intense and the butterfly took on mythic proportions in our minds. We began staking out a tumbledown abandoned farmyard where other nymphs were drawn to rotted manure. Finally, on a warm May afternoon, we cornered the goatweed butterfly near the old stables.

As he flickered about the yard, I somehow held back. A false lunge would have sent him into the next county before I could blink. After each sally around the yard, he returned to the same basking perch on the ground. Jack began to stalk the goatweed like a farm cat watching a granary mouse, while I covered the open gateway to the canal. The brilliant butterfly shot out and back time after time. Jack crept nearer and nearer, then struck—and got him! The flaming male flapped its last in Jack's net. I didn't even mind that I hadn't caught him myself.

While the better netman (as that goatweed proved), Jack had never been quite as keen on butterfly study as I was. For him the chase was the thing; the curating had less appeal. More than once he threatened to pull out of the operation, taking his goatweed butterfly with him, and most of the swallowtails, too. Once we actually divided the collection, until Jack realized how bad the PDB in the bug boxes smelled, and he brought them back.

The usual trigger for our spats was jealousy. Down the block lived Jack's other best friend, Bill Sampson. Bill was into baseball cards as I was into butterflies (so much so that he operated a baseball card shop out of his garage after school) and, like Jack, he was also a keen golfer. Jack might decide to peddle baseball cards or swing golf clubs with Bill instead of swinging nets with me. Or maybe I would choose to fling the platter with my discus-throwing buddy, Chuck Dudley, when Jack wanted to go to the canal. Later we all became great pals—Chuck, Bill, Jack, and I. But in those vulnerable years when the terrors of testosterone were just making themselves known, loyalties were all-important. Caught in the middle, our butterfly bond stretched ever thinner.

A day came when I decided to head for the canal by myself. The closest way lay through the park. To get there I had to pass through Jack's yard. He was there with Bill and some golfing friends of his dad's, putting golf balls around the lawn and drinking Cokes. Net in hand and gritting my teeth, I opened the gate in the chain-link fence and entered the Jefferses' backyard. "Hey, is that a butterfly net?" called one of the men in golf shoes.

"Sure looks like it," laughed another.

"Catch some for me, butterfly boy," said the first.

Jack started to say something, but Mr. Jeffers interrupted. "You wanna go with Pyle?" he asked. "I'll take your club if you want to run get your butterfly net—but we won't hold up the tee time."

"Heck, no," Jack replied, hunched over his putter, eyes on the ball. "I wouldn't be caught dead with one of those things."

That stung, like the time I made the mistake of collecting by the hollow tree as Jack and friends were basking by the new pool, and they had a laugh at my expense. I would become used to such taunts. They were a foretaste of something I would encounter all my life: the wild array of attitudes—curiosity, incomprehension, envy, indifference, wonder, mockery, mirth—directed at naturalists by others. This is nothing new. One of the things we loved about Holland's *Butterfly Book* was the series of "Digressions and Quotations" interlarded among the text. One such piece, "Uncle Jotham's Boarder" by Annie Trumbull Slosson, tells of a fellow who "just spent/His hull days in loafin' about/And pickin' up hoppers and roaches and flies/ Not to use for his bait to ketch trout/But to kill and stick pins in and squint at and all./He was crazy's a coot, th'ain't no doubt." In fact, the poet concluded, he was just "a nat'ral histerrical feller."

"Dumb jerks," I mumbled as I left Jack and the gawking golfers behind and headed off across the park. I knew that Jack was only distancing himself for self-preservation. But that wasn't the whole story. Our butterfly nets were not considered cool by our peers, and when grade-school kidding grew into mild ostracism in junior high, I assumed that Jack dropped out under the peer pressure. Yet as I later learned, his defection owed at least as much to the increasingly scientific tack my interest was taking. As Jack saw it, the butterflies themselves were being eclipsed by a flurry of Latin names, the adventurous by the academic, the casual by the curatorial. Jack would become a better scientist in college than I, and eventually, a professional mathematician. But our days afield in search of Olympia marblewings and goatweed butterflies meant more to him for the thrill of the chase than for the facts of the matter. It wasn't just the jeers that put him off.

I was mad at Jack for a while. But I would miss him, too.

I remember a winter walk to the hollow tree from my father's house. Snow newly diapered the suburban expanse, so you couldn't tell the difference between the cornfield that had been and the playing field that was. This was night. I was lamenting the flight of the vacant lots before shopping malls and some of life's other losses. Snow flurried, all but blocking out streetlights and carlights. I slipped out of the cold into the belly of the big cottonwood—a snugger fit than when I was a kid, but a fit still.

Once again the wet char smell filled my nostrils. I felt as protected as ever, and for a little while both the changed-up scene and my personal concerns faded into the furrows of the cottonwood bark, all wounds snow-gauzed.

Winters and winters later, I walk a snowy stretch of the High Line east of Potomac Road. My father lies dying downtown in Saint Joseph's, a victim of the evil trade in *Nicotiana*. Earlier, I met some of my old teachers in a doughnut shop. We shared coffee and revisionist memories of good old times. Then I walked to the police station beside the canal to report a theft, for my car had been burgled and something special taken. A bleak day. Rigid twigs crack underfoot, like the ice that clamps them to the edge of solid puddles. My breath makes white puffs through a woolen muffler; I wiggle my fingers to keep them from freezing. The canal curves into the middle distance, where its white stripe blends into the bland winter sky. I pick up the pace.

The warmth is hard to find this time. Just the same, I walk the path a while longer before returning to the hospital and the empty house. With my father gone, there will no longer be a home to bring me here. Visits to the canal will have to be made on their own pretense. I wonder if I will. Just a cold dirt ditch on the edge of someone else's town. Why bother?

The afternoon darkens, going colder. A raw wind comes up. Withered yellow rabbitbrush stirs, brittle beside the frozen ditchbank. A whiff of woodsmoke from a condo fireplace brings to mind a campfire of cottonwood twigs and a distant High Line weenie roast, when my father was young and fit.

Dad wasn't a naturalist, but he helped me to be one. He bought me books and took me to see the old lepidopterists in town and the younger ones in the mountains who made all the difference in my life. He took me to the hills, to the plains, to the museum. With my stepmother, Pat, he took me to Crested Butte for several summers, where he fly-fished as I chased butterflies. His smile when he angled a rainbow in the East River was the same as mine when I netted a rainbow on the wing. Dad was not indifferent.

The Luckies got him at only sixty-six. I've come back to see him through the last of his cancer. Earlier, when he learned he was ill, we spoke of many things. We talked about family, travels, ambitions, about history and hopes. We spoke of Ernie Pyle, and how Dad had met him in the Philippines during the war, shortly before Ernie was shot; of fish and flies, and even of butterflies. He is beyond talking much now.

Dad will die tonight. Over his fading rasp I'll remind him of a sunrise that he saw and drew from the deck of a Liberty ship in the Mediterranean. I'll try to take him back to Big Thompson Canyon. To paint the East River meanders in his mind's eye.

I turn back into the canal's chill breath, and it gives me heart. This is where the tortoiseshells come to life in spring. It is hard for me to believe that they're here somewhere now, butterflies in winter.

11

A Grand Surprise

To think/that every brain is on the brink of nameless bliss no brain can bear/unless there be no great surprise.

—Vladimir Nabokov, "Restoration"

When I handle a cocoon or a chrysalis, or when I roll the euphonious names of butterflies around in my mouth, I often think of my mother. I see her working the warm spring soil, weeding among the violets. Her yellow sunsuit shows the skin of her back already brown. I am three or four, impatient, but I like the worms and the smell of Mother and the earth she disturbs with her garden claw. She reaches down with her other hand and pulls a small golden sphere out of the soil. I take it, roll it gently between my fingers, hold it to the sunlight. It is thin and papery, nearly round, and shiny. Mother says, "That's a cocoon, Bobby. Something pretty will come out of it."

I don't remember if anything ever did come out. It was very likely a spider's egg case, anyway. But an egg and a pupa are much the same thing: life gathered within a papery caselet, to emerge when it's ready. This is why the butterfly farmers of New Guinea call their chrysalides "eggs." A name, too, is like an egg. Compact, shiny, it contains the seed of meaning that the namer had in mind. My mother didn't have a name for what that cocoon contained, but her love of life and language made her want to know about such things. From that minute packet was to come a shared passion for cocoons and their contents. Years after that earliest of memories, we learned their names together.

Like a butterfly, a name goes through changes as it finds its final form. A butterfly's name has metamorphosed doubly, once in its own right, once before in the skin of the creature that carries it. Every giant swallowtail used to be an orange dog. A monarch has not only been a tiny green egg, a striped caterpillar, and a jade chrysalis with gold spots; it has also been a milkweed butterfly, a storm fritillary, and a wanderer.

Mom and I found that we both liked the old-fashioned names used by bygone authors and common country folk before the modern monikers arose. For example, the butterfly commonly known as the red admiral (*Vanessa atalanta*) has also been called alderman or nettle butterfly, and before that, red admirable or simply the admirable. This old name, a simple aesthetic judgment, seemed better suited to a butterfly (in spite of its scarlet epaulettes) than the standard martial title, especially as it is not a true admiral (genus *Limenitis*). The other three North American *Vanessa*s also had their aliases. The painted lady (*V. cardui*) has been the thistle butterfly, Cynthia of the thistle, and the cosmopolite, for its worldwide occurrence. The alias of *V. annabella*, the West Coast lady, is the malva butterfly. The American painted lady (*V. virginiensis*) has gone by Virginia lady, marbled Cynthia, and Hunter's butterfly. The mourning cloak, too, was once considered a member of the genus *Vanessa*. Now known formally as *Nymphalis antiopa,* it has been called Camberwell beauty, Antiopa, yellow edge, willow butterfly, and, best of all, the name Vladimir Nabokov preferred for it: the grand surprise.

Dutch still-life paintings of the eighteenth century often contained a red admirable, a painted lady, a mourning cloak, or another insect among their extravagant flower arrangements. I've often wondered if they were included to surprise complacent viewers as much as for their decorative value. Certainly these animals have surprised me again and again as they have decorated my life.

RED ADMIRABLE

When I was nine, my mother went away.

One gray afternoon a Yellow Cab came to the house. "Grab a few things," Mom told me gently, "and come on. We're in a hurry."

"Are we going to Grammy's?" I asked.

"No," she said. "Farther."

The taxi took us to Stapleton Airport. "We're going to Seattle," Mom said. "I want to show it to you."

We were leaving the ticket counter, on our way to the gate to board a Constellation for Boeing Field, when my father found us. "Where do you think you're going?" he yelled, grabbing my hand. Mother held the other one firmly.

"We're going to Seattle," Mom said, "and you can't stop us."

"Try me," said Dad. He pulled me in the other direction.

I started crying, and people stopped to watch. Mom and Dad were yelling, and she was crying, too. They struggled over me, and a pair of glasses came off. A small crowd gathered. The tug-of-war went on until an airport official came and said we couldn't have a scene right there in the airport. Security arrived and we were led off to a quiet room. Mother left for Seattle alone, and I didn't see her for years.

In fifth grade, I had a penchant for monsters of all sorts. My teacher, Mrs. Frost, growing weary of this preoccupation, insisted that I do something else for a butcher-paper class mural of a country scene. When even a vampire bat was rejected, I cast about for a subject among a pile of magazines Mrs. Frost had brought in for our inspiration. Between Jersey cows, red barns, and oak trees, the rural mural was nearly filled, so I was obliged to choose a small subject. A butterfly caught my eye. Coal black with fiery orange-red bars and blue spots, it was labeled "Red Admiral." I painted a passable likeness in tempera.

"That's so much nicer than those bloody-fanged things you always draw, Robert," said Mrs. Frost. I was very taken with it myself and wondered whether I might ever see such a beast in real life.

Butterflies soon swept my interest from both seashells and monsters, leaving Dracula in the dust. When Jack Jeffers and I went out at night it was to collect moths at lights and flowers rather than to play werewolf games. Still, a spooky sense accompanied certain dark forays, never more than on one particular night's walk along the High Line Canal.

We were netting pale gold miller moths on the yellow blooms of rabbitbrush along the ditchbanks when we approached a lone farmhouse. This big, blocky red brick building was well known to us by day. Occasionally we had trespassed to snatch apples from its orchard or swallowtails from its big old lilacs. No one had ever challenged us, but once or twice I was aware of someone watching, a woman, her face blurred by the back porch screen. Local kids had told us that this lonely mansion was occupied by a witch. Our recent obsession with monsters and such was fresh enough that we were not inclined to ignore the tale altogether.

We intended to slip quickly past the red house, but in the lonely corona of the pole lamp by the driveway dozens of moths were dancing with bats. We shrugged and walked over to check it out. The moths circled crazily in the repetitious rendezvous, bats diving at them like dark meteors across their orbits, sometimes making contact, often not. A few moths alighted on the pole where we could reach them with our nets or collecting jars.

Looking over my shoulder, I saw the screened veranda of the old house standing out like a lighted island in the dark sea of night. Myriad moths flapped about inside this illuminated cage. Jack saw them too; our nets twitched nervously. We longed to get at the captive abundance of moths, but how? We didn't want her calling the sheriff—he'd noted our nocturnal prowls more than once and warned us not to bother anyone—and besides, what if she *were* a witch?

Nudging each other, we got up the nerve to open the gate and approach the porch. "Maybe we can sneak in and get a few without her seeing us," I whispered to Jack.

"You do it," he said, "and hand them out before she gets you."

I turned the squeaky handle on the porch entrance just as the heavy front door of the house opened wide. Before we could turn and run, a grandmotherly voice asked, "Can I help you, boys?"

The woman stood in the doorway, clad in a flowered dress and looking younger than we expected. Her face was luminous in the porch light, her hair drawn back in a silver bun, her lips drawn back, too, in a thin smile. Stammering, I asked, "May we catch some moths here, ma'am?" I added, "We have a collection . . . for school." I thought "for school" made it sound more official. Actually, that might have helped. Far from a witch, Miss Margaret Robina Smith, a retired teacher and nurse, was a generous benefactor of education. Her father, William Smith, had been on the school board for fifty years. Furthering the schooling of young people was her greatest love, even if it involved moths. But we didn't know that.

She scrutinized us for a moment, then looked up at the moths flitting and banging all around us, smacking the windows, screens, and lights, making a nuisance. "By all means," she chuckled, shaking her head. "Take 'em all."

Jack and I swung and batted away at the horde, their scale-covered wings loosing a drift of sparkling powder into the light. Soon we realized that they were almost all army cutworm moths, a kind of noctuid miller that breaks out in vast numbers some years. About an inch across, their forewings were brown, their hindwings smoky gray. One was not unattractive; hundreds were boring. Our jars were full, our hunters' hunger for the kill overwhelmed. We finished, having made little impact on the moth population.

The woman had stood in the doorway, watching us, with folded arms. We showed her some of the prettier species: a red, white, and black tiger moth, a snowy ermine moth, a striated orange geometer, a yellow underwing. She displayed interest and not a bit of witchiness. Then she told us to sit, and brought out lemonade and cookies. The scents of hay and running water and the High Plains at night filtered through the broad screens as we sat and sipped and talked. Rich, dark wooden trim in the parlor of the red house showed through the lace curtains of the windows. Miss Smith said she was the daughter of the pioneer who had built the house and planted the cottonwoods. I asked if she would mind if we spread a bait of stale beer, brown sugar, and bananas on the tree trunks one night to attract underwing moths, and if we might chase butterflies there by day. She said, "Why yes, you may." And then she said, brushing a miller off her face, "But I wish you could have caught a few more of these."

One day after school that fall, Jack and I returned to the red house. Miss Smith was apparently out. We explored the big barn next to the house and netted West Coast ladies on rabbitbrush. Then in the late-day sun, basking in the warm, nettle-strewn barnyard, flat-out against a paving stone, appeared a vision from that butcher-paper mural: cinnabar bands on ebony wings, lapis lazuli set in obsidian—a red admirable.

It proved one of the most difficult butterflies to catch. One of the *Vanessa*s, known for both fleetness of wing and quick reactions, it would bask invitingly and then vanish at the first approach. These brush-footed butterflies are considered highly evolved and quite intelligent as insects go, as well as keenly perceptive. *V. atalanta* has a reputation for landing on people in their gardens, in fact singling out the same person, among several present, to alight on repeatedly. I suspect these traits have as much to do with its being called "admirable" as its gorgeous looks. In later years, after I'd had the experience of one landing on me a few times and watching it up close, I grew incapable of collecting a red admiral, or admirable, ever again.

Unable to overwinter in freezing climes, Atalanta appears from the south most years in May. Her larvae consume stinging nettles, clustering in midsummer among the leaves in webs pebbled with their own black frass. There were nettles by the barn, and red admirables seemed to come back there each spring until Miss Smith died. Then her orchard and fields were cut up into lots and sold off, and the barnyard became a backyard. When the next spring's journey brought them back to a destination no longer nettled, the red admirables flew on.

HUNTER'S BUTTERFLY

When my mother came back from the coast, after numerous adventures, another marriage, hard trials, and a lot of illness, she lived in my grandmother's house in East Denver. We got to know each other again by walking the flowered parkways, alleys, and old parks—Cheesman, Congress, City—searching for the butterflies I had newly discovered. Bright diurnal moths, black-and-white eight-spotted foresters and rust-and-yellow nessus sphinxes, let us catch them on the sweet rocket. I was shy with her, but we both loved nature, and that quickly broke down the silence of years.

Helen Lee had always been a closet naturalist. A splendid gardener in her younger years, she later became an enthusiastic mushroom hunter, though too wary to eat much of what she found. She was a meditative angler, too. Looking over their smiling photos in fishing togs, taken during their honeymoon at Grand Lake, I wondered why angling hadn't been a better bond between Mom and my fly-casting father. Now we two were finding a bond in butterflies.

When Jack drifted off, Mom came home just in time to take his place as my field partner. During my last year in junior high school, Mother regained the house and custody of her children. My father and stepfamily moved elsewhere in town. Susan had grown and gone off to college and marriage. Tom, Bud, and I lived with Mom again in Hoffman Heights. She worked in downtown Denver as a banker's secretary.

On the weekends we went to the mountains with Bud when time and cash permitted, or we would dash off to the Denver Botanical Gardens, to Kiowa Creek on the plains, or to the High Line Canal. Most often, the old ditch was our destination. While it might not have had the checkerspots and fritillaries of Rabbit Ears Pass or the hairstreaks and skippers of the Front Range canyons, it offered its own surprises. Mom took her time and netted fewer individuals, but she often found rarities and novelties.

On a summer day in 1964, we parked Mom's blue and white 1959 Chevy in Fairmount Cemetery and headed southwesterly along the canal. Butterflies speckled its weedy shores. Mother lagged behind to attend to a Weidemeyer's admiral as I chased ahead after a swallowtail. When I turned back I could see her broad smile from a distance. Her curled hair was silver, tinted light brown. She wore baggy jeans and a loose print shirt with pockets for specimen envelopes. As I approached, she eagerly held out her net with a butterfly trapped in a fold for me to examine. "What is it?" she asked excitedly. "It looks like a painted lady, but it's different."

So it was. Mother had netted an American painted lady. Rarest of the four species of *Vanessa* in Colorado, its salmon wings stood apart for their bright pink bars, soft purple patches, and big blue eyespots. She'd spotted it gracing a canalside thistle.

"It's a Hunter's butterfly," I said. "*Vanessa virginiensis*—our first!" She laughed with the pleasure of it, then coughed. Mother looked older than her forty-eight years, except for her outdoor smile. The catch, new for the High Line list, was something to celebrate. It would go into our collection with a label commemorating the day. Hunter's butterfly—the name suited her. Sublimating her own cares in the search, Mother was a keen hunter. And her enthusiasm revived and fired my own, keeping it alive through the ennui of adolescence.

Next, we crossed over into a weedy zone where lupines grew among wild barley. This was the only lupine patch in the neighborhood. We knew that where you see the blue of lupine flowers, blue butterflies might be found as well. We thrashed through the weeds, swept the gray and azure domes of the lupine plants, and lo, emerged with bits of blue in our nets—butterflies that looked as if they'd been distilled directly from lupine blooms, skipping the caterpillar stage, far from their usual mountain haunts.

Back at the car, we didn't want to go home. As long as we were out, our nets and the sun kept the other side of life at bay: no homework for me, no bills or pills for Mom. We followed a two-tailed tiger swallowtail past the crematorium and deeper into the cemetery before it disappeared. A dappled green place, cool on a hot day, Fairmount might well have been a park with an unusually sedate public. Rows of green ash and hackberry trees shaded the roads and paths among the gravesites. Magpies swooped between markers, calling urgent queries, grieving for all the good carrion buried deep out of reach.

We spotted the tiger's larvae, thumb-size snakes with blue and yellow eyespots, grazing brazenly on green ash trees, and the pale green caterpillars and chrysalides of hackberry butterflies cryptic against rough and pungent hackberry leaves of their same color.

The swallowtail reappeared, gliding like a great yellow sailplane between two ashes. A brown blur darted out from a white tombstone toward the two-tail and circled the swallowtail like a pestering bat. When the larger species left, the other returned to its perch. A hackberry butterfly, its narrow wings were warm brown above, tan and lilac below, spotted with bright eyes. Mother began to go for it, then noticed another nearby, and another. We chased them between two obelisks into a memorial glade, where the still air was alive with *Asterocampa celtis*. We'd hit the peak of their flight period in a year of unusual abundance: hundreds of hackberries swooped through the glade in agitated encounters, basked on the boughs of blue spruces, and decorated the headstones. Catching and papering one after another, still surrounded by the quick brown insects, we looked at one another and giggled, a little embarrassed by our gluttony.

Taking a break in the shade of a Colorado blue spruce, we pondered the incredible numbers of the hackberries and the contrasting scarcity of the Hunter's lady. Neither species was numerous in eastern Colorado when Europeans arrived. Common in the East, the Hunter's thins out westerly in spite of the near omnipresence of its pearly everlasting and pussypaw food-plants. Hackberries, confined to the foliage of the tree by that name, originally occurred sparsely in a few Front Range canyons. But *Celtis* trees were planted in large numbers as shade trees in the cities, enabling the butterfly to spread and, in places like Fairmount, to become preternaturally abundant. Hunter's butterfly, meanwhile, continued to follow its own peculiar rhythm of rarity.

I'd been sending hackberry butterflies, both dried and alive, to a specialist in Tennessee who was working out their biology. This was our rationale for collecting so many—not that we really needed one. We were gathering in the closeness that the years apart had stolen. Butterflies were our medium, the canal our meeting place. The low sun cast long shadows behind the carved stones, and we had to go home. But we'd be back.

Early the following summer, we were catching pair after pair of fresh little painted crescentspots in a low weedy field beside the canal at Chambers Road when a heavy thunderstorm arose. The crescents meant money for college, since I was now collecting professionally for a New York dealer. I was paid in pittances—four cents for a sulphur, ten cents for a swallowtail, maybe a dollar for a rare alpine satyr—and having Mom along added measurably to the bag. We both disliked the bloodthirstiness of commercial collecting, and it took a toll on our pleasure ("All those little lives," as the Alaskan poet John Haines remarked of his trapping days), but it offered a way to be out together in places like this green meadow while working for my tuition.

Mother had finally managed to take me to Seattle, if only for a visit. I liked it and determined to go to the University of Washington. Once accepted, I had to earn my share of the fees. I'd given up another summer job in favor of the dealer's offer so I could spend my time chasing butterflies with Mom whenever her work permitted.

We hurried for home as the rain came in torrents. Once there, the power went out. Jack dashed across the street with a black swallowtail he'd found trying to take shelter in a little elm in the park. We studied her by candlelight and fed her sugar water as we listened to a battery radio. A tornado had struck Plum Creek, near the source of the High Line in Platte Canyon, sending a wall of water down the Platte River toward the city.

Listening from our front porch we could hear the advancing flood several miles away. When the water fell back, the field of the painted crescents had been scoured by the overflowing canal. Railroad tracks lay twisted near the Thunder Tree, and the old wooden flumes over Toll Gate Creek and Sand Creek had been destroyed. When it stopped raining and the sun came out, Jack made me let the swallowtail go in our yard. He was right. Having survived the storm, she did not need to die for a dime.

After my high school graduation, the Aurora house was sold. Mother, Bud, and I moved back to Grammy's house. Almost daily I drove up the Front Range canyons of Deer Creek, Turkey Creek, Coal Creek, and Boulder Creek to collect in places such as Genessee Park, Mother Cabrini Shrine, and Parmalee Gulch, then dropped back down with my full collecting bag before the mountain rains began. In the late sunshine I worked over my catch and my accounts outside on my balcony, surrounded by the redolence of Gram's tall mock oranges, as the evening came on and Denver cooled. The mountains that were the source of my bounty flamed off to the west. When my mother came home from the bank, we walked Detroit Street to Seventh Avenue Parkway and back on the alleys in between, where we had discovered a species of peace, butterflying together.

Around the alley hollyhocks, we often saw painted ladies of one sort or another. All the *Vanessa*s are immigrants, showing up here and there, leading adventurous lives. Also called the cosmopolite, the painted lady follows the thistles north, where we found her and her sisters on dandelion lawns in April or May. West Coast ladies appeared on the canal in Aurora each September or October, having come from who-knows-where. Late spring was the time to watch for red admirables, whose offspring would still be flying till the frosts of fall.

But of Hunter's butterfly, we never found another.

THE GRAND SURPRISE

Flashing open its bark-black cowl, the butterfly revealed its inner wings—maroon and chocolate, blue spotted, with a butter-yellow border. I had never seen anything so beautiful. When my knees worked again, I gave chase. Gliding in and out of the dappled shade of cottonwoods, this chimerical creature appeared, disappeared, and reappeared. I followed it back and forth, its wings closing into ashes, spreading into live cinders, and seeming to pause before my eyes momentarily as if it were mounted on the air. I swung my net, disturbing it, and the big insect vanished over the towering crown of the Thunder Tree.

I knew it was a mourning cloak from one of my favorite books. *Nature's Wonders in Full Color* depicted an array of seductive butterflies and moths, including a dogface sulphur on clover, tortoiseshells among autumn leaves, and Cynthia moths on forsythia. Another bright photo showed an open mourning cloak resplendent against red sumacs. "The mourning cloak spends the winter tucked in a hollow tree," read the caption, "and is one of spring's first butterflies." Now here it was, beside my hollow tree, a grand surprise if ever I'd seen one.

I would follow mourning cloaks through the coming years. In March, on the first warm days, they would appear along the ditch among patches of dirty snow with their smaller relatives, Milbert's tortoiseshells. In June I might find masses of their red-and-black spiny caterpillars making tatters of our backyard weeping willow. I reared them, and by midsummer their gray chrysalides, thorny pellets like diabolical bullets, hung upside down inside my jars and from the eaves of our house.

June would see the fresh new cloaks on the wing, and by schooltime their offspring would be bedding down for their winter-long sleep. Occasionally, on a sunny walk in winter, I spotted a tatty Antiopa dodging between the naked trees.

When Jack and I went out on the first warm days, hungry for butterflies, we'd see dozens of cloaks. But we both had difficulty catching them, as they never seemed to sit, instead patrolling the canal bed up and down, down and back. We had many chances to swing at them as they sailed past, but without fail they swerved over the net rim at the last second, like a tennis ball with radar. Finally I thought of letting one get past me and then swinging from behind, and it worked. I had one at last! But when I removed the big female from my net, the big surprise was to find her pallid and worn. Hers were hardly the "purple-brown wings edged with creamy yellow" described by Brown in *Colorado Butterflies.* We should have known better. As we'd already seen with the tortoiseshells, these winter-nymphs emerge from their hibernatoria both early and diminished. Even a mild winter takes its toll on those velvet vanes. We would have to wait until June to see the insect that moved the English to call it the Camberwell Beauty.

Something about the mourning cloak made me averse to killing it. Like the red admirable, it held a kind of totemic value for me, having been among the ones that thrilled me from the very start. Too, being big and exceedingly strong bodied, cloaks didn't die easily, and I hated to see them struggle. The spring individuals were never perfect enough for specimens, and the bright ones of high summer had a mission to perform. I wondered whether, growing a little jaded from the professional collecting, I was also getting soft. In any case, the cloak was so common that it brought a tiny price, entirely disproportionate either to the effort of catching it or its own great size and beauty. Letting one go was no loss at all.

I cashed in my butterflies and went off to college. Mother and Bud moved into a small apartment in East Denver near Gram's. Mom seldom drove her old Chevy but took a bus to work when she could, or a taxi. On foot, she carried her net only as far as City Park, and her mushrooming was confined to the lawns and old maple stumps of the parking strip.

By coincidence, the apartment stood across the street from the home of a young doctor who was also an avid lepidopterist. When Ray Stanford saw the nets my mother had placed in the hands of neighborhood kids, he knew there must be another collector around. They met, and Ray helped maintain Mom's zest for the hunt in my absence.

When I came home for visits, we drove to the old haunts. Sometimes, with Ray and other friends, we organized expeditions in search of rarities. They always knew that Helen Lee was likely to find them, though she couldn't walk far or fast. In March we chased green hairstreaks among the red rocks of the canal's headwaters. In June we found the once-flooded field repopulated with painted crescents. I spent the summer in Denver working as a postman. Weekends afield with Mom, Bud, and my fiancée JoAnne were almost as before. We found the scarce Nokomis fritillary in a desert seep in western Colorado, and a gully alive with tens of thousands of blues thronging the milkweed bloom near the Black Canyon of the Gunnison.

JoAnne and I married in 1966 and returned to Seattle in the fall. I hoped the butterflies and mushrooms would invigorate Mom, though I knew her health was getting worse and her bills bigger. The next summer I stayed in Seattle to work for the Sierra Club. But I was worried when Mother didn't write, and she sounded bad on the phone. I hitchhiked back to Colorado through a hot, dusty August.

The sagelands of southern Idaho made Denver seem cool. I found my mother ill with an infection on her legs that GrandPop's cheeseweed poultice couldn't cure. Bud, only in junior high school, was at a loss to help her. I felt I should stay with Mom, having come so far to see her, but the close, smoky apartment, the disease, and her tears were oppressive.

I had been writing a piece on the ditch and hoped on this trip to find its terminus at last. I'd imagined Mother and me doing that together, and things being as they had been, but she couldn't walk. So I took Bud, who was depressed by her condition, and after doing what we could to make Mom comfortable, we drove east with our friend Chuck Dudley.

Out on the High Plains northeast of Aurora, the canal vanishes into a many-headed hydra of prairie watercourses. Ditches and creeks and gullies all intersect, and all look about the same. The maps were unclear as to the ultimate end of the High Line. Bud, Chuck, and I planned to walk it right through.

As we drove north on Tower Road, a western kingbird flew into the Chevy's windshield. I recovered it, and we stroked its soft, hot, pale yellow breast. Blood ran from one corner of the bill. Stilling this voluble and lively prairie singer seemed a bad start.

We plowed through mud behind emerald frogs, crisscrossed the mile roads north of Colfax Avenue, and got all hot and sweaty following gullies stuffed with tumbleweeds. By midafternoon we still hadn't found the end and felt we'd better get back. But we stopped off at the A & W for a Frosty Mug before heading into the city, and when we finally got back to the apartment, Mom was lying on the floor, sobbing in pain and frustration. She'd left her chair, fallen, and couldn't get back up.

"Where have you been?" she cried as strong Chuck lifted her onto a couch. I told her about our day, but the stories that once would have cheered her seemed to make it worse. She didn't even say that she wished she could have been with us. I didn't understand what she knew: that she would not be walking on the canal with me again.

I ambled south along the High Line toward the scruffy lupine patch near the mausoleum and Masonic plot. Hackberry butterflies followed me along the row of stickery blue spruces. Golden skippers flew out from pink inflorescences of milkweed. A small mourning cloak haunted the hems of peachleaf willows overhanging the water, laying eggs in masses on the branches. I came to the spot where my mother had caught the Hunter's butterfly.

A bit beyond, I paused and looked through a gap in the blue spruce wall, into the cemetery. I saw the rounded granite stone that read PHELPS and walked over to it. My father and his father were buried a mile across the lawns, in a newer part of the cemetery where upright stones were not allowed. But here, in the old section, obelisks, stones rugged and smooth, and small mausoleums stood among mature trees.

Sitting on a curved concrete bench in the shade of an arched juniper, I read the names of my grandmother's parents on the marker: "Hannah and Edward Phelps." Between them, Grammy and her sister, Aunt Helen, lay interred in their urns. Their names were inscribed on brass plaques attached to the memorial stone. "Grace Phelps Miller, 1894–1977," said one. The other, shiny and new, read "Helen Bailey Phelps, 1896–1989."

I went around to the other side, where the stone was blank but for a single brass plaque facing the canal above the grass and clover. "Helen Lee Pyle," it read, nothing else. Her legal name was Lemmon, but Grammy never recognized my mother's second husband. Her dates would have read 1916–1967. Mom's ashes were not there either: some had gone into Puget Sound, some to her favorite ravine in Seattle, and some had merged with the muddy flow of the High Line Canal.

Eventually I did find where that flow ends up, in a tiny tributary of Second Creek. It was in the autumn. I had Mom in mind as I wandered a lateral ditchlet to an empty, weed-filled little reservoir near the canal's mouth. Once it held a share of High Line water for a ghost farmstead signified by a few dead locusts. Dried-up salsola and goatsheads filled the parched hollow, and young cottonwoods lined the lee side, dying for want of water. A magpie nest six feet up in one of the saplings had been abandoned.

The reservoir had become an ad hoc firing range. Brass shells lay everywhere, and fragments of shattered black clay pigeons littered the dusty ground among fall leaves. A row of tall old cottonwoods along the inlet ditch had been shoved over; the only one left standing, a broken snag, was peppered with lead. No wonder the magpies departed.

The prone cottonwood trunks lay about like femurs in a bone-yard, hardly rotting in the desiccating air. I walked out the longest one. Its bark had fallen away and little thornlike prickles covered the pale bare wood. I came to the root mass of the log, where old mud once surrounding burned-out roots had lithified into hollow casts. They were brown as the fields that stretched into the distance on all sides. The scene seemed lifeless except for horned larks lurching behind clods of earth and the contrails of jets scratching the blue sky.

The decaying base of the tree had the same charred smell as the Thunder Tree in storm. It took me back. And just then something dark blew out of the hollowed root wad. It was a grand surprise! Had it planned on spending the winter there? Mahogany vanes spread in an instant's hesitation, flashing sapphire spots and yellow bands before my eyes, then sailed away.

The mourning cloak flew northeasterly across the open plain. I watched it with my binoculars as far as I have ever followed a butterfly in flight, maybe a mile. Then it disappeared. Not below the horizon—I could see the curvature of the earth—but up above it. Into a point.

12

The Thunder Tree

They laugh at our Cottonwoods. That, we can't help. It's better to laugh than cry. They call our Cottonwoods a cheap tree. It is along the Missouri River, but it has not been a cheap tree in Denver. Our people have paid large prices for Cottonwoods, and larger sums for water to make them grow . . . The Cottonwood has been a necessity, nay more, it has been a luxury and a living joy—a luxury and joy no people can experience who live in a timbered country, no matter how beautiful or graceful or ever renowned their trees for shade may be.

— W. G. M. Stone, *The Colorado Handbook,* 1893

There are stars in the cottonwoods. If you grasp a cottonwood twig, neither too green nor too rotten, and snap it at a wrinkled growth node, a perfect five-pointed star may be revealed on the broken ends. The star is the darker heartwood contrasting with the paler sapwood and new growth. Carl Crookham, a great Colorado teacher who used the Platte River Greenway in Denver as his classroom, told me about the stars and how they got there.

The Arapaho people believed that the stars in the sky, like all else, came from the earth. They moved up through the roots and trunks of the cottonwoods to wait near the sky at the ends of the high branches. When the night spirit desired more stars, he asked the wind spirit to provide them. She then grew from a whisper to a gale, thrashing the cottonwoods in her tempest. Many twigs would break off with her force. Each time they broke, first from the branch and again on the ground, they released stars from their nodes. When the night spirit had enough, the wind spirit calmed again to a whispering breeze. Looking about beneath cottonwoods after a storm, you might find one of these star sticks.

As the only tall tree encountered frequently by the Arapaho and Cheyenne Indians, the plains cottonwood naturally assumed a powerful and procreative role in their cosmos. They observed how summer brought snowstorms of "cotton" from the trees' catkins, which gave rise to ranks of new cottonwoods along the prairie watercourses. They found that its white wood could be easily worked and hardened by fire. Maker of stars and trees, giver of starlight by night and welcome shade by day, provider of bowls, bows, and arrows, the cottonwood must have inspired reverence and affection among the High Plains' first residents.

European settlers, too, took pleasure and comfort from the plains cottonwood, adapting it as well to many uses. In *A Natural History of Trees*, Donald Culross Peattie related that Missouri River pirogues were fashioned from them, and that two such craft lashed together could transport ten to fifteen tons on the river. He went on to describe the wagon trains' dependence on the great trees:

> *This cottonwood grows naturally in low moist ground, in the vicinity of streams, water holes, and old buffalo wallows. So in the days of prairie schooners immigrants sighted their way on the Santa Fe trail and the Oregon trail, from one grove of the Great Plains Cottonwoods to the next, sure that they would find water, fuel, and shade in the burning day. Upon that shelterless sea of grass 400 miles wide, these Cottonwood groves were the wayside inn, the club, the church, the newspaper, and the fortress when the wagons drew up in a circle beneath the boughs. Whether the traveler "nooned it" or by night sent the sparks of Cottonwood logs flying to the stars, here he was sure to meet other travelers and with them exchange the vital news of the trail. And these trees, whispering among each other, must have heard the talk of the women, exchanging immemorial secrets of their kind.*

The Arapaho had long since been herded off to Oklahoma by the time the Thunder Tree was a sapling. In 1890 or so, Aurora pioneer William Smith wanted to green up the district of his arid homestead. The Lowland Scotsman missed the spreading oaks of home. In the absence of oaks, he teamed up with ditching contractor H. H. Nickerson to plant cottonwoods along their new High Line Canal. Nickerson took the stretch from the Denver city line to Alameda Avenue, while Smith planted from Alameda out to his spread's eastern edge at Peoria Street. They pulled up seedlings at Cherry Creek and carried them back in saddlebags of wet sand. One of these saddlebag saplings was to become the great hollow poplar that graced Smith's farm until long after his death in 1946.

Season by season, the sinuous rows of trees grew from sprouts into monuments. Some curved, making broad arches over the bed of the canal, overpasses for the commerce of squirrels. Others launched straight up, their branches meeting in a leafy bower far above the slow water. By chance advantage of soil, moisture, or superior genes, certain trees in favored sites grew larger and faster than the others. And a few, subject to a range of stresses and forces, became hollow. The greatest of the cottonwoods in William Smith's domain also became the hollowest, and for years after the devastating hailstorm in which this tree saved my life and my brother Tom's, I'd assumed it was hollowed chiefly by lightning. Then longtime High Line ditchrider George Swan told me what really happened.

About half a century after William Smith planted the cottonwoods on the Sand Creek Lateral, George Swan was riding ditch on that branch of the High Line. He knew the cottonwood in question, since it was already a giant. It bore round woodpecker holes, since like many of the cottonwoods it provided lodgings for flickers. One of the galleries had rotted into a cavity large enough to attract a swarm of wild bees. By 1938 the hollow tree was a flicker tree and a bee tree, though not yet very hollow.

On that particular day, George Swan saw smoke along the lateral and hurried to check it out. Flames leaped from the old cottonwood. A knot of farm kids broke up and ran when they saw him coming. George figured that they had built a fire in a small cavity at the base of the tree, hoping to smoke out the bees and snatch the honey. But the woodpecker holes and insect workings caught fire from sparks, acted like flues to fan the flames, and turned the whole tree into a blazing chimney. The hot draft sent flames twenty to thirty feet into the air, and the hive and its honey were burned up. The tree survived but smoldered for two days. That was when the reaming of the hollow tree began in earnest. Ever since, as Swan put it, "the hollowing of that old tree just went on."

Summer winds and winter gales scraped and planed the ebony cracked throat of the great tree. Rot and insects ate away at the bole. Tom and I, sucked out of the storm and into the belly of the hollow cottonwood that day in July of 1954, were just another minor tool of erosion. Rubbing up against the wet charcoal within, we helped the wind and the rain and the rot to shape the graceful contours of this grand plant we came to call the Thunder Tree.

The plains cottonwood is otherwise known as *Populus sargentii*. The genus *Populus* belongs to the willow family and includes the black, silver, and willow-leaved cottonwoods, the Lombardy and other poplars, and the aspens of montane and northern boreal forests. The specific epithet *sargentii* honors Charles Sprague Sargent, author of the classic *Manual of the Trees of North America* and cousin of the artist John Singer Sargent. America's greatest dendrologist of the day, Sargent served as professor of arboriculture at Harvard University and director of the Arnold Arboretum. His impressive career received a fitting tribute in the naming of this equally imposing species of tree.

Consulting Sargent's 1905 manual about "his" tree, I learned that *P. sargentii* normally grows sixty to ninety feet in height, often becoming six or seven feet in diameter. The Thunder Tree neared both these maximum dimensions. The species grows erect, with spreading branches forming a broad, open head, its profile not unlike that of an English oak: William Smith should have felt at home among them. Pale brown bark, thick and deeply fissured into broad ridges, ascends the stout trunk. The leaves are ovate, almost heart shaped. They can be two or three inches long, three or four broad. Light green above, bluish below, and lustrous as they quiver on the prairie wind, the leaves bear rounded teeth along their margins. They spring from sticky buds coated with balsam, a fragrant, volatile resin.

Cottonwoods bear their sex in catkins on separate trees. They are thus said to be dioecious—to have two households. The male trees put out two-inch staminate catkins, fuzzy-caterpillar-type danglers that seed the spring skies with vast batches of pollen. Pistillate catkins launching four to eight inches from twigs on the female trees are lined with green capsules that burst when fertile, releasing masses of minute brown seeds tufted with fine white hairs. These seeds float great distances from their mothers, filling the summer sky with the cottony fluff that gives the trees their name while making soft summer snow. The Thunder Tree was a female.

Like thistledown or dandelion parachutes, cottonwood seeds are capable of spreading the species across areas of many miles. Spiderwebs and pools become clogged with the sheer mass of kapoklike stuffing released at seed time. Any patch of suitable soil is likely to receive one or many seeds. It seems surprising that cottonwoods do not cover the plains, given this fertile fallout, until one realizes that they cannot grow except where sufficient moisture exists—in other words, along the watercourses. And these tend to be so thickly vegetated that potential new ground for seedlings is severely limited.

Nor do cottonwoods rely strictly on their seeds. Like willows, their frequent consorts, they possess a second elegant mechanism of colonization. The trunks, branches, and twigs of cottonwoods tend to be brittle. As the Arapaho legend confirms, storms rend pieces from the trees and scatter them over the ground. Some spear the rain-soft soil, rooting directly. Or should they fall into the stream below, the orphaned branches might be swept far downstream. Coming to rest on a muddy bank not yet occupied, such a castaway might take root, giving rise to a new cottonwood tree. Stumps send up new shoots, and bright red suckers spring from waterside roots. So one way or another, cottonwoods are pretty likely to take hold wherever their potential habitat occurs. Growing in the riparian zone assures these trees not only the moisture they require, but also a means of dispersal. Cottonwoods and willows play both ends against the middle, sending out their adaptable genes by wind as well as water.

The plains cottonwood ranges through the foothills and the plateaus on their hems from Saskatchewan and the Dakotas to Texas and New Mexico. It is the signature tree of these zones. In fact, the lowland riparian ecosystem characterized by the South Platte River, its tributaries, and the High Line and similar canals is often called the cottonwood community. This plant association, in addition to the dominant cottonwoods, includes peachleaf and sandbar willow, sand plum, wild rose, snowberry, milkweed, poison ivy, Virginia creeper, and many other shrubs, herbs, and grasses. Since Europeans arrived, American and Chinese elms, green ash, and tamarisk have moved into many cottonwood communities. The actual amount of cottonwood has changed, varying with the width of the floodplain, agriculture, grazing, logging, and burning. On certain rivers such as the lower South Platte, forests of plains cottonwoods grow along the floodplains—broad galleries of pallid trunks meeting in a closed canopy of shining green. Some consider these galleries an artifact of settlement. Even so, their distinct domes, clumped or single-filed in loopy lines, trace the path of moisture through the drylands. Following water across the plains, the green ranks of cottonwoods define a countryside otherwise nearly featureless.

Populus sargentii not only backs the fabric of the riparian plant community but provides homes for many animals as well. Tiger swallowtails and Weidemeyer's admirals are only the most conspicuous of the hundreds of species of insects that feed on its foliage. Many birds nest here, among them Bullock's orioles in their woven scrotal bags hanging from branches over water; magpies in their flimsy stick tenements; and red-shafted flickers in holes of their own making. The flickers dig for wood-boring beetles, part of an insect medley performed beneath the bark. Kestrels, chickadees, and many other cavity nesters occupy abandoned woodpecker holes. Such hollows grow through influence of fire, fungi, and insects into homes for owls, bees, spiders, and raccoons. Mourning cloaks hibernate in hollows, while thirteen-lined spermophiles dwell in burrows among the massive root systems. Squirrels tumble leaves and twigs into nests among the branches. Ants, beetles, and other invertebrates flourish among fissured bark, feather, and fur. Whether gallery forests along the broad sand streams, or the lone tree stranded on some forgotten lateral, cottonwoods are magnets for the life of the High Plains.

Mirrors, too, for the seasons. First the bud bracts break away, shiny and brown, sticky and sweetly aromatic, though not as cloying as the balsam poplar of the North Woods. Gray-green leaves unfurl, growing shiny as their toothed triangles spread. Catkins shove their way out. The males' pollen storm coats the styles of the females, triggering the cottonfall to come. The leaves grow heavy with high summer, the green dulls, photosynthesis finishes its job, and chlorophyll withdraws. The leaves of autumn go bright yellow, warm dirt brown, or the color of old gold, and fall away. Underfoot, they give off an aroma of cured tobacco sweetened by the slightest tincture of balsam. Then the tree stands bared, silvery, shadowed by its own deep furrows. Almost luminous, it blends into the winter sky, and only against snow at a distance or the moonlit night does it look dark. In the gaunt days before spring, the cottonwood makes a gray frame for the black and white magpies who have nowhere else to light, or a perch for the survey of rough-legged hawks, immigrants who will disappear before the buds swell with balsam and tender green leaves once more.

Cottonwood seasons, scents, and spectacles have inspired writers from Willa Cather to Wallace Stegner to Bruce Springsteen ("I love to see / the cottonwood blossom in the early spring"). Once, in a writing class, I tossed a handful of autumn cottonwood leaves onto my students' desks and asked them to write what the leaves evoked. Dodie spoke of the leather hearts of leaves, their golden hearts in fall. Claire caught the scents: a hint of balsam still on the dry fall smell, combining in a sweet scent of fresh bread. John thought of a leaf's decomposition—"helping its mother to grow." To Lee, the leaves, dark above, silvery below, were like the clouds with silver linings. But Claire thought them "like dry hands . . . the kind they'd use in a Vaseline Intensive Care commercial." Jennifer saw through the leaves to the trunk, with its "multitudinous hues of earth that colored your sinews . . . I held you," she wrote, "smelled you, and smiled at you. I remembered you as I had known you before. Strength, love, freedom, knowledge, survival, and joy, all thoughts and emotions brought to me by the momentary touch of your dried crackled yellow leaf."

Cottonwoods and willows are the natural lineaments of the prairie waterways. Often the mere presence of one or two great poplars gives away the location of a buried lateral ditch or a long-forgotten homestead. Their winding ranks let your eyes chart the track of the canal far into the distance. They changed the complexion of the land, these trees, providing sinuous avenues of cool green shade. Endless windbreaks have been erected of cottonwoods and their tall, slender relatives, Lombardy poplars. Groves of cottonwoods on the lone prairie almost always secrete a farmhouse, or its remnants. And to these groves, the abandoned ones, generations of farm-town youths have gone in their own season to mingle catkins.

Indeed, everyone who travels the High Line Canal admires it largely for those prominent plants along its banks. Everyone, that is, except the ditchriders, who travel the canal more than anyone and who love it more too, in their own way. Not that the ditchriders don't admire a beautiful tree or take their lunches in islands of cottonwood shade. But on the whole, the old trees mean trouble to the watermen. A certain number is tolerable, but from their perspective many of the cottonwoods should be removed, even though the work falls to the ditchriders.

The beauties of the big trees are easy to appreciate. Their faults are less obvious, unless you have to deal with them. To the hydrologist, cottonwoods and willows are phreatophytes—water thieves. Denver Water Board personnel once estimated that the trees growing along half of the canal consume three million gallons per day. Some believe the mature cottonwoods can take over a thousand gallons each per day or, collectively, more than one third of the canal's overall flow. All can agree that these figures, if accurate, represent a substantial drain on water rights. But they might disagree on whose rights come first. The trees' basic offense, according to the water managers, is their wrongful taking of an allocated commodity. Commercial fishermen tend to regard salmon-catching seals in the same light. Seals and trees can thus become scapegoats when there isn't enough of a high-demand resource to go around.

Anyway, the figures have holes. The trees survive just fine for the hundred to three hundred days or so per year when the canal goes dry, presumably drawing their needs from the groundwater; perhaps they do so whether or not the canal is running. The trees transpire a great deal of water, much of which returns to the local microclimate as humidity and dewfall. The water taken up by cottonwoods should not be considered lost, but rather stored and recirculated. In any case, the poplars' draw may be less than the amount ditchriders turn out as overflow at the wasteways, the accumulated runoff that has to be tapped at the flumes, or the tailwater running out the end during times of heavy flow.

Water theft is not the department's sole grudge against the big trees. Their roots sometimes puncture the canal bed, causing leaks. Branches fall in storms, endangering people and blocking the waterway. Leaves contribute to the debris load, clogging drops and flumes. Neighbors complain about the "messy cotton" broadcast when the big trees send forth their seeds. Dead trees create a liability, and hollows can attract wild bee swarms, subjecting users to the threat of stings and managers to complaints.

But the roots also help to stabilize the banks from erosion. Snags provide necessary habitat for woodpeckers and other cavity-nesting wildlife that give the canal much of its interest and ecological value, just as the living crown of the tree furnishes nest sites for others: a canal without flickers, magpies, and kestrels is unthinkable. Hollows harbor squirrels, raccoons, and small boys. And many people take pleasure in the scent of balsam in spring, the cotton, the crisp and fragrant dead leaves in autumn, and the bee trees.

Controversy broke out in the seventies when cottonwood lovers began to resist the strip-cutting of trees. Each time I came home to Aurora, more and more splendid cottonwoods were missing from sections I knew well, leaving bleak, bare banks. The loss of these hoary monuments seemed to go along with the development of nearby fields, and each exaggerated the other. As the plains cottonwoods went, so went the plains.

Unofficial vandals reinforced the city crews, heightening losses. In 1971, one Jack Bisgard hired three men to cut nearly thirty tall cottonwoods from the canal banks near Cherry Creek. His motive: he wanted a clear view of the night lights of Denver. Bisgard and his hit men were convicted and aptly punished. The community service portion of the felons' sentence included extensive tree planting. Fortunately, such crimes have been rare. The cottonwoods' champions have greatly outnumbered their enemies.

Stella Marker lives beside the canal. I first knew her as mother of Eddie, a fellow butterfly enthusiast of my boyhood days. Stella used and enjoyed the canal as much as any latter-day settler, and she took a proprietary view of the cottonwoods and willows. When she noticed them going, there was sure to be hell to pay. A vibrant brunette, Stella greeted you with a warm and genuine smile. But she could fix you, too, in a formidable frown when the situation called for it. Once, when I tried to peddle Eddie a bunch of beat-up butterflies for his entire allowance, I got that look.

So did the Denver Water officials who met with Stella and her compatriots, several women dedicated to protecting the High Line cottonwoods. Unmollified, Stella suggested that the best solution might be for the women to "lay our bodies across the trees" and offered to chain herself to one of the jeopardized cottonwoods. She never had to do so. Eventually the Water Board and the several parks departments backed off, left her favorite trees intact, and implemented a process of environmental review prior to cutting cottonwoods all along the canal.

Stella Marker's willingness to stand between the chain saws and the cottonwoods anticipated the Earth First!ers of today. It showed the devotion of those who love the earth enough to place its well-being above personal safety or comfort. When conservationists are committed to protecting the last of the ancient trees of the temperate and tropical rain forests, the fate of a few cottonwoods along a manmade canal might seem trivial. But in the land of little rain and few trees, each green tower seems as important as an acre of old growth elsewhere.

The entire issue of vegetation management along the High Line Canal is under review, thanks to the tree huggers. Fewer big trees are likely to fall in the future, although removal does go on and replanting promises to green some of the barren zones. Yet some of the new policies, while better than the free-form cutting of old, make me wonder. For example, few of the new plantings are native trees and even fewer are cottonwoods. What few cottonwoods are newly planted belong to a sterile cottonless hybrid variety developed to assuage homeowners obsessed with tidiness. This is weirdly parallel to a measure proposed to protect the new trees from abundant beavers: neutering the beavers.

Cottonless *Populus,* barren beavers: the naturalist recoils from these aberrations of modern management, whose practitioners insist that efforts to maintain the benefits of an artificial canal are bound to involve further artifice. Maybe this is the best we can get, when the plants and animals must share the plateau with more than a million people, but we don't have to like it. In any case, the best efforts to keep the canal green will fail without adequate irrigation, as William Smith knew when he first set out the Thunder Tree and its cohorts. Many of the replanting efforts have seen their saplings die for want of water, while the beavers thrive.

This brings to mind the settlers' endeavors to green the streets of early Denver and how farmers had to be petitioned to give up ditchwater to save the city trees in times of greater than usual aridity. Trees just don't grow in the Great American Desert without help until they get their taproots into the groundwater. They alone decide where they can make it on their own. Cottonwoods and willows are good at that, being well adapted for dryland creek banks. Landscape managers should keep these successful natives in mind. Then, perhaps, cottonwoods and willows will come to be regarded not as water thieves but as green gifts—trees for the aridlands, where the elm, the oak, and the maple merely wither.

I have long carried on my summer walks a massive butterfly net respectfully named Marsha after a strong and loyal friend. My brother Bud carved it first as a walking staff from a High Line cottonwood pole, and I appropriated it for a net. But I too use it as a staff at least as much as for netting insects. Marsha's crook, oiled and burnished from years of use, just fits my grasp. In its strength I feel the power of all the cottonwoods.

One recent summer, Marsha in hand, I waded Toll Gate Creek not far east of the Thunder Tree. My legs, scratchy from cheatgrass, welcomed the cool creekwater. Shadows in the gully muted the insistent July sun, but where it fell butterflies flashed—hairstreaks, skippers, coppers, crescents. I rested against a skinny cottonwood to watch hundreds of whites and sulphurs nectaring on pale blue veronicas. Overhanging the stream, this scraggly little tree gave shade to the wader and resistance to the current. A flood-ripped colonist from somewhere upstream, judging from its rough root wad clinging to the sheer bank, this tree would likely surrender something of itself to the next high water. Over my head a dead, swooping sickle twig enclosed a spiderweb upholstered with seeds, like cotton batting in a silken quilt.

A very different cottonwood grows beside the canal many miles upstream, where it crosses South Broadway. I knew this loop of the ditch when it bore only the remains of an old homestead and a profusion of wildflowers. When I returned recently, the meadows were entirely infilled with apartments, but this big old tree still stood. Its roots formed steps down into the dry canal bed. By walking there, I could ignore the changes above the brilliant red fringe of poison ivy and cherry leaves. The massive bank tree stood seventy-five feet or higher, its trunk was as broad at chest height as I am tall, and its root mass spread thirty feet along the shoreline. Looking out from the eye of an old fallen branch, it reached up with four trunks from its ten-foot crotch. The bark furrowed into plates and channels of tan, beige, and brown, like some Middle Eastern landscape that once knew water. Many thousands of leaves shimmered green and gold, spinning in the breeze like those of the related quaking aspens up in the Front Range.

Box elders line the uppermost reaches of the High Line Canal where it emerges from the Rockies. If you start there and walk down to Plum Creek in high summer, you will find the canal banks hung with ripe fruits: the sweet, small, wild sand plums of orange and purple that give the stream its name, apples escaped from old orchards, grapes, haws, hips, and hops. You will see the wild clematis (or old man's beard or maiden's bower), its starry flowers growing woolly, twining over all still things, including the tall stalks of wild asparagus. Then, passing under cottonwoods, you might come upon the barkless remains of a tree that someone felled, bucked, and left long ago. The clematis trails over each log, turning the sun-bleached wood a whiter shade of pale, glinting like snow in the hot afternoon beams.

Each of these trees, and many another, has given me its particular gifts. But of all the master poplars, only one offered life itself. For though tree holes are common in cottonwoods, they tend to be of a size suitable for squirrels or kestrels, raccoons at most. Hollowing trees usually fall to the current or the cutters before their holes get big enough for kids. The Thunder Tree made a spectacular exception, and Tom and I were its beneficiaries.

In the spring of 1979, a quarter century after the lethal hailstorm, I visited my father in Aurora, arriving at night. The next morning, as he drove me around Del Mar Circle on an errand, I looked across the park to take in the familiar comforting form of the beloved cottonwood. But it wasn't there. Instead of the great green globe of its canopy, I saw a hole in the horizon with Mount Evans showing through. Lesser cottonwoods around the site still stood, but the Thunder Tree was definitely gone.

I was incredulous, then inconsolable. It was the first time my father had seen me cry for years. He held my shaking shoulders.

Back home, I wrote the Aurora Parks Department inquiring of its decision to remove "the historic hollow cottonwood." Bruce Waldo, Parks director, wrote back:

Sometime in the early spring of 1979 the city was hit with a severe windstorm accompanied by heavy snow. Due to the wind and the weight of the snow, the large cottonwood literally split down the middle. One half of the tree fell across the High Line Canal [Sand Creek Lateral]. The other half was leaning to the west in a very precarious position. It was the decision of the City Forester that the tree could not be saved and presented significant danger to any person in the area. I concurred with his decision to remove the tree inasmuch as there was no possibility for it to be saved.

Waldo enclosed the work orders that documented in clipped and clinical terms the cutting, brushing, and removal of the Thunder Tree. The foreman's notes revealed that the diameter at twelve feet was forty-nine inches. A three-foot stump was left at first. Sadly, they cut this too, flush to the ground, where the diameter expanded to seventy inches. The remains of the great tree were disposed of without ceremony. The work order reads: "Level 1 cottonwood & haul logs to dump."

Every July a group of naturalists meets in Del Mar Park for a butterfly count along the High Line Canal. They used to gather beside the hollow tree, the designated center of the count circle. Now nothing of that tree is to be seen. But a ring of lesser stems, scions sprung from root sprouts of the Thunder Tree, partly encircles the place where the old tree grew. Here the counters rendezvous to begin their census. First they pause to recall the ancestor tree and to take a snapshot on the spot to which the count's founder owes his life and his love of butterflies.

On my desk sits an orange basket, like a small pumpkin. It serves as a sort of reliquary for a few special things. Opening it, I find a couple of leaves from the Thunder Tree and a fragment of its heartwood recovered during that sad visit. The tan wood shows the circular marks of the chipping saw running in one direction, the wavy flow of the grain in another. The leaves are the color of October earth. Remarkably, they still give off the sweet balsam smell.

Once, while researching the history of the High Line Canal, I pressed a large leaf from the Thunder Tree between sheets of a photocopied document. Shuffling through these materials many years later, I was surprised by the ghost of the leaf. There on the page referring to President Grant's support for the canal, and for several pages following, appears the clear gray shadow of a cottonwood leaf. Apparently the chemicals released by its tissues excited the photoreactive copier bond, leaving the image as sharply inscribed in the text as the words themselves.

When I finger these relics or inspect the pages with the leaf's stigmata, something of the life of this one cottonwood comes back to me, and through it the lives of all the trees that ever grew tall beside some prairie ditch. I place the chip and the leaves back in the basket and add one more relic: a twig, broken at a node, showing a perfect five-pointed star.

Last summer I took Bud back to the site of the hollow tree to show him the cottonwood stars. We searched together, and he found some good ones. Then we gazed up at the gape in the skyline where that gaping tree once stood. I thought of the hundreds of descendants it must have left all the way to Nebraska from branches carried downstream, the thousands from its copious cotton seeds. And I thought of all the stars released into the winter night when the wind spirit finally brought the Thunder Tree to earth.

Travels in the Aftermath

Out, away to the world with hope . . .

—William Kittredge, *Hole in the Sky*

We walk the curved line of Toll Gate Creek on a hot July morning, counting butterflies. Bulldozers grind down the plateau behind us as we salvage the last sightings to be made here before the condos come. Russet skipperlings and golden skippers adorn the pale pink bells of snowberry clumps in mortal thickets beside the stream.

Jan nets a question mark, a rich fox-red anglewing butterfly of mostly eastern occurrence, a rarity here. We reconnoiter on the gully rim to examine the prize before releasing it, speaking above the background din of the 'dozers. Just then a rusty smear writes itself on our periphery. Is it another *Polygonia interrogationis*?

But no, it is an actual fox running it knows not where. We watch, entranced, then appalled, as the fox dashes from place to place, pursued everywhere by the roar of construction and the blind light of day, unable to find its customary coverts: they are gone. The butterfly, a wanderer, can fly away to seek another patch of suitable ground. But where will the fox go?

When I walked on the canal twenty years earlier with Tom and Jack, we sometimes found what we took for fox prints. Hoofmarks of deer showed up in the hard mud of the ditchbed in winter, and once we were certain we'd found a bear's track. Animals surely moved up and down the corridor of the canal from mountains to plains and back, pausing to feed and rest in thick spinneys of wild plum and young cottonwood groves. The land at that time went on and on, and the canal was how you got there. We knew there were foxes, all right, but I never saw one until that day when the bulldozers flushed the fox before our eyes.

*ATTENTION: to anyone who rejoices in a walk along a wooded trail;
who appreciates the natural aspect of the land and its inhabitants; who
realizes the value of an outdoor laboratory and classroom with a bit of the
ecological picture intact, for education and research; and most especially,
to anyone who would wish to preserve such a place—WITHIN THE
CITY LIMITS OF AURORA.*

So began a letter I sent to the newspapers and everyone else I could
think of in 1967. I'd moved away for college, and each return visit made me
weep. I wanted to try to galvanize some action on behalf of the vanishing
canal landscape. With the support of city manager Robert O. Wright and
mayor Norma Walker, I petitioned the Aurora Parks Department and the
Denver Water Board to open a public trail along the closed service road, for
a start. When back home I went before the city councilors, who patronized
me as a hometown boy with an admirable, if quaint, request.

Almost no one responded to my dittoed letter, but I was not the only
one haranguing the powers-that-were for canal conservation. In time—
some would say just in time—our voices had an impact. About sixty
miles of the canal right-of-way were dedicated as public pathway and part
of the National Trail System. It was what I'd wanted but it seemed too
little, too late, as the prime habitats along the trail dropped out in favor of
condominiums and shopping sprawl.

The birdwatchers of Aurora were keenly aware of the retreat of natural
diversity. My high school Ecology Club advisers, Ed Butterfield and Keith
Anderson, confirmed my impression that the best spots were going fast.
Ed had worked for the only formal nature reserve in those parts, the Plains
Conservation Center out near Buckley Field. Its owners watched helplessly
as the educational reservation became more and more hemmed in, an island
losing its species right and left. Bird bander Mildred Snyder had observed
nearly a hundred and fifty species of birds at her home near the Thunder
Tree, beginning in 1960. As the birds dwindled, she said it was hard to
realize she had once been on the edge of "new territory."

Denver Audubon Society members, especially ornithologist Lois
Webster, agitated for the protection of remnant semi-wildlands in the

heart of Aurora. The best of these survived within a broad wreath of ditch that crossed Toll Gate upstream from the fox's run and in another of our butterfly-counting areas, where the canal and Sand Creek run parallel and cross, farther out where the town was just arriving. We butterfly-and-bird people hoped against reason that these bits might be spared. But as local extinctions mounted, we awaited the 'dozing of our little Edens one by one, along with the expulsion of their occupants.

Given the attitude of growth for its own sake that had dominated Aurora and other canalside suburbs through the past decades, one could be forgiven a fatalistic attitude. Each time I sent another letter and more maps urging protection of certain special habitat nodes, as I did from time to time, it was with little hope of success. Bit by bit, my optimism eroded like prairie soil running away from the scraped banks of the ditch.

So we were pleasantly surprised on a certain butterfly count to find the Toll Gate fields intact. The following March, my sister Susan and I picked our way through the past year's cheatgrass to see the old round barn while it was still standing. Chilly sun shone on Toll Gate Creek, where mallards dabbled and a kingfisher shot its blue rattling dart. Purple crossflowers bloomed in the battered soil, their mauve petals reflected in the breasts of rock doves sunning on the roof of the barn. They boomed off as we approached, and a prairie dog reported nearby.

Inside the round barn, debris lay all about and the walls were glyphed with graffiti. We crawled up a slanted board to reach the high loft. Overhead, sixteen rafters spoked from the crown, three thinner radii between each two rafters, the whole radiating in a dramatic sunburst. An elegant spiral of slats supported the porous skin of green shingles that let in the sun. Back outside, we saw the rock doves return to the ball-capped cone of the roof.

When we approached the spruced-up ranch house to inquire after the fate of the barn, we found rangers instead of ranchers. Ranger Pete Taylor and manager Ellen Rice explained that the entire tract—fields, stream, and barn—had been acquired by the city of Aurora as a natural and historical preserve known as the DeLaney Farm. John and Bridget DeLaney had emigrated from Tipperary in the 1860s, eventually raising cattle and crops along the High Line Canal. The creek gave them a backup source of water, and the tollgate they operated gave the creek its name. It was a descendant of theirs who had plucked Tom and me from the aftermath of the great hailstorm. Now their farm had been rescued from the maw of development at the eleventh hour.

The gracious farmhouse built nearby by Bridget's parents, Thomas and Temperance Gulley, had been moved onto the site and restored. As for the round barn, it was soon listed on the National Register of Historic Places and its restoration begun. Ellen told me there was to be a nature center installed in the ranch house; my offer to provide a representative collection of High Line Canal butterflies, in remembrance of my mother, was warmly accepted. (Though this latter plan has not yet come to pass, the enthusiasm and clear intention to conserve things that shouldn't be lost were real.) How had all this come about?

City councilwoman Peggy Kearns was among those who foresaw the need for open space and pursued it aggressively. Assistant parks director (later, senior environmental planner) Linda Strand took measures to set aside the first four open space preserves and to create new wetland habitat on damaged farmland through mitigation. Aurora parks director Bruce Waldo supported her efforts. "It's unusual," he said, "for a city to have this decision to make . . . Many cities have developed without regard to maintaining open space near their core."

The Aurora attitude had apparently softened. And so it should have. Waldo was right: cities everywhere were scrambling for open space. Even Seattle and Portland, famous for their urban forests, were working hard to plug the green leaks in their violated Olmsted plans. Overgrown and growing still, Aurora was smart to save something of its prairie creekside setting. An Open Space Master Plan, ratifying these setasides, was later approved by the city council.

According to island biogeography theory, artificial islands of remnant habitat, like the Plains Conservation Center, are bound to lose diversity through progressive extinctions. One of the best ways to get around this is to create an archipelago of nature reserves—safe havens linked by corridors of hospitable habitat to permit species movement among them—such as these open space reservations strung along the High Line Canal. That two of the reserves corresponded with our highest-priority nominations, as indicated by the butterflies and the birds, was gratifying but not surprising. My letters doubtless had long been filed away and forgotten when Ms. Kearns and Ms. Strand went to work on open space. But the good places have a way of suggesting themselves to observant people; there are just not that many of them left.

Not that the success of these good intentions is yet assured. Funding needs to be maintained. Growth goes on, and the momentum of the open space effort will have to keep pace or the extinction of experience will continue inexorably. Once set aside, the land still requires stewardship to maintain its character. There is no magic in a master plan that guarantees survival of the features for which a place was singled out. For example, some dirt-bike and off-road-vehicle riders love nothing more than an open space tract to trash with knobby tires. Such abuse may meet a recreation need but is death on habitats, and must be resisted in sensitive sites.

So must the urge to manicure the canal banks be opposed. In too many places, the canal path is mown all the way from the verge to the ditchbank and over, ruining otherwise productive habitat for native wildflowers, pollinators, birds, small mammals, and other beneficial life forms. The Sand Creek Lateral by the site of the Thunder Tree brimmed with silvery blues and purplish coppers, milkweed and monarchs, when it was left alone. Now routinely mowed all the way across, it is but a barren groove of ragged lawn. Such overzealous cutting is both counterproductive and unnecessary. Even worse, one sees herbicides sprayed on what should be rich, teeming verges, or "tangled banks," in Charles Darwin's inspired term. No, it isn't enough just to designate open space, when a lamentable tendency toward obsessive tidiness can destroy the diversity of a park or preserve in no time at all. Overtidied parklands are about as interesting as parking lots.

Nothing will affect the future character of the canal more than the fate of its trees, especially the cottonwoods. I recall one Fourth of July butterfly count when we found our traditional lunchtime rest spot in Norfolk Glen Park bereft of the fine row of prairie poplars that had shaded our usual picnic table. With them went wildlife, as well as the trees' cool shadow on a hot day. Managers cite rot and liability implicit as causes of removal. Yet it is rot that makes the trees so valuable as habitat. On a recent canal walk, one stroller pointed up and said, "Those trees are diseased; they'll have to come down." She was referring to hollows and holes that are the very ensigns of diversity in any arboreal community. Later, she "oohed" over the kestrels and chickadees, making no connection until we gently pointed out where they nested. Open space managers should tag both live trees with cavities and dead snags as "animal inns," as some national forests do, and permit only those presenting a clear and substantial public danger to be removed or pruned.

In 1991 a group of canal lovers formed the High Line Canal Preservation Association to replace lost cottonwoods through replanting and to ensure the future of the ditch. They helped Volunteers for Outdoor Colorado plant over fifteen hundred trees and shrubs along the canal in spring 1993, and in 1996 installed mile markers along the length of the High Line Canal Trail. But instead of indigenous cottonwoods, the well-intentioned workers planted a mix of American and exotic trees chosen to make life simpler for ditch managers, while blending into suburban neighborhoods. Green is green, but the native birds and other wildlife know the difference, and so do people who love the canal for its long and winding rows of massive poplars. Lacking taproots, many of these out-of-context ornamentals died for lack of water in subsequent seasons. The fact is, *Populus sargentii* is the keystone species of the ecosystem everyone wants to conserve here. If the High Line is to maintain its character, culturally and biologically, plains cottonwoods simply must remain a large part of the picture.

But the ongoing battle between those who would cut cottonwoods and those who would save them seems to have shifted in favor of these grand stems, too many of which have already been lost. On my latest visit, I learned that high-hazard trees are now identified on a tree-by-tree basis with specified standards, and that cottonwoods will no longer be felled without strict environmental review and cause. And in the *High Line Canal Future Management Plan,* much of the emphasis is on how to get enough water to the cottonwoods to ensure their survival.

For in the end, it all comes down to water, a matter that has marked all these pages. The value of the High Line Canal Trail and all its associated habitats depends entirely on the flow of Platte River water through the ditch. A resource originally designed and still operated chiefly for the conveyance of water, the canal has become something more besides. It cannot be helped: the greater worth of the ditch today is for recreation and the connection with nature it affords the people of the towns. What if this green umbilicus, this lifeline, loses its water? The High Line today represents one of the major recreational resources in the entire Denver metropolitan area. To Crawford Scott, author of the popular guide *Wogging the High Line,* the canal represents "mysterious and exotic destinations." A lot of people would be seriously upset if the canal were allowed to wither.

So what is to become of it? After a lot of idle speculation and rumor, the *High Line Canal Future Management Plan* was commissioned by a consortium of interested agencies and groups called the High Line Canal Partners, funded by Great Outdoors Colorado and published in 2002. As of 2011, it still comprises the joint will of the parties and Denver Water's formal canal policy. Several alternatives were considered, depending on water supply prospects. Full, annual watering of the whole canal was considered infeasible, but the desire was clear to water as much of the ditch as possible, as often as possible. Here's what the plan proposes.

As of 2010, Denver Water, for purposes of water conservation, ceased to use the lower twenty-two miles of the sixty-six-mile canal for water distribution beyond Cherry Creek. The Upper Canal is still considered a water conveyance foremost, with recreation and habitat to be honored within that framework. The Lower Canal, from Cherry Creek to Sand Creek, will be devoted to recreation, natural resources, and existing public access to the canal, with ownership turned over to the underlying jurisdictions. A strong effort will be made to furnish sufficient water to maintain vegetation as far as the Arsenal Lateral, using sources that may include direct flow, groundwater, reuse water, irrigation return, or stormwater, all of which involve complex water rights issues. (The former Arsenal has contracted with Denver Water to use recycled water instead of original High Line Canal water for irrigation, so its lateral will have to fend for itself. Now that Rocky Mountain Arsenal has become a great national wildlife reserve, we can only hope that the lateral to Derby Lake will remain a rich riparian corridor instead of a desiccated relic.)

In the previous editions of this book, when the future of the canal was less clear and the prospect loomed of dewatering it altogether, I offered a radical proposal. "Now that the water courts have ruled in favor of in-stream flow as an option to diversion for beneficial use," I wrote, "how about a consortium of wildlife and recreation agencies acquiring the rights in order to maintain in-canal flow? Perhaps the rights could be transferred to the High Line Canal Preservation Association—or to the ditch itself? Supreme Court Justice William O. Douglas proposed a Wilderness Bill of Rights and legal standing for trees; Roderick Nash wrote of the 'rights of rocks.' How about water rights for a watercourse—are we ready for that?"

Something of the sort may be coming to pass. Without transferring any water rights, Denver Water has guaranteed minimal flow for the Upper Canal (assuming adequate rainfall and river flow); and has offered, at its cost, to furnish water for twenty-eight days of flow in the Lower Canal (two weeks in the spring, two in the late summer and fall) in order to water the cottonwoods and other trees. Denver Water has actually been sponsoring a study with Colorado State University researchers for several years in order to quantify the trees' needs. What a shift from the days when cottonwoods were demonized as water-thieving phreatophytes! This change of policy shows that the agency fully recognizes the importance of the canal as habitat for humans and others, as well as a source of supply for paying customers.

Not that ill-advised growth hasn't raged on. For example, some residents of Highlands Ranch, a big, upscale subdivision that replaced the actual ranch by that name, requested an exit from the E-470 beltway. The interchange was unnecessary, but would take a few minutes off a few folks' commutes—while displacing many gracious big trees, causing diversion and concrete channeling of the canal, creating noise and danger for trail walkers and riders, and further maiming a beautiful section of the waterway, above McClellan Reservoir. Led by the High Line Crossing cohousing community, many lovers of the canal objected valiantly. But permits were issued and bulldozers rolled. Thanks to developments like these, certain sections of the canal path no longer resemble their descriptions in these pages.

But there have been gains as well. A few years ago I learned about a cattail marsh, ringed by woodland, that lay just outside the bounds of my boyhood haunts. I sought out Jewell Wetlands, got lost in the pollen storm of its cattails, and wrote letters on its behalf. Happily, the Trust for Public Land (TPL) bought the site to protect its marshy charms for local kids and creatures. Since then, the TPL has protected the clear mountain views and wildlife habitat of twenty-acre Highline Farm, abutting the canal in Greenwood Village; with several partners, saved the last four acres of undeveloped land adjacent to the Marjorie Perry Nature Preserve, long beloved of walkers, joggers, equestrians, and birdwatchers; and along Big Dry Creek, helped safeguard three acres of land where a six-unit subdivision was planned, thus connecting the Big Dry Creek and High Line Canal trails at the junction of Littleton and Greenwood Village.

A good start to be sure, yet there's still more. Through the new "Tip-to-Tail" campaign, TPL and collaborators hope to preserve many of the last best bits of habitat and open space along the entire canal, source to mouth. It's like a reprieve after the fact; just when I thought the best was already lost, here come TPL and friends to save special places along the canal that I didn't even know were still extant. Meanwhile, the multi-jurisdictional partnership known as the High Line Working Group hopes to find a broad consensus over the future of land surrounding the canal.

If these intentions work out; if enough of the sweet, wet flow maintains; if the keepers of these precious shards will hear and heed the gentle counsel of the cottonwoods, well, then maybe the old wriggly snake may yet stay green and wild. In spite of all the change, something of value may survive here ... something more than one expected, maybe even something truly significant. For the true significance of the High Line Canal is this: if wild nature can make it here, it can make it anywhere.

Ron Wahl and I walk through the wooded edge of the meadow that occupies an old farm pond. It is July, but the morning is foggy and cold. Where we usually strip to thin cottons by midmorning, this year we wear wool. Surrounded from the world by the cottonwood curtain, we try to kick up some butterflies in the damp, surprising chill. All we see are thousands of cabbage whites, roosting on the undersides of weeds, clinging to tall grasses, or lumbering off before our footfalls in clumsy, chilly flight. There are so many, they remind me of the monarchs on their overwintering grounds in Mexico. The temperature here is similar, too. Weedy, alien butterflies, these European whites proliferate in leftover spots like the old DeLaney Farm, and they don't mind the cold as much as other butterflies do.

We see little else on our count this morning. But as I scan the red seed heads of giant dock, I halfway expect to see a fox of the same hue. I know we could, because the rangers at the old ranch house told me that at least a pair of red foxes occupies this protected land. Pearl crescents and Acadian hairstreaks, two small, bright butterflies long thought to be gone from the canal in Aurora, have turned up here too, though we don't see them this gray morning. They dwell in the willowed bottoms of the Toll Gate floodplain, near where the creek and the canal meet and cross in the heart of the new preserve. But it is the fox I think about now, here among the spatter of white butterflies and red dock.

A fox, I think, with a place to live.

Afterword for the 2011 Edition

Early last spring I returned to Denver to take part in an event for the Trust for Public Lands. Driving away from Denver International Airport, I decided to visit the current terminus of the High Line Canal. The outflow used to be a steep culvert running into Second Creek just south of where the airport, a city in itself whose white tents loom across the plains, now stands. Denver Water recovered the rights from the last farm or two and ceased supplying water beyond Green Valley Ranch, where the canal now debouches into the little Platte River tributary called First Creek. I expected my visit to be elegiac, the actual ranch now buried beneath sheetrock and bluegrass, the canal unceremoniously truncated at the edge of the huge subdivision.

When I entered the new town of Green Valley Ranch, I saw that I might have been too harsh on it in my chapter "Of Grass and Growth," where I grouse about its imposition onto the prairie. I found the houses tidy, the yards kempt, the community maturing and much more ethnically diverse than the one I grew up in on the previous edge of the Great Plains. Beside a pond on the nearby golf course, seven white pelicans preened.

The willows were just leafing out, the ditchbank lined by purple crossflowers. The High Line, narrower now than the path beside it, disappeared into a concrete sluice sliced on the bias, dove underground, and then reissued into the creek—or would have, had there been any tailwater in it. The creekbed too was dry, redolent of the May blossom of sand plums, quiet but for the lamentation of mourning doves. Across Piccadilly Avenue lay a once-complicated site where the High Line Canal, the Dougherty Ditch, and First Creek all met and crossed in a symphony of sluices and channels beside a venerable slatted farmhouse where old John Petty and his sister, Mrs. Merry, once lived. Hammered by a perfect storm of a flood some years back, the tract was now absolutely flat and simple: every sign of each feature had been eradicated by the flood and a D-9 Caterpillar tractor preparing that section for the next advance of Green Valley Ranch. Except, that is, for one enormous cottonwood that still stood, marking the place where all those watercourses had once met.

And then I met Rolando and Clyde. I was standing in the creekbed, beneath a footbridge, when a kid up on the railing called, "Mister, would you like to buy a chocolate bar?" I told him no thanks, but I'd love to hear what they thought about this place. They'd been playing all over the bridge, poking all through the sand plums and blue willows, same as Tom and I used to do. "We love to come down here," said Rolando.

Clyde, from Mississippi, which he missed, said he loved it too. "There aren't any gangs here," he said, unlike places they've lived before.

"No matter how angry I get," said Rolando, "I calm down when I get out here."

The boys called me "sir" or "Mr. Bob," and when I told them I'd studied butterflies around there for a long time, and some had disappeared, Rolando asked, "What's your hypothesis?" They shared all sorts of wildlife encounters of their own: coyotes, foxes (including an albino), a robin's nest with blue eggs. We compared notes on magpies, which (just like me) they'd considered shooting, but couldn't do it in the end. They had many adventures to share, and I swapped the amazing tale of the Thunder Tree, which they loved—they had their own favorite cottonwoods. What pleased me most was that they had the freedom to wander, just as we'd enjoyed (so rare today!), and that they cared to do so. The dwindled canal, the creek, the bridge—the whole place—meant everything to them, just as the bigger ditch upstream had to me. They hadn't an earbud or an electronic device between them, and they didn't care. They were just so happy to be out there! So was I. Elegiac, my foot: it still goes on.

From the beginning, I hoped this book would be a spyhole into the long-left, often-lost special places of its readers. In this I have been richly rewarded. A continuous stream of letters, calls, and personal approaches, modest in absolute number but immodest in passion of expression, has let me know that my ditch indeed speaks of everybody's ditch. A surprising number of the people who approach me after lectures or readings, or who take precious time to write, testify to their acquaintance with the actual ditch of my own dreams, the High Line Canal of Colorado. Many more speak of the subtle but nourishing qualities shared by all hand-me-down lands that they have recognized in these pages, recalling their own long-ago Valhallas and vacant lots.

Thus gratified by readers' responses, I am especially pleased that Oregon State University Press is bringing *The Thunder Tree* into print again. May these cottonwood leaves shimmering in a summer ditch continue to remind us of the worth of the wildness residing at the edges of our homelands, and prick our memories of the particular places that made us who we are. It has been out of print too long, right through the first few years of the revolution in the arena of kids-and-ditches brought about by Richard Louv's essential *Last Child in the Woods: Saving Our Children From Nature-Deficit Disorder.*

A literature of the exurban wild has been slowly and solidly growing, from Richard Mabey's *The Unofficial Countryside* to Scott Russell Sanders's *Paradise of Bombs*, from Janisse Ray's *Ecology of a Cracker Childhood* to Robert Sullivan's portrait of the trashed marshes of New Jersey, just outside Manhattan, *The Meadowlands. Last Child* is the capstone to them all. Each of these testimonies to the love of damaged lands comes down to this: we can't throw the land away, so why not love it, make the best of it, and make it better? More and more, we discover that the deep wilderness of mountains and deserts, though utterly essential, is not enough to provide for a largely urban and overbloated population of humans. We need to keep some of the so-called vacant lots, some big old hollow trees, some brush and scrub. We need the Country in the City, and the balm of the "accidental wild." I am hopeful that this new edition will further foment such radical ideas.

I am also happy that this book has bolstered the efforts of canal conservators and their counterparts in other communities, and that in this new form it will continue to back up the lovers of local wildlands—who are more and more all the time, as people realize what they have lost and what they still stand to save. And that's good, because the extent to which curious children will still be able to find what I found along the canal will depend upon the degree of love, care, and action exercised on its behalf. One group of activists defeated a plan to pave and widen one stretch of the canal path, to turn it from a flowered rural track into just another road. The citizen clientele for the High Line, and places like it, grows stronger each year as more people walk, ride, bicycle, and otherwise get out on them.

At my thirtieth high school reunion, in 1995, organizers and old pals Terry Truman and Greg Bradshaw asked me to lead a nature hike along the canal. My initial response was "Oh, sure!" I figured about as many people would come as used to accompany my canal rambles those many years ago: like, none (unless my old butterfly compatriot Jack Jeffers rejoined me). But in the end, more than fifty of the attendees walked with me, including Jack all right, and the mothers of two former classmates. I was amazed.

The times truly have brought an increased appreciation both of the secondhand lands and of the place they should hold in our denser and denser communities. As we sauntered, I heard from my fellow alums (as from other old friends, at other times and places) about their own relationship with the canal and their personal ditchwater adventures, completely unknown to me before. Again and again, I learn how people who care about the world outside remember particular places that made a difference in their apprehension of the earth. And again and again, that place turns out to be modest, like some scruffy Denver ditch, rather than anywhere grand.

I wrapped up that recent trip to Denver with another walk along the High Line trail. This time, far from the working-class gumbo of Green Valley Ranch, I strode a section through its polar opposite: Cherry Hills Village, the early-days retreat of the affluent from the noise and heat of the city, still a gracious, dispersed settlement on high ground south of town, with grand views of the Front Range and one of the comeliest sections of the watercourse winding through it. Large houses sprawl above the banks, both older ones of stone, slate, and tasteful proportion, and vast and vulgar new grandiosities thrown up by people with too much money and an edifice complex. In between stretch great expanses of open space crossed by streams and dotted by ponds, some of it recently set aside, much of the rest belonging to the sprawling campus of the Kent School.

I'd never seen Denver prettier. It had been a wet spring, the air was clear and bright and cool in the sun, and every verge and vale seemed pink or white with the blossoms of crabs and apples. House finch song almost drowned out the beeps of nuthatches, the soft conversation of bush tits, the quiet whistles, burbles, and warbles of an eastern blue jay (a new resident since my day). A flicker worked inside a cottonwood trunk, a downy woodpecker on the outside. The air was fragrant, and many bicyclists, runners, horseback riders, and a few amblers like me were out to enjoy it all. Raccoon tracks impressed the mud in the bed, and cottontails dashed across the path.

One of the great things about the High Line is that it is ultimately democratic. Just as the jays and swallowtails are free to work their way up and down the vegetated corridor, so Rolando and Clyde could hop on the bus, make a couple of transfers, and walk this section in Cherry Hills Village if they so wished. Likewise, folks from this neighborhood could point their Volvos out to Green Valley Ranch and stretch their legs on the canal's final run down to First Creek. Running as it does through every socioeconomic stratum of Greater Denver, the High Line allows the people to mix and match and mingle, not only among themselves, but among the magpies, the orioles, the kingfishers, and the prairie dogs. It might even be that this humble canal could conquer fear, providing a patch of common ground among people, through shared love of its green and snaking way.

It is my hope that this revivified book will bring a few more folks to know the preciousness of what remains in the wildling fringes of our towns, to love and enjoy the natural fragments, and to act to keep them present, connected, and lively around us. Only then can we trust that the cool, fresh air will still and always go sweet in spring with the balsam breath of cottonwoods, the feathered brush of the birds, the glide of butterflies.

Acknowledgments

This book belongs to all those who have walked the High Line Canal with me and helped me to see it more clearly, especially my mother, Helen Lee Lemmon, who was my boon companion; and notably Tom Pyle, Howard (Bud) Pyle, Susan and Ted Kafer, Bruce Campbell, JoAnne Heron, Jack Jeffers, Charles Dudley, Robert H. and Robert C. Pyle; my 4JBC companions, Jan, Ray, and Amy Chu, Mary Jane Foley, Ron Wahl, Ray Stanford, Paul Opler, Andy Warren, Josie Quick, Molly Muller, and Carol, Lynelle, and Lauretta Jones; also Don Phillipson, John Halverson, Eddie Marker, Tim Hartman, Marc Epstein, Don Eff, Risa Rosenberg, and Mary Hathaway; Sarah Anne Hughes, who introduced me to English canals and performed valuable research on the High Line's history; and many others, named in the text or not. Susan's, Tom's, and Bud's memories enhanced my own.

I received essential assistance from the following individuals and their institutions: Virginia Steele and Bobbie Pepper, Aurora History Museum; Judy Henning, High Line Canal Preservation Association; Mary Brown and Mary K. Ayers, Aurora Public Library; Eleanor Genres and Lynn Taylor, Denver Public Library's Western History Room; Mercedes Buckingham, the Stephen H. Hart Library of the Colorado Historical Society; Ric Peigler and Kristine Haglund, Denver Museum of Natural History; Longview Public Library; Anne Musché, Naselle Timberland Library; Timberland Regional Library System; Cambridge University Library; Caryl Winn and staff, Manuscripts and Archives, University of Washington libraries; and Christopher Meyer, National Wildlife Federation.

These parks department people helped beyond their public duty: Linda Strand, Bruce Waldo, Ellen Rice, and Pete Taylor, Aurora; Dan Wolford, South Suburban; Neil Sperando, Denver; and Susie Trumbull, Paula Ehresman, and Gary Buffington, Colorado State Parks. In the Denver Water Department I was abundantly assisted by Gil Martinez, John Peterson, Ray Edwards, Rusty Simon, Kerker Bryant, Pete Reinhart, Rusty Christiansen, Manuel Bachicha, Bob Shroeder, Doris Kaplan, Glen Wilson, Ed Ruetz, Bill Miller, Lois Haugen, and especially Bob Rosendale and George Swan.

For sharing their personal histories and knowledge, I thank Norma Walker, Laura Corliss Sabados, Charles Corliss, Evelyn Iritani, Ellen Lanier-Phelps, Randy Sanders, Pete and Cindy Glasier, Don Sampson, Rich Bolenbaker, Mildred Snyder, Cherry Tippie, Ruby Olmsted, Jim Pinnell, Jim Knopf, Margaret Maupin, and Joanne Ditmer and all the other authors quoted in the text. For memories of my past in common with theirs, without their permission or verification of my personal version, I strongly thank Mike Snodgrass, Mike Tatum, Gary "Mike" Beasley, and Jack Jeffers.

Early support of High Line studies and conservation came from Philip Poch, Julius A. Korman, Ed Butterfield, Keith Anderson, Dick Beidleman and the Colorado/Wyoming Academy of Science, Alfred M. Bailey, Robert Niedrach, Walker Van Riper, F. Martin Brown, Raymond Jae, Richard Buchmiller, Bill Sieker, Robert O. Wright, Jim Fisher, Stella Marker, and Lois Webster, who also furnished kind hospitality during my studies in situ as well as inspiration with her total dedication to nature study and conservation. Maude Linstrom Frandsen stimulated an early interest in Colorado and natural history that was reinforced by Grace P. Miller, Helen B. Phelps, and Helen Lee Lemmon; all four encouraged me to write about my passion for place and its occupants.

Pat Campbell got me to Gothic, where I met Charles Remington, with whom (thanks to Spencer Beebe) I went to Pine Butte Swamp, where Al Haas put the witching wand in my hands: of such leaps across the years are essays made. Jim Fitzgerald and Jim Wright showed me the grasslands and cottonwood galleries of the Platte. Carl Crookham gave me the story of the stars in cottonwoods, Joel Fitts and Ronnie Theisz the Lakota Grass Dance.

Deep thanks go to Fayette Krause, Ron Cisar, Pat Miller, my writing group, Jane Elder Wulff, and Mathew Tekulsky for their endless encouragement. To Mike Houck for his long-standing enthusiasm for my theory of "the extinction of experience," and to him, Gary Nabhan, Richard Nelson, and Linny Stovall for penetrating discussion of the idea. To Harry Foster, Kim Stafford, and Tom Heidlebaugh for teaching me the sanctity of story. To Robert Adams, who knows the territory. To Terry Tempest Williams for giving me courage to write Chapters 10 and 11. Edwin Way Teale inspired the entire enterprise.

Important new information for the current edition was kindly provided by Jerry Foster of Denver Water. The Trust for Public Land's Sandra Tassel, Lea Parks, Scott Dissel, Justin Spring, and their colleagues acquainted me with TPL's accomplishments and hopes for canal conservation, as did Judy Henning for the High Line Canal Preservation Association and Debbie Wells for the High Line Working Group.

I am obliged to everyone at Houghton Mifflin who gave the book first life. I cannot imagine an editor of greater patience and empathy, wiser direction and advice, or kinder authorial care and concern than Harry Foster showed over seven years to this book; it owes everything to him. To Lilly Golden and Jennifer McDonald, I am grateful for the Lyons Press edition. My agent Laura Blake Peterson kindly assisted with this edition, also championed by Panayoti Kelaidis, Mike Houck, Gene and Polly Reetz, Steve Kellert, and Richard Louv. For this beautiful new OSU Press incarnation, I owe acres of appreciation to Mary Elizabeth Braun, Tom Booth, Jo Alexander, to David Drummond for his fine cover art, to Laura J. Westlund and Nancy Barbour (the proofreaders), and to Richard Louv for his kind and wonderful foreword.

I remain especially grateful to my stepdaughter, Dory Hellyer, for her inspired suggestion for the name of the book. She, her brother, Tom Hellyer, and their step-cat Bokis Volkilla deserve my loving appreciation for their patience with the writing and my preoccupation with it. Finally and foremost, their mother, Thea Linnaea Pyle, has my profound thanks for her beautiful magpie woodcut, for reading every word of every draft with close and helpful attention to detail, for getting me away from my desk and into the field, and for her perpetual faith in a sometimes-faltering project and its servant.

Sources

Words, facts, and thoughts from dozens of written sources have found their way into these essays. Following are the essential citations, documentation, and some places to look for additional information on the topics brushed in each chapter.

PROLOGUE: EVERYBODY'S DITCH

Don Berry's *Trask* is available in paperback from Oregon State University Press. The Kim Stafford quotation comes from his fine book *Having Everything Right,* published by Confluence Press, 1986 (in paperback from Sasquatch Books). "The Study of the High Line Canal" by Laura Corliss was privately published in Denver (May 6, 1975). Vladimir Nabokov's remarks on time come from his elemental essay on butterflies in the memoir *Speak, Memory: An Autobiography Revisited* (Capricorn Books edition, 1970, Chapter 6; in paperback from Vintage).

I: THE HAILSTORM

The epigraph arose in Lyall Watson's book *Heaven's Breath: A Natural History of the Wind* (William Morrow, 1984). The history of Hoffman Heights is nicely told in the booklet *Historic Aurora House Tour: Hoffman Heights, September 15, 1984,* by Elizabeth Johnson, published by the Aurora Historical Society. The hailstorm was recorded in the *Denver Post,* July 28, 1954, and the *Aurora Advocate,* July 29, 1954. An excellent discussion of hail and hail-caused fatalities among humans and livestock may be found in *It's Raining Frogs and Fishes: Four Seasons of Natural Phenomena and Oddities of the Sky* by Jerry Dennis (HarperCollins, 1992; paperback from HarperPerennial).

2: THE WATERCOURSE

The Wind in the Willows by Kenneth Grahame was published by Scribner in 1908 and in many editions since. David Wagoner's phrase is the title of his novel, *The Road to Many a Wonder* (Farrar, Straus and Giroux, 1974, available in paperback from Avon). Harvey Manning's great *Walking the Beach to Bellingham* was published by Madrona Publishers (Seattle) in 1986 (paperback, Oregon State University Press). I refer to the novel *Milagro Beanfield War* by John Nichols (Holt, Rinehart and Winston, 1974; available in paperback from Owl Books). Joanne Ditmer's article "What Makes a City Park?" appeared in the *Denver Post,* February 15, 1973. Her column "Raising the Roof" often focused on the High Line over the years.

3: THE RIVERS OF APRIL

The epigraph was spoken in D. H. Lawrence's *The Rainbow,* available from Viking Penguin. The title comes from an untitled verse written by Thomas Hornsby Ferril and inscribed beneath a series of water murals in the rotunda of the Colorado State Capitol Building. Ferril was a good friend of Walker Van Riper, referred to in Chapter 10, and with him a member of the exclusive Cactus Club. His lines are placed in the context of the modern water debate in the article "Amendment Would Alter State Water Law" by Senator Bob Pastore and Richard G. Hamilton, in the *Pueblo Chieftain,* February 25, 1992. For a primer on water law, see Christopher Meyer's undated *Western Water Allocation: New Players in an Old Game* (National Wildlife Federation, Boulder). Early water-shifting history is discussed in *Northern Colorado Water Conservancy District* by J. R. Barkley, published by the district in Greeley, 1981.

Throughout this chapter appear quotations and facts from Marc Reisner's monumental *Cadillac Desert: The American West and Its Disappearing Water* (Viking, 1986; revised paperback available from Penguin). John Wesley Powell's experience and views are found in his *Report on the Lands of the Arid Regions* (U.S. Geographical and Geological Survey, 1878) and superbly elaborated and interpreted in Wallace Stegner's biography, *Beyond the Hundredth Meridian: John Wesley Powell and the Second Opening of the West* (Houghton Mifflin, 1953; paperback, Penguin). I also quote Willa Cather's *Death Comes for the Archbishop* (Knopf, 1927; paperback, Vintage) and Loren Eiseley's essay "The Flow of the River" from *The Immense Journey* (Random House, 1957; paperback, Vintage).

Stu Stuller's article "The Last Big Dam" appeared in an issue of *Wilderness* devoted to "Water and the Dimensions of Crisis" (Fall 1987, volume 51, no. 178). For other major discussions on the topic see the March/April 1990 issue of *The Nature Conservancy Magazine* and several titles from Island Press, including *Water in the West, Overtapped Oasis,* and *Western Water Made Simple.* The latter incorporates a series of articles from *High Country News,* whose February 25, 1991, issue discusses Aurora's water picture in "Colorado Enters a New Water Era" by Steve Hinchman and "Gunnison Fights Off the Front Range" by Gary Sprung, as does "A Year of Victories on the Waterfront" in the April 1992 *High Country Report,* the annual newsletter of the High Country Citizens' Alliance (Crested Butte, Colorado). Zorba's words are from Nikos Kazantzakis's *Zorba the Greek* (Simon and Schuster, 1952; available in paperback from Touchstone). I quote Mark Obmascik and Patrick O'Driscoll from a *Denver Post* series, "Colorado Water: The New Harvest," published July 19-22, 1992. Norma Walker was profiled by Angela Harris and Dick Friedrich in "A Mayor? In Ocean Park?" (*Chinook Observer,* Long Beach, Washington, February 15, 1989).

4: LILACS AND CROSSFLOWERS

Herbert Gold's "The American as Hipster" appeared in *Ten Masters of the American Essay* (Harcourt, 1966). Information on Baron Walter von Richthofen comes largely from Thomas J. Noel's very helpful *Richthofen's Montclair: A Pioneer Denver Suburb* (Pruett Publishing, Boulder, 1976). Details about William and Margaret Smith originated largely with the Aurora History Center, particularly the *Aurora Historic Preservation Inventory,* and *Aurora from the Beginning* by Dave Hicks, A-T-P Publications (Denver), 1977. *Roxborough: History Etched in Stone,* written by Paula S. Ehresman for Colorado State Parks in 1984, describes Roxborough Park and my family's connection with it. The history of the High Line Canal, including U. S. Grant's involvement, the English Company, and Henry Doherty, is illuminated in *History of the Denver Water System* by E. L. Mosley, privately published in 1966. The author, an engineer, protested that his opus was assembled "without undue regard for literary excellence," but I found it both readable and endlessly fascinating. Numerous other documents in the archives of the Denver Water Department and Colorado Historical Society expand on this history, including the department's *Water News* and its brochure "High Line Canal: Winding Through History" (1985). Also see "Henry L. Doherty: A Utilities Radical," by Gail Pitts (*Denver Post,* November 25, 1981); Jerome C. Smiley, *History of Denver,* as excerpted in the *Denver Times,* May 15, 1870; and *Denver in Slices* (Sage Books, Denver, 1959; paperback available from Swallow Press) by Louise Ward Arps. Lord James Barclay's article "Colorado" appeared in *Fortnightly Review* (January 1880, volume 157 [New Series]), excerpted in Robert G. Athearn's *Westward the Briton,* Scribner, 1953 (paperback available from Kessinger Publishing). Judge Stone's remarks were taken from Alice Polk Hill's *Colorado Pioneers in Picture and Story* (Brock-Haffner Press, Denver, 1915).

5: MAGPIE DAYS

The epigraph and other information on corvids originate with Tony Angell's *Ravens, Crows, Magpies and Jays,* University of Washington Press, 1978. Additional magpie notes came from John James Audubon, *Birds of America* (originally published between 1827 and 1830, published in many editions since); Roger Tory Peterson, *Field Guide to the Birds* (Houghton Mifflin, 1980 edition); Edward Armstrong, *Bird Display and Behavior: An Introduction to the Study of Bird Psychology* (1947, reprinted by Dover in 1965); Percy A. Taverner, *Birds of Canada* (Musson Book Co., Toronto, 1949); S. G. Jewett, Sr., et al., *Birds of Washington State*; and Jean Myron Linsdale, who submitted the magpie write-up in Arthur Cleveland Bent's *Jays, Crows, and Titmice,* volume 15 of *Life Histories of American Birds* (1946, reprinted by Dover in 1964).

6: MILE ROADS

For the source of John Haines's epigraph, see Chapter 11. Alfred Watkins's book *The Old Straight Track: Its Mounds, Beacons, Moats, Sites, and Mark Stones* appeared in 1925 and was reprinted by Abacus (London) in 1974. J. H. B. Peel's *Along the Green Roads of Britain* was brought out by Cassell (London) in 1976. The Kennet and Avon Canal is described in *Along the Canal: The Kennet and Avon from Bath to Bradford-on-Avon* by Valerie Bower (Ashgrove Press, Bath, England, 1985).

7: SNODGRASS, TATUM, AND BEASLEY

John Updike's *Of the Farm* was published in 1965 by Knopf; paperback available from Ballantine Books. I quoted Betty McDonald's *The Egg and I,* first published by Lippincott in 1945, currently available in a Perennial Library (Harper and Row) paperback. Historical notes on ditchrider dynasties were drawn from interviews with them and from Carl V. and Leona M. McFadden's *Early Aurora* (Aurora Technical Center, 1978).

8: OF GRASS AND GROWTH

The epigraph comes from Bruce Springsteen's song "Fourth of July, Asbury Park (Sandy)" on his album *The Wild, the Innocent, and the E Street Shuffle,* © 1973 Columbia Records. The Grass Song of the Lakota Sioux is on an album by Henry Crow Dog, *Crow Dog's Paradise: Songs of the Sioux,* Elektra Records, 1971. Books referred to are Charles Darwin's *The Origin of Species* (first published in 1859, finally revised in 1871) and Alexander B. Klots's *Peterson Field Guide to the Butterflies East of the Great Plains* (Houghton Mifflin, 1951). I have mined historical facts and opinions from *Aurora: Gateway to the Rockies* (Cordillera Press, 1985) by Steven F. Mehls, Carol J. Drake, and James E. Fell, Jr. Newspaper articles quoted were "Aurora's Malls, Condos Called Future-City Model," by Gary Delsohn, *Denver Post,* October 11, 1987, and a series of articles by Ron Dawson and others on growth issues in the September 30, 1987, *Aurora Sentinel.* Wallace Stegner's remark was voiced in the article "Land of Hope, Land of Ruin," which appeared in the *New York Times,* March 19, 1992. Alvin Steinel's epic *History of Agriculture in Colorado* came out in Denver in 1916. The Wendell Berry quote, typical of his writings on the subject of growth and scale, comes specifically from his article "Getting Along with Nature," from the June 1983 *Country Journal.* The Two Forks Dam issue was discussed in depth by Alex Shoumatoff in "A Reporter at Large: The Skipper and the Dam" (*The New Yorker,* December 1, 1986).

9: THE EXTINCTION OF EXPERIENCE

See Charles Darwin in the previous chapter for epigraph source. I refer to Dr. Klots's *Peterson Field Guide* (see Chapter 8) and to *Colorado Butterflies* by F. Martin Brown, Donald Eff, and Bernard Rotger, Denver Museum of Natural History, 1957. The listing of the migratory monarch as a threatened phenomenon is to be found in *The IUCN Invertebrate Red Data Book* (S. M. Wells, R. M. Pyle, and N. M. Collins, IUCN, Cambridge, England, 1983). H. H. Behr's letter about German chickens and Xerces blues resides in the archives of the Chicago Field Museum of Natural History. E. O. Wilson's Pulitzer prizes were awarded for *On Human Nature* (1979) and *The Ants* (1990, with Bert Holldöbler), and his thoughts on biophilia appear in a book by that name published by Harvard University Press in 1984. Valerie Martin's short story "The Consolation of Nature" was the title story in a collection published by Houghton Mifflin in 1988. *The Unofficial Countryside* by Richard Mabey came out from Collins in 1973; paperback available from Little Toller Books. For more about the urban habitat program in Portland, Oregon, see "Wildlife in the City" (Michael Jackson Reed, *Sunday Oregonian,* April 10, 1988) and proceedings of the various Country in the City Conferences (Department of Geography, Portland State University, edited by Michael C. Houck and Joseph Poracsky).

The fossil butterflies I mention are detailed in *Florissant Butterflies: A Guide to the Fossil and Present-day Species of Central Colorado* by Thomas C. Emmel, Marc C. Minno, and Boyce A. Drummond (Stanford University Press, 1992). Urban butterfly extinction rates come from "Urbanization and Endangered Insects" by Robert M. Pyle, in *Urban Entomology: Interdisciplinary Perspectives* (Praeger Publishers, 1984). Aldo Leopold's stunning sentence is from his manifesto, *A Sand County Almanac,* first published in 1946 by Oxford University Press with many editions since; it is the essential starting place for the revolutionary concept of a universal land ethic.

10: BUTTERFLIES IN WINTER

John Hay's *The Bird of Light* was published by W. W. Norton in 1991. Klots's and Brown's butterfly classics are cited above. The other one mentioned here is William Jacob Holland's *The Butterfly Book* (1898), published by McGraw-Hill; I had the 1930 edition. Vladimir Nabokov's quotation comes from the essay cited for the Prologue. My studies were summarized in "The Butterflies of the High Line Canal of Colorado," in *The Mid-Continent Lepidoptera Series* (volume 2, no. 24, February 1971). Subsequent data can be found in annual reports of the Xerces Society Fourth of July Butterfly Counts (www.Xerces.org, Portland, Oregon) and North American Butterfly Association, after 1993 (www.naba.org, Morristown, New Jersey).

11: A GRAND SURPRISE

Nabokov's epigraph-in-verse is from his poem "Restoration," included in *Poems and Problems,* McGraw-Hill, 1970. The quotation by John Haines graces *The Stars, the Snow, the Fire: Twenty-five Years in the Northern Wilderness* (Graywolf Press, 1990). *Nature's Wonders in Full Color,* edited by Charles E. Sherman, was published by Hanover House in 1956.

12: THE THUNDER TREE

Judge W. G. M. Stone's *The Colorado Handbook,* source of the epigraph, was published in Denver in 1893. Charles Sprague Sargent's *Manual of the Trees of North America* appeared originally in 1905, was revised in 1922, and reprinted in a Dover edition in 1961. I also quote Donald Culross Peattie's *A Natural History of Trees of Eastern and Central North America,* most recently brought into print by Houghton Mifflin in 1991. The plains cottonwood ecosystem is discussed in *From Grassland to Glacier: The Natural History of Colorado* by Cornelia Fleischer Mutel and John C. Emerick (Johnson Books, Boulder, 1984; revised paperback edition available from Johnson Books). Bruce Springsteen's line about cottonwoods comes from his song "I Wish I Were Blind" on the album *Human Touch*, © 1992 Columbia Records. Other cottonwood quotes were given me by Evergreen State College students Dodie Blair, Claire Littlewood, John Malcomson, Lee Burnett, and Jennifer Shafer. Key articles on the cutting and saving of cottonwoods came from reporters Whit Sibley ("Arapahoe Man Guilty of Felling Cottonwoods") and Steve Larson ("Their Bodies Will Shield Trees"), respectively, in the February 14, 1975, and February 5, 1976, issues of the *Denver Post*. Beaver management is discussed in "Safe Sex for Beavers?" by Robin Chotzinoff in the March 23–29 issue of *Westword*, a Denver weekly.

EPILOGUE: TRAVELS IN THE AFTERMATH

The epigraph comes from William Kittredge's wonderful *Hole in the Sky: A Memoir*, published by Knopf in 1992, available in paperback from Vintage. My letter to the *Aurora Advocate* was published on August 23, 1967. Numerous articles in Denver and Aurora papers cover the open space and DeLaney Farm preservation issues, among them "Aurora Council Seals Land Deal" (Sally Hekkers, *Denver Post*, March 30, 1982) and "A Past Preserved Means a Future Enhanced" (Tamra Tate, *Aurora Sentinel*, July 29, 1987). Among the more important articles on the canal trail, all in the *Denver Post*, were JoAnne Ditmer's "Canals Integral to Denver's Growth" (March 12, 1969); Dick Johnston's "Strip Park Planned Along Canal" (September 1, 1968); and Olive Knight's "Canal Trail an Oasis of Rare Quiet" (June 9, 1971); also, "High Line Canal Trail Proves Popular Year Round" (Denver Water Department's *Water News*, January-February 1980). Readers who want to explore the High Line Canal will enjoy Crawford Scott's chatty guide *Wogging the High Line* (Lord Publishing, Englewood, Colorado, 1986). For more on the rights of land, trees, and rocks, see William O. Douglas, *A Wilderness Bill of Rights* (Little, Brown, 1965) and Roderick Nash, *Wilderness and the American Mind* (Yale University Press, 1967). The *High Line Canal Future Management Plan* was published on August 1, 2002, by the High Line Canal Partners and was provided to me as a pdf file by Jerry Foster of Denver Water.